Building English Skills

Purple Level

Yellow Level

Blue Level

Orange Level

Green Level

Red Level

Gold Level

Silver Level

AQUA LEVEL

Brown Level

Plum Level

Pink Level

Kindergarten Level

Building English Skills

Aqua Level

McDougal, Littell & Company
Evanston, Illinois
New York   Dallas   Sacramento

Authors

Kathleen L. Bell, Assistant Director of Composition, Department of English, University of Miami, Coral Gables, Florida

Carol Dossa, Former Elementary Teacher, Cleveland Public Schools, Cleveland, Ohio

Frances Freeman Paden, Ph.D., Lecturer, Department of English and Communicative Arts, Roosevelt University, Chicago, Illinois

Susan Duffy Schaffrath, Consultant in Educational Materials for the Elementary and Middle Grades, Chicago, Illinois

Consultants

Linda Coleman, Teacher, District 109, Deerfield, Illinois

Phyllis W. Dole, Language Arts Consultant and Teacher, San Juan Capistrano, California

H. Kaye Griffin, Ed. D., Language Arts Coordinator, Klein Independent School District, Spring, Texas

Thomas C. Holland, Ed. D., Assistant Superintendent, Curriculum and Instruction, McKinney Independent School District, McKinney, Texas

Sue Cox Mays, Ph. D., Instructional Specialist, Fort Worth Independent School District, Fort Worth, Texas

Edmund Sullivan, Supervisor of Language Arts, Evansville-Vanderburgh School Corporation, Evansville, Indiana

Cathy Zollars, Director of Instruction, Grand Prairie Schools, Grand Prairie, Texas

Acknowledgments: See page 386.

ISBN: 0-86609-003-7

Copyright © 1984, 1981 by McDougal, Littell & Company
Box 1667, Evanston, Illinois 60204
All rights reserved. Printed in the United States of America

85 86 87 88 / 12 11 10 9 8 7 6

Contents

Chapter 1   Learning New Words   **1**

     Part 1   **Context Clues**   2

     Part 2   **Word Parts**   7

         More Exercises—Review   13

Chapter 2   Levels of Language   **15**

     Part 1   **Standard English**   16

     Part 2   **Slang**   18

Chapter 3   Getting Acquainted with Others   **23**

     Part 1   **Introducing Yourself**   24

     Part 2   **Introducing Other People**   26

     Part 3   **Carrying On a Conversation**   28

Chapter 4   Learning About Sentences   **31**

     Part 1   **What Is a Sentence?**   32

     Part 2   **Not All Groups of Words Are Sentences**   34

     Part 3   **Kinds of Sentences**   36

     Part 4   **Parts of the Sentence**   40

     Part 5   **More About the Parts of the Sentence**   43

         Sentence Patterns: Word Order and Meaning   47

         More Exercises—Review   49

Chapter 5 Writing Good Sentences   **53**

Part 1   **Keeping Thoughts Apart**   54
Part 2   **Putting Thoughts Together Correctly**   56

More Exercises—Review   59

Chapter 6 Using Nouns   **61**

Part 1   **What Are Nouns?**   61
Part 2   **Using Nouns as Subjects**   64
Part 3   **Common Nouns and Proper Nouns**   66
Part 4   **Singular Nouns and Plural Nouns**   68
Part 5   **Making Nouns Show Possession**   71

More Exercises—Review   74

Chapter 7 Using Pronouns   **77**

Part 1   **What Are Pronouns?**   77
Part 2   **Using Pronouns as Subjects**   80
Part 3   **Using *Me, Us, Her, Him*, and *Them***   83
Part 4   **Using *I* and *Me*, and *We* and *Us***   85
Part 5   **Possessive Pronouns**   87

Sentence Patterns: The N V Pattern   89

More Exercises—Review   90

Chapter 8 Using the Exact Word   **93**

Part 1   **Synonyms**   94
Part 2   **Using Words To Express Feelings**   97
Part 3   **Being Alert to How Others Use Words**   99

Chapter 9   Writing Paragraphs   103

Part 1   **What Is a Paragraph?**   104
Part 2   **Studying Paragraphs**   107
Part 3   **Reviewing Topic Sentences**   111
Part 4   **Pre-Writing: Planning a Paragraph**   115
Part 5   **Writing a Paragraph**   117
Part 6   **Revising a Paragraph**   118

Chapter 10   Improving Your Speaking and Listening Skills   123

Part 1   **Using the Telephone**   124
Part 2   **Making Announcements**   128
Part 3   **Giving Directions**   130
Part 4   **Listening To Learn**   132

Chapter 11   Talking in Groups   135

Part 1   **Sharing Ideas**   136
Part 2   **Disagreeing Politely**   139

Chapter 12   Using the Dictionary   143

Part 1   **Entry Words**   144
Part 2   **Finding the Word You Want**   144
Part 3   **Finding the Pronunciation**   150
Part 4   **Finding the Meaning**   153

     More Exercises—Review   155

Chapter 13   Using Verbs   157

Part 1   **Verbs That Tell About Action**   157
Part 2   **Verbs That Say That Something Is**   159
Part 3   **Main Verbs and Helping Verbs**   161

Part 4   **Using Helping Verbs**   163

Part 5   **Separated Parts of Verbs**   165

Part 6   **Using the Right Form of *Be***   167

Part 7   **Using Contractions**   169

Part 8   **Using Negatives Correctly**   171

Sentence Patterns: The N V Pattern   173

More Exercises—Review   174

Chapter 14   Using Verbs Correctly   179

Part 1   **Verbs That Tell About Present Time**   180

Part 2   **Verbs That Tell More About the Past**   182

Part 3   **Irregular Verbs**   184

Chapter 15   Telling Stories   187

Part 1   **Finding the Shape of a Story**   188

Part 2   **Getting People To Listen**   190

Part 3   **Telling a Story**   191

Chapter 16   Writing About Things That Happened   195

Part 1   **Pre-Writing: Choosing a Topic**   196

Part 2   **Pre-Writing: Making Your Plan**   199

Part 3   **Writing**   200

Part 4   **Revising**   201

Chapter 17   Taking Tests   205

Part 1   **Giving Information About Yourself**   206

Part 2   **Marking Your Answers**   208

Chapter 18 Using Adjectives   **211**

   Part 1   **What Are Adjectives?**   211

   Part 2   **Three Kinds of Adjectives**   214

   Part 3   **Using *A*, *An*, and *The***   216

   Part 4   **Using Adjectives To Compare People or Things**   218

       Sentence Patterns: The N L V Adj Pattern   222

       More Exercises—Review   223

Chapter 19 Using Adverbs   **227**

   Part 1   **What Are Adverbs?**   227

   Part 2   **Making Comparisons with Adverbs**   231

       More Exercises—Review   233

Chapter 20 Writing Descriptions   **235**

   Part 1   **Studying Descriptions**   236

   Part 2   **Pre-Writing: Choosing a Topic**   238

   Part 3   **Pre-Writing: Arranging Details**   240

   Part 4   **Writing: Using Details**   243

   Part 5   **Revising: Making Sure That Details Are Used Well**   246

Chapter 21 Writing Paragraphs That Explain Why   **249**

   Part 1   **Understanding Fact and Opinion**   250

   Part 2   **Giving Reasons**   252

Chapter 22 Writing a Story   **257**

   Part 1   **Studying an Example**   258

   Part 2   **Writing a Story**   260

Chapter 23   Using the Library   **263**

Part 1   **How Books Are Arranged**   264
Part 2   **Finding Books**   269
Part 3   **Appreciating Books**   273
Part 4   **Using an Encyclopedia**   277

Chapter 24   Enjoying Poetry   **281**

Part 1   **Getting To Know the Speaker in Poems**   282
Part 2   **Seeing the Pictures in Poetry**   285
Part 3   **Hearing the Sound Patterns in Poetry**   288
Part 4   **Hearing the Rhythm in Poetry**   290

Chapter 25   Writing a Report   **295**

Part 1   **What Is a Report?**   296
Part 2   **Pre-Writing: Choosing a Subject**   299
Part 3   **Pre-Writing: Learning About the Subject**   301
Part 4   **Pre-Writing: Planning the Report**   304
Part 5   **Writing the Report**   307
Part 6   **Revising the Report**   308
Part 7   **The Process of Writing**   314
Part 8   **Sharing a Report**   315

Chapter 26   Writing Friendly Letters   **317**

Part 1   **The Parts of a Friendly Letter**   318
Part 2   **Addressing the Envelope**   322
Part 3   **Writing Invitations**   323
Part 4   **Writing Thank-You Notes**   324

Chapter 27   Writing Business Letters   **327**

Part 1   **The Parts of a Business Letter**   328
Part 2   **Addressing the Envelope**   332

Handbook: The Mechanics of Writing

Chapter 28   ## Using Capital Letters   335

Part 1   **Names of People and Pets**   336
Part 2   **Names of Particular Places and Things**   338
Part 3   **First Words**   340
Part 4   **Titles**   342

   More Exercises—Review   344

Chapter 29   ## Using Punctuation Marks   347

Part 1   **The Period**   347
Part 2   **The Question Mark**   350
Part 3   **The Exclamation Point**   351
Part 4   **The Comma**   352
Part 5   **The Apostrophe**   356
Part 6   **The Colon**   359
Part 7   **Quotation Marks**   360
Part 8   **Underlining**   362

   More Exercises—Review   363

Chapter 30   ## Improving Your Spelling   367

Part 1   **Plan Your Study of Spelling**   368
Part 2   **Rules for Spelling**   370
Part 3   **Homonyms**   375   376

   More Exercises—Review   377

1. Balanced Coverage. *Building English Skills, Aqua Level* is a comprehensive text that presents balanced coverage of seven areas of language arts:

1. Vocabulary development
2. Speaking and listening skills
3. Grammar and usage
4. Composition skills
5. Study and research skills
6. Appreciation of literature
7. The mechanics of writing

2. Effective Teaching Method. Each chapter develops one topic completely through a combination of clear, readable explanations; examples that appeal to students at this grade level; and numerous exercises, at frequent, appropriate intervals, that directly reinforce the preceding lessons. Chapters of the grammar and usage strand and of the composition strand refer to and build upon what has been taught in the previous chapters of each of those strands. This steady development of grammar and composition concepts not only provides for meaningful maintenance but also makes possible an ever-growing awareness of the nature of language.

3. Emphasis on the Process of Writing. Chapters 9, Writing Paragraphs; 16, Writing About Things That Happened; 20, Writing Descriptions; and 25, Writing a Report, help develop and improve writing skills by leading the student through the process of writing. This process consists of three major steps:

Pre-writing, which includes choosing a topic and planning what to write

Writing, which includes writing topic sentences and developing paragraphs or reports according to a plan

Revising, which includes changing the ideas or organization of a piece of writing to improve its meaning and correcting the capitalization, punctuation, and other mechanics to make the writing more easily read and understood.

The text teaches that changing a piece of writing does not mean just correcting mistakes. Rather, it means expressing an idea more clearly or developing the idea more fully. The step of proofreading for mistakes comes after the idea and its expression have been developed as far as the writer can take them.

4. Useful Handbook for Student Reference. Chapters 28, Using Capital Letters; 29, Using Punctuation Marks; and 30, Improving Your Spelling, form the Handbook of the Mechanics of Writing. These three chapters list the basic rules likely to be needed by a student at this level, with easy-to-follow explanations, examples, and exercises. The Handbook is a practical reference tool for students, who should be encouraged to consult it independently throughout the year. It appears at the back of the book and is printed on lightly tinted pages for easy reference.

The Handbook will be most helpful if the teacher introduces and explains its use early in the year and reminds students of it at strategic intervals. The chapters may also be taught following the usual teacher-directed method, either an entire chapter at a time or one Part at a time.

Chapter 1

Learning New Words

Every day you hear or read new words. How can you find out what they mean?

One way is to look them up in a dictionary.

Another way is to look for clues to the meaning of a new word. When you are reading, these clues may be right in front of you.

This chapter will show you ways to find some of these clues. It will make it easier for you to discover the meanings of new words.

Part 1   Context Clues

When you find a new word in your reading, you find the word *in context*. **Context** means the sentence, or the paragraph, that has the new word. Very often the context of a new word helps you discover what the word means. A **context clue** is a word or group of words that leads you to the meaning.

King Henry was the *ruler* of England.
Susan used a *ruler* to measure her paper.

The word *ruler* can mean two things. It may mean "king" or "leader." It may mean "a flat measuring stick."

How did you know which meaning to use for *ruler* in each sentence? You could tell by seeing how the word *ruler* was used in the sentence.

You discovered the meaning by looking at the word in the context of the sentence. Writers give context clues to word meanings in several ways. Learn to look for these clues.

Context Clue 1   Definition

Sometimes a writer tells you the meaning of a word. He or she puts a *definition* of the word in the context. The definition may appear in the same sentence or the next sentence. Here are some examples:

Lava, which is melted rock, poured from the volcano.

The writer tells you that *lava* is melted rock.

Paul *hewed* the tree. That is, he cut it with an ax.

The writer explains that *hewed* means "cut with an ax."

2

The fishing pole was too *flimsy*. In other words, it was too thin and weak.

The writer explains that *flimsy* means "thin and weak."

There are certain words that help you spot a definition in the context.
Here are some of those words:

which is   **that is**   **in other words**

Remember these clue words.

An obelisk, **which is** **a pillar, stood in the park.**

The obelisk was askew, **that is,** **not straight.**

It inclined toward the right. **In other words,** **it slanted.**

Exercise   Using Context Clues

Each sentence or pair of sentences below has a definition clue in it. The clue will tell you the meaning of the underlined word. Write the word on your paper. Then write its meaning.

1. Joe had two tickets to an opera, that is, a play that is sung rather than spoken.

2. The sky was indigo. In other words, it was dark blue.

3. The walls were covered with mildew, which is a mold caused by dampness.

4. The photo was glossy. In other words, it was smooth and shiny.

5. Donna poured water on the embers of the fire. That is, she poured water on those coals that were still burning.

3

Context Clue 2   Restatement

A *restatement* is like a definition. However, it does not have the key words. Read the following examples.

Pioneers made bullets from *molten*, or melted, lead.
The old apple tree was *gnarled*—twisted and knotty.
Frank is a *mason*, a person who works with stone.

You can see that *molten* means "melted." *Gnarled* means "twisted and knotty." A *mason* is "a person who works with stone." The writer has restated the new word in a different way.

Here are clues for spotting a restatement:

the word *or*   commas   dashes

Remember these clues.

The artist drew fabulous, or imaginary, animals.

One was a unicorn —— a horse with a horn on its forehead.

Exercise   Using Context Clues

Each of these sentences has a restatement clue in it. The clue will help you find the meaning of the underlined word. Write the word on your paper. Then write its meaning.

1. Some rope is made from <u>jute</u>—a tropical plant.

2. The boys kept their rabbits in a <u>hutch</u>, or pen.

3. Joan saw a <u>marten</u>, a small animal like a weasel.

4. Venice has <u>canals</u>, man-made waterways, instead of streets.

5. Diana seemed very <u>subdued</u>, or quiet.

4

Context Clue 3   Examples

Another way a writer gives you clues is with *examples*. These examples list some things that are *like* the thing the new word describes. Here are some sample sentences.

> *Primates*—for instance, apes and chimps—often act like human beings.

The writer tells you that apes and chimps are primates. So *primates* must mean animals like apes and chimps.

> *Regulations* such as speed limits and other traffic rules save lives.

Speed limits and other traffic rules are examples of *regulations*. From this you can see that a regulation is a rule or law.

> The color of the prince's *garb*, for example, his shirt, cape, and boots, was dark red.

Can you guess what *garb* means? Since a shirt, a cape, and boots are given as examples, *garb* must mean "clothing."

Here are some words that will help you spot example context clues:

for example	**especially**	**like**
for instance	**such as**	

Notice these clue words.

Would you help collect properties ◁ **like** ▷ **tables, dishes, and curtains for the play?**

Look for old-fashioned eyeglasses, ◁ **especially** ▷ **monocles.**

Using Examples

Each sentence below has a context clue in it. This clue will help you figure out the meaning of the underlined word. Write the word and its meaning on your paper.

> Example: Some unusual fruits, like papayas, grow in tropical countries.
>
> papayas—unusual fruits

1. Marcus played several musical instruments, for instance, the oboe.
2. She teaches Polish dances, such as the mazurka.
3. The style of headgear, such as caps and helmets, changes through the ages.
4. Gilda liked sweet desserts, especially chocolate mousse.
5. All reptiles—snakes and lizards, for example—are cold-blooded.

Review Exercise **Using Context Clues**

Each sentence or pair of sentences has a context clue in it. Number your paper from 1 to 6. Write the underlined word and its meaning.

1. The old woman loved to reminisce—talk about her past.
2. The author is anonymous. In other words, the author's name is unknown.
3. We collected pictures of Indian habitations, for instance, longhouses, tepees, and pueblos.
4. This material is flammable. That is, it will catch on fire quickly.
5. Dr. Silver studies arachnids, such as spiders, scorpions, and daddy longlegs.
6. School rules prohibit, or forbid, running in the halls.

uncontrollable

Part 2   Word Parts

What do you do if there is no context clue to help you with a new word? Don't give up!

You can look at the word itself to find its meaning. Did you ever take apart a toy to find out how it worked? You can do the same thing with words.

Many words that look strange are built from words you already know.

Sometimes they are made by adding a **prefix.** A prefix is a word part added to the front of a word. It changes the meaning of the word.

Prefix		Base Word		New Word
un	+	happy	=	unhappy
re	+	paint	=	repaint
mis	+	behave	=	misbehave
non	+	stop	=	nonstop

Prefixes

Some of the most common prefixes are these four:

un- This prefix means "not" or "the opposite of."
un + fair = unfair
Unfair means "not fair."
un + clean = unclean
Unclean means "the opposite of clean."

necessary
fair
happy
wanted

re- This prefix means "again" or "back."
re + visit = revisit
Revisit means "visit again."
re + turn = return
Return means "turn back."

usable
visit
read
paint

mis- This prefix means "wrong" or "wrongly."
mis + spell = misspell
Misspell means "spell wrongly."
mis + behave = misbehave
Misbehave means "behave wrongly."

understand
pronounce
spell
step

non- This prefix means "not."
non + sense = nonsense
Nonsense means "not sense."
non + living = nonliving
Nonliving means "not living."

sense
profit
living
stop

When you see a word that starts with one of these prefixes, break the word into its two parts. You may know what the prefix means. You may know what the base word means. Put the two parts back together. Then you can get a good idea of what the new word means.

8

Be careful. Many words look as if they have prefixes, but they do not. When you take off the letters that you think make a prefix, look at the word that is left. Does it make sense? If it does not, the word does not have a prefix.

<u>Exercises</u> **Prefixes**

A. Copy each word. Draw a circle around the base word. Underline the prefix. Then write a meaning for the whole word.

Example: reappear

<u>re</u> (appear)—appear again

1. misjudge 5. mislead
2. rewrite 6. recall
3. unbutton 7. unsure
4. nonstop 8. nonsolid

Word	Prefix?
redraw	√
red	x
reindeer	?

B. Copy these words on your paper. Underline each prefix. Circle each base word. If the word cannot be broken into parts, write *No* after it.

1. miscue 5. rent
2. none 6. unlock
3. redo 7. nonsmoking
4. under 8. mission

C. Answer the following questions.

1. If *inform* means "to give correct information," what does *misinform* mean?
2. If *skid* means "slip," what does *nonskid* mean?
3. If *gain* means "to win," what does *regain* mean?
4. If *view* means "to look at," what does *review* mean?
5. If *tried* means "tested," what does *untried* mean?
6. If *conform* means "to act like everyone else," what does *nonconform* mean?

9

Suffixes

Sometimes a new word is made by adding a **suffix** to a base word. A **suffix** is a word part added to the end of a word. A suffix changes the meaning of the word.

Base Word	Suffix	New Word
joy	+ ful	= joyful

Notice that when *-er* is added to a word, the last letter of the base word is often doubled.

swim + er = swimmer

Also, when *-ful*, *-able*, or *-less* is added, the *y* or silent *e* at the end of the base word often changes.

beauty + ful = beautiful
love + able = lovable
penny + less = penniless

Rules for these spelling changes are given in Chapter 30, Improving Your Spelling, pages 370 to 374.

Word	Suffix?
swimmer	√
under	x
water	?

Words are not always made of base words and suffixes. You might guess that the *er* in *under* is a suffix. However, if you take away *er*, *und* is left. It is not a real word. Be careful. If you take off a prefix or suffix, look at the letters that are left. They must form a real word. If they do not form a real word, you cannot break the word into parts.

Some of the most common suffixes are these four:

paint
sing
loud

-er

-er (or **-or**) This suffix means "someone who does something." The suffix -er can also mean *more*.

dive + er = diver
A *diver* is someone who dives.
act+ or = actor
An *actor* is someone who acts.
loud + er = louder
Louder means "more loud."

score
hair
help

-less This suffix means "without."
score+ less = scoreless
A *scoreless* game is a game without a score by either team.
hair + less = hairless
Hairless means without hair.

-less

break
burn
wash

-able This suffix means "can be."
break +able = breakable
A *breakable* cup can be broken.
burn + able = burnable
A *burnable* thing can be burned.

-able

hope
hand
spoon

-ful This suffix means "full of."
hope + ful = hopeful
A *hopeful* person is full of hope.
hand + ful = handful
A *handful* of snow is as much snow as a hand can hold.

-ful

11

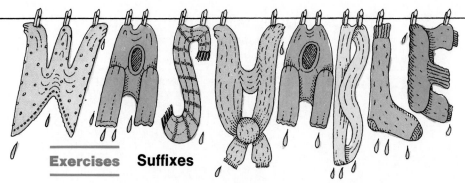

Exercises Suffixes

A. Copy each word. Draw a circle around the base word. Underline the suffix. Write a meaning for the word.

Example: hitter

(hit)ter—one who hits

1. scornful
2. drummer
3. thoughtless
4. workable
5. climber
6. drinkable
7. dropper
8. restful

B. Put the base word with the suffix. Write the new word.

1. train+ er
2. end + less
3. success + ful
4. rest + less
5. reason + able
6. direct + or
7. care + less
8. lead + er

C. Answer these questions.

1. If *cease* means "end," what does *ceaseless* mean?
2. If *bounty* means "plenty," what does *bountiful* mean?
3. If *observe* means "to notice," what does *observable* mean?
4. If *compose* means "to write music," what does *composer* mean?
5. If *instruct* means "to teach," what does *instructor* mean?
6. If *reuse* means "use again," what does *reusable* mean?

Learning New Words

A. Context Clues

Write the meaning for each underlined word.

1. I've always wanted to see a heron, which is a large bird that lives in marshes.

2. The doctor was frank, or honest, about the problem.

3. The pony was piebald—spotted.

4. The cook uses lots of herbs, like sage.

5. George is a skeptic. That is, he doubts nearly everything.

6. I like to eat all kinds of seafood, such as scallops.

7. The shirt was made of velour, a cloth that looks like velvet.

8. The sailboat heeled, that is, tilted, when the wind blew.

9. We saw hansoms and other carriages in the museum.

10. Our steak was served with morels, brown mushrooms.

B. Word Parts

Write the base word for each word. After the base word, write a definition for the word that is given. Watch out for words that do not have suffixes or prefixes.

Example: careful
        care, full of care

1. refill	5. undo	9. curable
2. player	6. real	10. misplace
3. heartless	7. undone	11. spoonful
4. union	8. speechless	12. missile

13

Chapter 2

Levels of Language

When you speak, you use different levels of language. You do not always speak the same way.

You choose words to fit your situation. When your words are on the wrong level of language, they sound out of place.

Let's look at an example.

Katy and Mark were walking to school. They saw their principal coming down the sidewalk.

MARK: Good morning, Mr. Wood. How are you?

KATY: Hey, man! Everything cool?

Mark used language that fit the situation. He was talking to an older person. It was right for him to be formal.

Katy's greeting would have been good for a friend of her own age. However, in this case, her language did not fit.

Part 1 Standard English

Standard English is language that most people understand easily. There are different kinds of standard English. Sometimes you need to choose your words very carefully. At other times, you can be more informal.

When To Choose Words Carefully

Suppose you have something special to say or to write. You must think about the language you use. Here is an example.

You are asked to make an announcement about the school talent show at the PTA meeting. You say this:

"On Wednesday evening, October 25, the boys and girls of Jefferson School will present their annual talent show. The program will be presented in the auditorium at 7:30 P.M. All parents, relatives, and friends are cordially invited to attend."

In this announcement, you are careful to make your thoughts clear. You use words in a way everyone will understand. You use complete sentences. This is formal standard English.

Here are some other special situations. In these situations, you will want to choose your words carefully.

1. You are giving a book report to your class.
2. You are writing a letter to your town newspaper.
3. You are applying for a job to mow lawns.

Can you think of other times when your words should be chosen carefully?

When To Speak Informally

Informal language is everyday talk. It is another kind of standard English.

Here is an example of informal language.

> You tell your cousin about the show. You say this:
>
> "Doing anything next Wednesday night? How about coming to my school talent show? It should be pretty good. Everyone's in it. It's in the auditorium at seven. Want to come?"

In the example above, your grammar is correct, but your language is informal. Although you leave out a few words, your friend understands you. You are speaking simply and naturally.

To speak or write in standard English, follow these guides:

> **Guides for Using Standard English**
>
> 1. Use correct grammar.
> 2. Choose words that most people understand.
> 3. Fit your words to your situation.

Exercises **Using Standard English**

A. Suppose you meet the mayor of your town. You want to invite him or her to speak to your class. Write down three things you would say to the mayor. Write in standard English. Choose your words carefully.

17

B. Imagine that you are going to an amusement park. Invite a friend to go with you. Write down three things you might say to your friend. Write in standard English. Use informal language.

Part 2 Slang

Slang is speech that uses new words, or new meanings for standard words. Many times, slang is not understood by everyone. Often it is colorful. If it is not used too much, slang makes your language lively.

Here are some words that are considered slang.

jive	klutz	kooky
snazzy	zilch	rip-off
dopey	wacky	roughneck

These slang words are listed in the dictionary. The newest words are not in the dictionary yet.

After a slang word has been used for a while, one of two things usually happens. Sometimes everyone comes to understand and use the word, and it becomes standard English. Other times, people who use it get tired of it, and it is forgotten.

18

Words That Work on Two Levels

Many times standard words are used in new ways, with new meanings. These words work on more than one level of language. Their meaning depends on how you use them.

For example, think about these words:

cool   turkey
dig   neat

All the words above have at least two meanings. Each word is used as a slang word. Each word also has a meaning in standard English.

Let's look more closely at *cool*. Read these sentences:

1. It's *cool* outside today.
2. Nina's plan for the picnic is *cool*.

In the first sentence, *cool* means "not warm." The level of language is standard English. In the second sentence, however, *cool* means "just right." *Cool* is used as a slang word.

Now look again at the other words. Can you think of two meanings for *dig, turkey,* and *neat?*

Was the play good?

This play is a bomb.

Let's split.

Some Dangers in Using Slang

Some people almost always speak in slang. It becomes boring to listen to them. Their words lose meaning. Sometimes you cannot tell what they mean to say. Look at this conversation.

JOE: We watched the Mets beat the Cubs last night.

TONY: Crazy, man!

JOE: They both got home runs in the fifth inning.

TONY: Crazy!

JOE: Are you a baseball fan, too?

TONY: Blows my mind.

Tony always responds in slang. Can you tell what he means?

Sometimes people use slang because they are lazy. Here is an example.

MOM: Marta seems to be a special friend of yours. What's she like?

JAN: She's really neat.

Jan hasn't told her mother anything. Perhaps you can help. Imagine that you know Marta. How would you describe her?

Guides for Using Slang

1. Use slang in small amounts.
2. Avoid words that are used too often.
3. Use language that has meaning for the listener.

Can you change the slang words into standard English?

The **dude** helped himself to a **freebie**

Exercises Using Slang

A. Make a list of slang words. After each word, explain its meaning in standard English.

B. Read the sentences below. Then rewrite each sentence. Change the slang to standard English.

1. I *loused* up my airplane project.
2. Jim won't come because he's *chicken*.
3. The fish tank is getting pretty *yucky*.
4. Arithmetic tests make me *uptight*.
5. Chuck wants to *do his own thing* today.
6. Alonzo's big sister really *turns me off*.
7. That's a *groovy* shirt, Maria.
8. The contest was too hard, so I *copped out*.

21

C. Read your new sentences from Exercise B out loud. Discuss them in class. Which slang words mean the same thing to everyone? Which ones mean different things to different people?

Chapter 3

Getting Acquainted with Others

Friends talk together easily. Talking with someone you have just met may be difficult. What do you say to someone new? Are you able to keep a conversation going? Can you disagree without hurting the person's feelings?

Think about these questions. The next few pages will help you find some answers. Let's begin with making introductions.

Part 1 Introducing Yourself

Sometimes you may be shy when you meet someone new. Introducing yourself helps you relax. Say your name clearly. Be sure you understand the other person's name. Then say something friendly to the other person. Here is an example.

Today Nora met a new girl at school. The new girl's name is Patty. She lives only two houses away from Nora. Nora wants to get to know Patty. She decides to go to her house after school. An older girl comes to the door. Here is what they say.

NORA: Hi. I'm looking for Patty Jackson.

TERRY: Hello. I'm her sister Terry. What's your name?

NORA: I'm Nora Stone. I'm glad to meet you, Terry. Is Patty home?

TERRY: Yes, she is. Please come in, Nora. I'll call Patty.

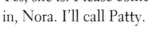

Nora and Terry introduce themselves. They tell each other their names. Nora says, "I'm glad to meet you, Terry." Her words are friendly. How does Terry make Nora feel welcome?

Here are some guides to remember.

Guides for Introducing Yourself

1. Say your name clearly.
2. Listen to the other person's name. Remember it.
3. Look directly at the person you are meeting.
4. Say something friendly.

Exercises   **Introducing Yourself**

A. Work in pairs for these exercises.

1. Using your own names, act out the scene between Nora and Terry.

2. Introduce yourself to your partner. Follow the Guides for Introducing Yourself.

B. Read this conversation. Then do the exercises.

PETE: Hi. Aren't you José?

JOSÉ: Yes. So what?

PETE: I saw you at the ball game.

JOSÉ: Right. I remember you.

PETE: My name is Pete.

JOSÉ: Hi, Pete. See you around.

1. Ask two people to act out the parts of Pete and José.

2. Discuss the conversation. What do Pete and José do wrong? List at least three mistakes that they make.

3. Correct the boys' mistakes. Follow the Guides above.

Part 2 Introducing Other People

You can help others get acquainted. It is fun to introduce one person to another. Once they meet, the people may become friends.

Let's look at an example.

Chico's grandmother has come for a visit. Chico wants his grandmother to meet his friend Tony.

CHICO: Grandma, I'd like you to meet Tony. He's our neighbor. Tony, this is my grandmother, Mrs. Peréz.

MRS. PERÉZ: Hello, Tony. I'm so happy to meet Chico's friend.

TONY: I'm glad to meet you, Mrs. Peréz. Chico talks about you all the time. He says you live near Disneyland.

Now try to answer these questions.

1. Chico says both names clearly. What is his grandmother's name?
2. What does Chico say about Tony?
3. Mrs. Peréz wants to be friendly. What does she say?
4. Tony repeats Mrs. Peréz's name. Why?
5. How does Tony make Mrs. Peréz feel welcome?

It's best to tell people what to call an adult member of your family. For example, Chico says, "Tony, this is my grandmother, Mrs. Peréz." Tony now knows what to call Chico's grandmother.

At the top of page 27 are some guides. Try to remember them.

> **Guides for Introducing Other People**
> 1. Say both names clearly.
> 2. Tell something about the person you introduce.
> 3. Show your interest in each person.
> 4. Listen to what the people say to each other.

Exercises   **Introducing Other People**

A. Holly has a new friend named Steve. She wants him to meet her brother Carl. Read her introduction.

HOLLY: Steve, this is my brother.
CARL: Hi, Steve.
STEVE: Hi, Carl.
HOLLY: Do you think you'll be friends?

Holly has made several mistakes. What are they? Discuss your answers in class.

B. Bob introduces Liz to his mother. Read what they say.

BOB: Mom, here's Liz. She lives on the third floor.
MOM: Hello, Liz. Are you in Bob's class?
LIZ: Yes, I am.
MOM: Would you like some cocoa?
LIZ: Sure. Thank you.
MOM: Do you want some, too, Bob?
BOB: Some what? I didn't hear you.

What are Bob's mistakes? Discuss them in class. Then correct the mistakes.

27

C. Form groups of three. Take turns introducing each other. Follow the Guides for Introducing Other People.

Part 3   Carrying On a Conversation

Conversations help people get acquainted. To carry on a conversation, you must listen. You will learn new things. When you can, ask questions. Questions make conversations lively.

Here is an example of a lively conversation.

SOPHIE:	Are you going to try out for the talent show?
BLAKE:	I guess so. I can do some magic tricks.
SOPHIE:	Really? Where did you learn them?
BLAKE:	My uncle taught me. He used to work in a circus.
SOPHIE:	I've never met anyone from a circus.
BLAKE:	My uncle is a lot of fun. Would you like to see a magic trick?
SOPHIE:	Sure. Then I could do my tumbling act for you.
BLAKE:	What's tumbling? Turning cartwheels?
SOPHIE:	That's right. I can do other things, too. Watch my backward flip! (She does a backward flip.)
BLAKE:	Terrific! Wait here a minute, Sophie. I'll go get my things. I'll show you a magic trick.

Now answer these questions. Discuss your answers in class.

1. Sophie and Blake both asked questions. Do you think they were good questions? Why?

28

2. Look at how Sophie and Blake answered questions. They never said just "yes" or "no." Instead, they added new information. Discuss each new piece of information. How do their answers keep the conversation lively?

Remember these guides.

> **Guides for Carrying On a Conversation**
>
> 1. Speak in a pleasant voice.
> 2. Look at each other. Listen.
> 3. Ask questions. Your questions should show the other person that you are interested in what he or she said.
> 4. Answer questions completely. Try to add new information.
> 5. If you interrupt, say "I'm sorry."

Exercises   Carrying On a Conversation

A. Below are three samples from conversations. Something is wrong with each of them. First, decide what is wrong. Then correct each mistake. Discuss the exercise in class.

1.   SUZI: Let's go get my bike. We could ride to the lake.

    ANDY: I'm tired. Why do you wear that funny hat?

    SUZI: It's not funny! I'm going home.

2.   PETE: Didn't I see you at the ball game?

   MARIO: No.

3. MANUEL: I can't wait for Jon's party.

    TOM: I can't go. We're moving that day. Will you come over to our new house sometime?

  MANUEL: I wonder what the movie will be. I hope it's not cartoons. They're silly.

B. Form groups of three. Make up a topic, or choose one from this list. Have a lively conversation with your group.

a class project	a recent storm	problems with pets
a hobby	a new game	your favorite books

Chapter 4

Learning About Sentences

When we talk or write, we use words. We try to choose words that will make our thoughts clear to others. We are also careful to use the words in groups that make sense.

For example, read this group of words:

likes Eric milk

This group does not make sense. In English, words do not go together this way.

Now read the same words in a different order.

Eric likes milk

This group does make sense. It follows rules for our language.

This chapter will talk about some of the rules of our language. It will help you to follow the rules. This will make it easier for you to share your thoughts with other people.

Part 1 What Is a Sentence?

A **sentence** is a group of words that tells a whole thought.
Read these groups of words. Each group is a sentence. Each sentence tells a whole thought.

1. Gerry loves chocolate chip cookies.
2. Tony pulled weeds.
3. We waited at the bus stop.

> A **sentence** is a group of words that tells
> a whole thought.

The Two Parts of a Sentence

Every sentence has two parts. One part tells *who* or *what* did something. The other part tells *what happened*.
Read each sentence. Find the part that tells *who* or *what* did something. Then find the part that tells *what happened*.

1. Angela painted a picture.
2. Mickey Mouse starred in movies.
3. The fastest runners won the relay race.

Now check your answers with the chart below.

Who or what did something?	What happened?
Angela	painted a picture.
Mickey Mouse	starred in movies.
The fastest runners	won the relay race.

Who or what?	What happened?

Exercises Finding the Two Parts of a Sentence

A. Make a chart like the one above. Draw a straight line down the middle of your paper. At the top of the first part, write *Who or what.* At the top of the second part, write *What happened.*

    Read each sentence below. Decide which words tell *Who or what.* Decide which words tell *What happened.* Write the words of each sentence in the correct part of the chart.

1. Mom poured the milk.
2. Your puppy barked at me.
3. Doug made a wagon.
4. Rosa wished on a star.
5. My brother raked the leaves.
6. The children danced.
7. Jenny threw the football.
8. Three red birds flew past.
9. Our Scout leader started a fire.
10. The kettle whistled.

B. Follow the directions for Exercise A.

1. Kenny's dad makes good spaghetti.
2. The wind lifted my kite.
3. Paulette joined the Campfire Girls.
4. Dinosaurs lived long ago.
5. The teacher thanked Marco.
6. My grandmother judged the contest.
7. The dentist gave me a new toothbrush.
8. Fran broke her hockey stick.
9. The fireworks exploded loudly.
10. Noreen takes pottery lessons.

33

Part 2 Not All Groups of Words
Are Sentences

Not all groups of words are sentences. Some groups of words do not tell whole thoughts. They are not sentences.

Read this group of words. Look for the two parts of a sentence.

The player in the red shirt

Does the word group tell *who* or *what* did something? Does it tell *what happened?* Does it tell a whole thought?

This group of words answers *who* or *what* did something. But it does not answer *what happened.* It does not tell a whole thought. It is not a sentence.

You can add words to the group to make it a sentence. The words you add must tell *what happened.* Here are a few ways you could complete the sentence.

The player in the red shirt threw the ball.
The player in the red shirt caught the pass.
The player in the red shirt counted to twenty.

Is this group of words a sentence?

Swam in the pool

This group of words answers the question *what happened.* However, it does not tell *who* or *what* did something. It does not tell a whole thought. It is not a sentence.

Can you change this word group into a sentence? The words you add must answer the question *who* or *what* did something. Here are some ways you could complete the sentence.

Hal swam in the pool.
My uncle Fred swam in the pool.
Three girls swam in the pool.

Exercises Making Sure That Sentences Are Complete

A. Number your paper from 1 to 10. Read each of the following groups of words. Decide whether the word group answers both questions, *who* or *what* did something and *what happened.* If it does, write *Sentence.* If it does not, write *Not a Sentence.*

1. Jeff's mother runs a grocery store.
2. Does cartwheels.
3. The large black crow.
4. The small dog chased a squirrel.
5. Many of Carl's friends.
6. The goldfish in the bowl.
7. The baseball costs two dollars.
8. Pushed the boat into the pond.
9. Mice like cheese.
10. The creatures stepped out of the spaceship.

B. Follow the directions for Exercise A.

1. Needs very little help.
2. Mr. O'Neill gave me some lettuce seeds.
3. The old book on the desk.
4. Cheetahs can run very fast.
5. A wet slippery rock.
6. A wheel came off my skate.
7. Plays the trumpet in the band.
8. Clara has a cast on her arm.
9. The principal introduced the visitors.
10. A speedboat on the lake.

Part 3   Kinds of Sentences

When Martha lost some money, she said several sentences.

I lost my quarter.

This sentence told what had happened.

Will you help me find it?

This sentence asked for something.

Look under the chair.

This sentence told someone to do something.

There is my money!

This sentence showed Martha's excitement.

Each of Martha's sentences did a different job. Each was a different kind of sentence.

When you write sentences, show where each new sentence begins. Use a capital letter at the beginning of each sentence.

> Use a capital letter at the beginning of every sentence.

Statements

A sentence that tells something is a **statement.**

I lost my quarter.   Ice is frozen water.

> A **statement** is a sentence that tells or states something. Use a period (.) at the end of every statement.

Questions

A sentence that asks something is a **question.**

Will you help me find it?   What is an android?

> A **question** is a sentence that asks something.
> Use a question mark (?) at the end
> of every question.

Commands and Requests

A sentence that tells you to do something is a **command.**

Look under the chair.   Please look under the chair.

Usually you use a period at the end of a command. However, if the command shows strong feeling, use an exclamation point.

Watch out for that car!   Don't touch the oven!

> A **command** is a sentence that tells you to do
> something.
> Use a period (.) at the end of most commands.
> Use an exclamation point (!) at the end of
> a command that shows strong feeling.

In each of the commands above, look for *who* or *what* should do something. You will not find any words that answer these questions. In these sentences, the word *You* is understood. It is meant but not said.

37

(You) Look under the chair.
(You) Watch out for that car!

Exclamations

A sentence that shows excitement, surprise, or other strong feeling is called an **exclamation.**

> There is my money!
> What a fine day this is!

An **exclamation** is a sentence that shows strong feeling.

Use an exclamation point (!) at the end of every exclamation.

Exercises   Using the Four Kinds of Sentences

A. The following list of ten sentences has five statements and five commands. Write each sentence correctly. Then write *Statement* or *Command* to tell what kind of sentence it is.

1. Dan has a twin brother
2. please be on time tomorrow

3. water the plants twice a week
4. Sally's favorite flavor is chocolate
5. check the air in the bike tires
6. Gilberto's family just moved in
7. dolphins can't breathe in water
8. remember your math homework
9. that dog is Jewel's best friend
10. bring in the mail

B. This list of sentences has six questions and four exclamations. Write each sentence correctly. Your end mark will tell what kind of sentence it is.

1. how much pizza did you eat
2. you're standing on my foot
3. did Kate get a new guitar
4. where are the colored pens
5. the soup is boiling over
6. are you coming to the Scout meeting
7. my snake is loose
8. when will Tim's party begin
9. there's a raccoon in our tent
10. what is the name of that record

C. This list has all four kinds of sentences mixed together. Write each sentence correctly.

1. how hot this room is
2. can Joshua carry that box home
3. please bring a sack lunch tomorrow
4. Debbie and her grandfather built a bird feeder
5. the toaster is on fire
6. my cousin drives a bus
7. does Mrs. Robinson live near the school
8. bring extra socks on the hike

Part 4 Parts of the Sentence

In Part 1 of this chapter, you learned that every sentence has two parts. They tell *who* or *what* and *what happened.*

The Subject

The **subject** is the part of the sentence that tells *who* or *what* did something. Sometimes it tells *who* or *what* is something.

Read these sentences. The subject of each sentence has a line under it. Notice that a subject may have one word or more than one word.

<u>Jess</u> plays the drums.
   (Who does something)

<u>This heavy book</u> hurts my arms.
   (What does something)

<u>The vase on the window sill</u>
   is very old.
   (What is something)

The Predicate

The **predicate** is the part of the sentence that tells *what happened.* It tells about the subject. It can do one of these two things:

Tell what the subject does or did
Tell what the subject is or was

Read these sentences. The predicate of each sentence has two lines under it. Notice that a predicate may have one word or more than one word.

Lois walks to school.
(What the subject does)

Heavy snow fell.
(What the subject did)

Mr. Garcia is my teacher.
(What the subject is)

The **subject** of a sentence tells who or what does something. It sometimes tells who or what is something.

The **predicate** of a sentence tells what the subject does or did, or what the subject is or was.

Every sentence must have a subject and a predicate.

Here are two more sentences. Decide by yourself which words belong in the subject. Decide which words belong in the predicate. Then check yourself against the following chart.

1. The bus is late.
2. Your little brother went for a walk.

Subject	Predicate
1. The bus (What)	is late. (What the subject is)
2. Your little brother (Who)	went for a walk. (What the subject did)

41

SENTENCE
SUBJECT & PREDICATE

Exercises **Finding Subjects and Predicates**

A. Copy these sentences. Draw one line under the subject of each sentence. Draw two lines under the predicate.

   Example: Ms. Lee hung our best papers on the board.

1. My guppy had four babies.
2. The principal asked for Vincent's help.
3. The band was too loud.
4. Rain stopped the school picnic.
5. Yuriko's father brought the fruit.
6. William's mother is a police officer.
7. The TV picture was blurry.
8. Workmen cut down the huge oak tree.
9. This book is about snakes.
10. The chain on my bike slips.

B. Follow the directions for Exercise A.

1. That truck ran into a post.
2. Brenda's grandmother teaches her old songs.
3. Eduardo left his lunchbox on the bus.
4. The whole class learned a folk dance.
5. Our tadpole is growing legs.
6. Michelle lost her allowance.
7. The janitor was busy all day.
8. My sister won a trip to Disneyland.
9. Tracy sent a card to Mrs. Settles.
10. Eli is a fast skater.

Part 5 More About the Parts of the Sentence

In Part 4, you found out what the subject of a sentence is and what the predicate is. When we divide a sentence into these two parts, we call the subject part the **complete subject**. We call the predicate part the **complete predicate**.

The Simple Subject

As you know, the complete subject of a sentence may have one word or more than one word. If it has more than one word, there is one word that is more important than all the others. This important word is called the **simple subject**.

If you leave out the other words of the complete subject, the sentence still makes sense. However, if you leave out the simple subject, the sentence does not make sense. It does not tell a whole thought.

In the sentences below, the simple subject is underlined. Other words are added to the subject.

Complete Subject	Complete Predicate
The <u>birds</u>	flew away.
The three <u>birds</u>	flew away.
The three <u>birds</u> on the branch	flew away.

43

Now notice how other words can be taken away from the complete subject. As long as the simple subject stays the same, the idea in the sentence stays the same.

Complete Subject	Complete Predicate
Mother's favorite lamp with the blue shade	broke.
Mother's favorite lamp	broke.
The lamp	broke.

Exercise **Finding the Simple Subject**

Copy each sentence. Draw a line under the simple subject.

1. The long green coat didn't fit me.
2. The policeman on the corner blew his whistle.
3. Bright red roses are my favorite flowers.
4. Jean's little brother had a birthday party.
5. That man with the beard looks like Santa Claus.
6. The two brothers wore matching shirts.
7. The winner of the race got a prize.
8. My uncle's old brown horse is still strong.
9. Everybody in my class likes popcorn.
10. The three girls in that family share a bedroom.

The Simple Predicate, or Verb

In the complete predicate of a sentence, there is one part that is more important than the rest. This important part is called the simple predicate, or the **verb.** In this book, we will call it the *verb.* Usually, a verb tells of an action.

In the sentences below, the verb has two lines under it. Notice how other words can be added to the verb.

Complete Subject	Complete Predicate
Tim	climbed the mountain.
Tim	slowly climbed the mountain.
Tim	slowly climbed the steep mountain.

In this next set of sentences, notice how other words in the predicate can be left out. However, the sentence will not be a sentence if the verb is left out. Every sentence must have a verb.

Complete Subject	Complete Predicate
Carol	quickly answered the question.
Carol	answered the question.
Carol	answered.

Not all verbs show action. Some verbs say that something is. Some verbs that do not show action are these: *is, are, was, were.*

R2D2 is a robot.

Exercises **Finding Simple Subjects and Verbs**

A. Copy these sentences. Draw one line under the simple subject. Draw two lines under the verb.

Example: The clown in the circus rode a donkey.

1. Sarah sang at her aunt's wedding.
2. The Scouts pitched the tent.
3. Jonathan runs very fast.
4. Mrs. Gomez is the school nurse.
5. Joey's father makes the best kites.

6. The little shaggy dog waited for its owner.
7. My new bookbag fell into the mud.
8. Wanda was the messenger on Tuesday.
9. Cora ate eggs for breakfast.
10. That big present is a surprise.

B. Follow the directions for Exercise A.

1. This chair belonged to my great-grandfather.
2. Liz's father sent her a new record.
3. Andrew practices piano every day.
4. The children on my street play stickball.
5. Julie is a new student this year.
6. Everyone in the theater cheered for the dancer.
7. That little boy jumped over two tires.
8. David's older sister broke her arm.
9. Each child brought something for the party.
10. That little gray squirrel lives in our tree.

C. Draw a line down the middle of your paper. In each sentence, find the simple subject and the verb. Write the simple subject at the left of the line. Write the verb at the right.

Example: The old tree shed its leaves.

tree | shed

1. Four boys joined the stamp club.
2. The oldest elephant at the zoo died yesterday.
3. Matt dives off the high board.
4. A sparrow built a nest in our mailbox.
5. Ira's mother fixed the broken chair.
6. The other campers swam in the lake.
7. Victoria's dog barks at squirrels.
8. Two firemen came to our school for the fire drill.
9. The little brown toad hopped under the bookshelf.
10. Some boys from my class sang in the talent show.

Sentence Patterns   Word Order and Meaning

Sentences are made of words. Each sentence must make sense. To make sense, the words must be in a special order. Read the groups of words below. Which group makes sense? Which group does not make sense?

Lisa stood up.
Stood Lisa up.

The second group does not make sense. The first group does make sense. The words are in the right order. They make an English sentence. You have heard many English sentences. From them you have learned what the right word order is. You can tell that the words in the second group are not in the right order. You can tell that the words in the first group are in the right order.

Sometimes a group of words can be put in more than one order to make a sentence. Each order makes sense. Each order expresses an idea. However, the ideas may be different if the word order is different. Read the two sentences below.

Rosa called Andy.
Andy called Rosa.

The words in each sentence are the same. The word order is not. The difference in word order makes a difference in meaning.

Remember that meaning in a sentence comes from the words in the sentence and the order of those words. If the words are not in the right order, the sentence may not make sense. A difference in word order can make an important difference in meaning.

47

Exercise   Word Order and Meaning

Read each sentence. Then change the order of the words to change the meaning. Write each new sentence on your paper.

1. Sam saw Donna.
2. The bag held the box.
3. Elaine helped John.
4. Some drivers are men.
5. Some cats are pets.
6. Max waited for Vicky.
7. My brother ran past my sister.
8. Clare found Rob.
9. Jackie thanked Marsha.
10. The storybook is under the notebook.
11. The salt is behind the pepper.
12. The hunter chased a bear.
13. Barbara likes pets.
14. Fred phoned Dan.
15. Lee followed the dog.

More Exercises — Review

Learning About Sentences

A. Finding the Two Parts of a Sentence

Draw a straight line down the middle of your paper. At the top of the first part, write *Who or what.* At the top of the second part, write *What happened.*

Read each sentence below carefully. Decide which words tell *Who* or *what.* Decide which words tell *What happened.* Write the words of each sentence in the correct part of the chart.

1. Our snowman melted.
2. Connie swam across the pool.
3. The band led the parade.
4. Don picked an apple.
5. My sister played the piano.
6. Laura rode her skateboard.
7. The rain flooded the basement.
8. Angel wrapped his gift.
9. The crowd cheered loudly.
10. Mr. Yamada bought a new car.

B. Making Sure That Sentences Are Complete

Number your paper from 1 to 10. Read each group of words. Decide whether the group of words answers both questions, *who* or *what* did something and *what happened.* If it does, write *Sentence.* If it does not, write *Not a Sentence.*

1. Flew through the window.
2. The hungry dog.

3. Judy slept.
4. Delivered the newspaper.
5. Curtis read a book.
6. The movie began.
7. Fell on the ice.
8. The school bus.
9. My kitten chases butterflies.
10. Several children.

C. Using the Four Kinds of Sentences

This list of sentences has all four kinds of sentences mixed together. Write each sentence correctly. Use a capital letter at the beginning. Use the correct end mark (period, question mark, or exclamation point) at the end.

1. what a scary movie that was
2. what is your name
3. my brother does magic tricks
4. what an exciting game that was
5. please answer these questions
6. where is your ball
7. i live on Ridge Road
8. catch that puppy
9. how hungry I am
10. do you know the answer

D. Finding Subjects and Predicates

Copy these sentences. Draw one line under the subject of each sentence. Draw two lines under the predicate.

50

Example: A stingray is a dangerous fish.

1. The ball bounced.
2. Jill laughed at the clown.

3. The train stops at every station.
4. My balloon floated away.
5. The girls formed a chorus.
6. My boots are muddy.
7. The floor was slippery.
8. Mr. Crane packed his suitcase.
9. Rich makes delicious ham sandwiches.
10. Ann was class president.

E. Finding Simple Subjects and Verbs

Number your paper from 1 to 10. Draw a line down the middle of the paper. In each of the following sentences, find the simple subject and the verb. Write the simple subject at the left of the line. Write the verb at the right of the line.

1. The tall boy found a quarter.
2. Dark clouds filled the sky.
3. A light shone brightly.
4. The girl at the counter ordered a Pepsi.
5. Olga wrote a long letter.
6. A small dog ran down the street.
7. Charles always wins at checkers.
8. Lupe's little brother lost a tooth.
9. The angry lion roared loudly.
10. My favorite color is yellow.

Chapter 5

Writing Good Sentences

When you talk, you use words. You put your words together to make sentences. Your sentences tell people what you are thinking.

You know that every sentence has a subject and a predicate. A sentence tells a complete thought.

Often, when you talk or write, you may want to put two complete thoughts into one sentence. This chapter will help you to do this correctly.

Part 1 Keeping Thoughts Apart

Read this group of words. How many thoughts does it tell?

> Sam drew a picture the picture showed animals in a farmyard.

Did you find two complete thoughts? Here they are:

1) Sam drew a picture
2) the picture showed animals in a farmyard

Was there any word in the sentence to connect the two thoughts? No, there was not. The two thoughts were simply run together.

This group of words is called a **run-on sentence.** A run-on sentence contains two or more complete thoughts that are not connected. These thoughts should not be run together in one sentence. Each of them should be a separate sentence.

This is how the sample sentence should be written:

> Sam drew a picture. The picture showed animals in a farmyard.

When you separate the thoughts in a run-on sentence, remember to begin each new sentence with a capital letter. Put a period, question mark, or exclamation point at the end of each complete thought.

Keeping Thoughts Apart

A. Some of the following groups of words are good sentences. Others are run-on sentences. Number your paper from 1 to 10. If the word group is a good sentence, write **S.** If the word group is a run-on sentence, decide where the first thought ends. Write the word group as two correct sentences. Use two capital letters and two end marks in the correct places.

1. Linda told a joke to her friends the joke was funny.
2. The Webers' barn is old they might build a new one.
3. Terence showed his new football to his friends.
4. These lemon cookies are good I ate four of them.
5. Marta lives on Park Street her house is yellow.
6. Charles had a nightmare last night about giant ants.
7. The girls had tickets for the baseball game the game was rained out.
8. Mr. Yee owns a hardware store down the street from our school.
9. Larry and his family took a trip to Arizona they saw the Grand Canyon.
10. There are sixty minutes in an hour.

B. Follow the directions for Exercise A.

1. I have a new pair of shoes the shoes are black.
2. Garnet likes to listen to records she likes to dance, too.
3. Ramona's baby sister is learning how to walk.
4. Summer is my favorite season of the year.
5. The snow covered all the cars and buildings.
6. It's raining hard I wish I had an umbrella.
7. Ryan is a good friend of mine.
8. Diane is good in sports she wants to be a basketball player.
9. Cheri is going to Detroit for a visit with her relatives.
10. Wayne mowed the lawn today he is a hard worker.

Part 2   Putting Thoughts Together Correctly

Sometimes you may put two complete thoughts in one sentence. However, you should remember these guidelines:

1. The two thoughts must be about the same topic.

For example, these two sentences could be combined in one good sentence:

> My coat is red. It has gold buttons.

These two sentences could not be combined:

> My coat is red. The phone is ringing.

2. You must use one of these words to connect the two thoughts: *and, or, but.*

Here are some examples:

> My coat is red, *and* it has gold buttons.
> I may buy a new coat, *or* I will use my old one.
> I like my old coat, *but* it is too short.

3. Use a comma before the word that connects the two thoughts.

Reread the sample sentences for Guideline 2. Notice where commas are placed.

4. Do not combine more than two thoughts in one sentence.

A sentence with three or more complete thoughts is called a **stringy sentence.**

Many people use *and* to connect several thoughts without a stop. Here is an example:

> Jean is learning how to cook and she can fix baked beans and she can make peanut butter cookies.

This stringy sentence has three complete thoughts. It should be broken into at least two shorter sentences:

> Jean is learning how to cook. She can fix baked beans, and she can make peanut butter cookies.

When you separate thoughts in a stringy sentence, leave out the connecting *and*. Begin each new sentence with a capital letter. End each new sentence with a period, question mark, or exclamation point.

If you leave two complete thoughts together, be sure you have used a connecting word, and a comma before it.

Here, once more, is the corrected form of the stringy sentence above. Look at how the ideas are organized. Notice where the sentences use capital letters, periods, and a comma.

> Jean is learning how to cook. She can fix baked beans, and she can make peanut butter cookies.

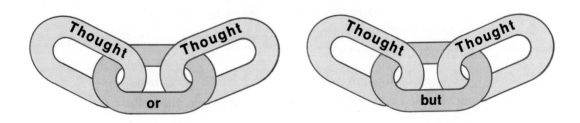

A. Each of the following stringy sentences has three complete thoughts. Rewrite each one as two or three shorter sentences. Be careful to use capital letters, commas, end marks, and connecting words in the right places.

> Example: I have a brother and his name is James and he's seven years old.
>
> I have a brother. His name is James, and he's seven years old.
>
> or I have a brother. His name is James. He's seven years old.

1. Paul was running and he fell and he broke his glasses.
2. We went to the park yesterday and Dad started a fire and we roasted wieners.
3. It was raining and I heard thunder and lightning and I was scared.
4. Sarah turned on the TV and she watched "The Electric Company" and that's her favorite show.
5. The children raced and David won and Maya came in second.
6. Alan planted vegetables and the lettuce is already growing but the carrots aren't up yet.
7. Mom drove to the store and I went along and we shopped all afternoon.
8. Sandy went fishing and she didn't catch a fish but she had a good time.

B. The following word group has several ideas strung together with several *and*'s. Rewrite the stringy sentence as three good sentences.

I went to the fair yesterday and I had a good time and I rode on ten rides and the best one was the roller coaster.

More Exercises — Review

Writing Good Sentences

A. Keeping Thoughts Apart

Some of the following groups of words are good sentences. Others are run-on sentences. Number your paper from 1 to 10. If the word group is a good sentence, write *Sentence*. If the word group is a run-on sentence, decide where the first thought ends. Write the word group as two correct sentences. Use two capital letters and two end marks in the correct places.

1. Brad made a peanut butter sandwich he likes peanut butter.
2. This car is too big for that parking space.
3. The windows are dirty I should wash them.
4. Edna walked to school in the rain her clothes are wet.
5. Ben and Dawn keep their bikes in the garage.
6. Greg moved to Atlanta he made some new friends.
7. Tomas wrapped the present for his mother's birthday.
8. Sally knew the answer she raised her hand.
9. Carla is a new member of our Girl Scout troop.
10. I woke up late I missed the bus.

B. Putting Thoughts Together Correctly

The following word group has several ideas strung together with several *and*'s. Read it carefully. Decide where you can break it into separate sentences. Rewrite the stringy sentence as three good sentences.

Yesterday I saw the movie *War of the Worlds* on TV and in the movie space ships from Mars landed on Earth and Martians climbed out of the ships and they attacked humans.

Chapter 6

Using Nouns

Part 1   What Are Nouns?

We can group people by the work they do. For example, there are carpenters, teachers, doctors, and police officers. We can group words, too, by the work they do.

Can you tell what job all the underlined words are doing?

> My friend has a garden. Roberto grows vegetables and flowers in his garden. The garden is in his yard.

Did you see that all the underlined words have the job of naming? Some of them name a person:

> Roberto   friend

Some of them name places:

> garden   yard

Some of them name things:

> vegetables   flowers

Words that name persons, places, and things are called **nouns.**

Nouns are words that name persons, places, and things.

Here are some nouns that name persons:

     Jane Addams   driver   principal

Can you think of three more?

Here are some nouns that name places:

     school   Denver   forest

Can you think of three nouns of this kind?

Here are some nouns that name things:

     magnet   jeans   Venus

Can you think of three more?

Some nouns name things you can see. Other nouns name things you cannot see. Here are some nouns of this kind:

     friendship   thought   Thursday

Can you think of three more nouns of this kind?

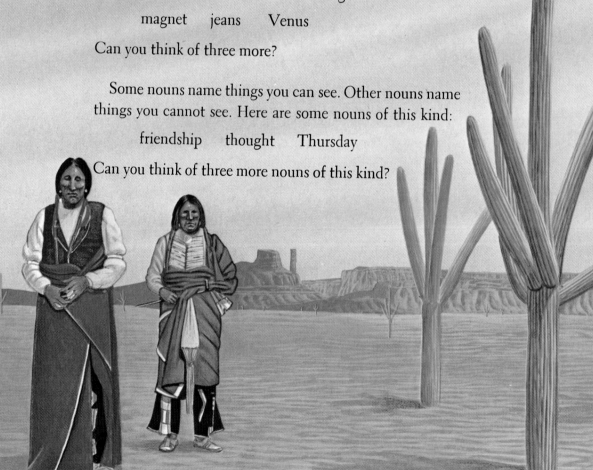

Exercises   Finding Nouns

A. Number your paper from 1 to 10. Find the nouns in each sentence. Write them on your paper.

1. This plum has a sweet taste.
2. Alice visited her cousins.
3. Marlene always tells the truth.
4. Carlos is the best player on our team.
5. June took an apple out of the refrigerator.
6. Dan wrote a letter to his friend in Georgia.
7. Kim rode her bike to school.
8. Clinton won a prize at the carnival.
9. There are only two giant pandas in this country.
10. Gina wrote a report about the Pilgrims.

B. On your paper, make four lists of nouns. Follow these directions.

1. Write the names of three things that you can hold in one hand.
2. Write the names of three things that you can eat.
3. Write the names of three friends.
4. Write the names of three persons, places, or things that you see in the picture below.

Part 2 Using Nouns as Subjects

In Chapter 4, you learned that the two parts of a sentence are the subject and the predicate. You learned that the simple subject is the word that tells *who* or *what* did something.

Nouns are names of persons and things. Nouns tell *who* or *what*. Therefore, nouns may be used as simple subjects. Nouns may also be used in other parts of the complete subject and in the predicate. This makes it hard, sometimes, to find which noun is the simple subject.

Read this sentence. Can you find the simple subject?

Linda hung a poster in our room.

There are three nouns in the sentence. However, only one tells who or what did something. The noun *Linda* tells who or what did something. Linda is the simple subject.

Can you find the noun that is the simple subject in this sentence?

The tallest girl in our room hung the poster.

This sentence has two nouns in the subject part: *girl* and *room*. However, the noun that tells who or what did something is *girl*. *Girl* is the simple subject of the sentence.

Exercises   Using Nouns as Subjects

A. Number your paper from 1 to 10. Find the simple subject in each sentence. Write only the noun that is used as the simple subject.

1. The Indians of the Northeast lived in longhouses.
2. Vera looked for the last piece of the puzzle.
3. Our phone at home isn't working.
4. The photos in your album remind me of last summer.
5. At the rodeo, the cowboys chased a runaway bull.
6. Annette rode her bike to the store.
7. Visitors to our classroom sign a guest list.
8. The star of the show is a dolphin.
9. The miners searched for gold.
10. The powerful winds blew down that old oak tree.

B. Number your paper from 1 to 10. Each sentence needs a subject. Think of two nouns that can be used as the subject. Write the two nouns you thought of.

Example: _____ can ride bicycles.

   Boys   can ride bicycles.

   Girls   can ride bicycles.

1. _____ grow in the spring.
2. _____ is my friend.
3. _____ eat worms.
4. _____ need sun and water.
5. _____ runs very fast.
6. _____ plays the piano.
7. _____ fly very high.
8. _____ can be scary.
9. _____ drink milk.
10. _____ work in hospitals.

65

Part 3 Common Nouns and Proper Nouns

Some nouns can be used for any member of a group. For example, *girl* stands for any girl. *Town* stands for any town. In the sentence *A girl lives in a town,* we cannot tell which girl lives in a town. We cannot tell which town she lives in.

Nouns like *girl* and *town* are called **common nouns.**

Other nouns name a particular member of the group. For example, *Nancy Chang* is one girl. *Los Angeles* is one town. In the sentence *Nancy Chang lives in Los Angeles,* we find out about a certain girl. We learn that she lives in a particular town.

Nouns like *Nancy Chang* and *Los Angeles* are called **proper nouns.** When we write proper nouns, we always begin them with capital letters.

> A **common noun** names a whole group of persons, places, and things.
> A common noun begins with a small letter.
> A **proper noun** names a particular person, place, or thing.
> A proper noun begins with a capital letter.

Many proper nouns are made up of two or more words. For example, *Nancy Chang* has two words. When a proper noun has more than one word, capitalize all the important words. You do not have to capitalize *of, on,* or *the.* Notice where capital letters are used in these proper names.

the Truman Library   the Declaration of Independence

Exercises Finding Common Nouns and Proper Nouns

A. Copy each noun. If the noun is a proper noun, begin it with a capital letter.

1. the united states
2. martin luther king
3. chocolate cake
4. mayor white
5. pacific ocean
6. newspaper
7. friend
8. actor
9. king kong

B. Copy these common nouns. After each one, write the name of a particular person, place, or thing that the word makes you think of.

1. day
2. city
3. month
4. singer
5. car
6. book
7. holiday
8. school

C. Turn to a page in a reader or a storybook. In one column, list all the common nouns that you find on that page. In a second column, list all the proper nouns.

Part 4   Singular Nouns and Plural Nouns

At this moment you are using one book. During the day, you use more than one book. How do you change the word *book* to mean *more than one book?*

Did you say you should add an *s*? When you add an *s* to the word *book,* it becomes *books. Books* means "more than one book."

A word that names one person, place, or thing is called a **singular noun.** *Book* is an example of a singular noun.

A word that names more than one person, place, or thing is called a **plural noun.** *Books* is an example of a plural noun.

When you change a noun from singular to plural, you are forming the plural of the noun.

> A **singular noun** names one person, place, or thing.
> A **plural noun** names more than one person, place, or thing.

68   **rider**

riders

Most nouns form the plural by adding -s. However, not all nouns change in this way.

Follow these rules for forming the plural of nouns.

1. To form the plural of most nouns, add -s.

    stars   boys   needles

    planets   girls   pins

2. When the singular noun ends with s, sh, ch, or x, add -es to make the plural form:

s	gas	gases
sh	brush	brushes
ch	match	matches
x	box	boxes

3. When the singular noun ends in a consonant and y, change the y to i and add -es.

    story—stories   baby—babies

    bunny—bunnies   candy—candies

4. For most nouns ending in f, or fe, add -s. For some nouns ending in f or fe, change the f to v and add -es or -s.

    belief—beliefs   leaf—leaves   shelf—shelves

    chief—chiefs   loaf—loaves   life—lives

    roof—roofs   half—halves   thief—thieves

5. Some nouns are the same for singular and plural.

    sheep   trout   deer   moose

6. Some nouns form their plurals in special ways.

    man—men   woman—women   child—children

    foot—feet   tooth—teeth   mouse—mice

Rules for Forming the Plurals of Nouns

1. **To form the plural of most nouns, add -s.**

2. **When the singular noun ends with s, sh, ch, or x, add -es to make the plural form.**

3. **When the singular noun ends in a consonant and y, change the y to i and add -es.**

4. **For most nouns ending in f or fe, add -s.**
   For some nouns ending in f or fe, change the f to v and add -es or -s.

5. **Some nouns are the same for singular and plural.**

6. **Some nouns form their plurals in special ways.**

Exercises   **Forming Plurals**

A. Copy each pair of nouns below. Then write the number of the rule that tells how the plural was formed.

    Example: ash—ashes, 2

1. knife—knives
2. mother—mothers
3. lunch—lunches
4. fish—fish
5. goose—geese
6. army—armies
7. moose—moose
8. crash—crashes
9. calf—calves
10. bus—buses

B. Copy each of these singular nouns. Then write its plural form.

1. milkshake
2. lady
3. strawberry
4. cowboy
5. butterfly
6. couch
7. life
8. daisy
9. fox
10. robot

Part 5 Making Nouns Show Possession

So far, we have talked about how nouns name people and things. Nouns can do more. They can show that certain things belong to certain people.

Read this example.

> Albert's dog does tricks.
> Who owns the dog? *Albert*

How was the name *Albert* changed to show that Albert owns the dog? Did you notice that *'s* was added?

Here is another example:

> I cleaned the hamster's cage.
> To whom does the cage belong? the *hamster*

How was the name *hamster* changed to show that the cage belongs to the hamster? Did you see that *'s* was added?

The words *Albert's* and *hamster's* are called **possessive nouns.** These nouns show ownership, or possession.

> A **possessive noun** is a noun that shows ownership.

Making Singular Nouns Show Ownership

To make a singular noun show that it owns something, add an apostrophe and *s*.

Singular Noun	Possessive Noun
builder	builder's
Sally	Sally's
Mr. Townes	Mr. Townes's

Making Plural Nouns Show Ownership

There are two rules for making plural nouns show that they own things. If the plural noun ends in *s*, simply add an apostrophe after the *s*.

Plural Noun	Possessive Noun
girls	girls'
boys	boys'

If the plural noun does not end in *s*, add an apostrophe and an *s* after the apostrophe.

Plural Noun	Possessive Noun
men	men's
women	women's

Adding the Apostrophe

Read these examples carefully. Notice where the apostrophe is added.

the miner's tools
This means tools belonging to one miner.

the miners' tools
This means tools belonging to more than one miner.

If you are not sure where to add the apostrophe, write the word by itself first. Then follow the rules.

When you write *'s* in cursive handwriting, do not connect the added *s* to the last letter of the word. The apostrophe should separate the two letters.

cook's hat

cooks' hats

Exercises Making Nouns Show Possession

A. In each sentence, one word is underlined. Write this word so that it shows possession. Write the word first. Then add the apostrophe, or apostrophe and *s*.

1. <u>Kevin</u> popsicle is melting.
2. The <u>dogs</u> tails are wagging.
3. <u>Randy</u> story was exciting.
4. Father gave me a ride to <u>Laura</u> party.
5. <u>Robins</u> eggs are blue.
6. Tracy borrowed <u>Cheryl</u> roller skates.
7. The <u>baby</u> eyes are brown.
8. <u>Superman</u> X-ray vision helped solve the case.
9. My <u>brother</u> hobby is collecting bugs.
10. The photographer took the <u>students</u> pictures.

B. Copy these sentences. Make the underlined words show possession.

1. Isabel is <u>Mario</u> sister.
2. Are you going to <u>Keri</u> birthday party?
3. <u>Giraffes</u> necks are extremely long.
4. The crowd watched the <u>aliens</u> spaceship land.
5. The shoe store is having a sale on <u>ladies</u> boots.
6. My <u>mother</u> flowers are all in bloom.
7. John followed the <u>doctor</u> advice.
8. The dew sparkled on the <u>spider</u> web.
9. The <u>Pilgrims</u> ship landed in America.
10. I saw <u>Darlene</u> cousin at the movies.

73

More Exercises — Review

Using Nouns

A. Finding Nouns

Number your paper from 1 to 10. Find the nouns. Write them.

1. There are fifty stars on the flag of our country.
2. The dog chased the squirrel up the tree.
3. Disneyland is in the state of California.
4. There is a clock on the wall in our classroom.
5. That car has a flat tire.
6. Kangaroos carry their babies in pouches.
7. My father gave a box of candy to my mother on Valentine's Day.
8. The people in the colonies fought for their freedom.
9. Ms. Jordan teaches her students good manners.
10. Lions and giraffes live in Africa.

B. Finding Common Nouns and Proper Nouns

Copy each of these names. If the noun is a proper noun, begin it with a capital letter.

1. spiderman
2. elephant
3. david ives
4. friend
5. boston
6. kathy walsh
7. street
8. name
9. the statue of liberty
10. doctor kiley
11. piano
12. texas
13. the amazon river
14. ship
15. bank
16. new york yankees
17. lake ontario
18. library
19. movie
20. leader

74

C. Forming Plurals

Copy each of these singular nouns. Then write its plural form.

1. bus
2. porch
3. candy
4. woman
5. city
6. box
7. child
8. letter
9. magazine
10. leaf

11. bush
12. country
13. roof
14. elevator
15. deer
16. dress
17. pirate
18. button
19. knife
20. wish

D. Making Nouns Show Possession

Copy the following sentences. Make the underlined words show possession.

1. Mr. Morgan sells <u>men</u> clothes.
2. Doreen returned <u>Beth</u> pencil.
3. The three <u>girls</u> experiment was interesting.
4. Have you seen <u>Alan</u> new bike?
5. Ms. Teller hung the <u>children</u> papers on the board.
6. The <u>woman</u> bracelet was stolen.
7. Lightning struck the <u>Conways</u> house.
8. Many <u>artists</u> paintings are in the museum.
9. <u>Ilona</u> uncle coaches our basketball team.
10. The <u>farmer</u> scarecrow frightened the crows.

Chapter 7

Using Pronouns

Part 1   What Are Pronouns?

Read this paragraph. What is wrong with it?

> Vicky earned money last summer. Vicky babysat for Vicky's aunt. Vicky helped Vicky's neighbors with yard work. Vicky also had a paper route.

Did the paragraph use the name *Vicky* too many times? Here is one way we could improve the paragraph.

> Vicky earned money last summer. **She** babysat for **her** aunt. **She** helped **her** neighbors with yard work. **She** also had a paper route.

What word was used instead of the name *Vicky?* What word was used instead of *Vicky's?*

The words *she* and *her* are called **pronouns.** Pronouns are words used in place of nouns.

77

> A **pronoun** is a word used in place of a noun.

Pronouns are used in place of these three kinds of nouns:

1. Your own name

    Kitty practiced skating on **Kitty's** new skates.
    I practiced skating on **my** new skates.

2. The name of the person you are talking to

    Paul, would **Paul** show us **Paul's** magic trick?
    Paul, would **you** show us **your** magic trick?

3. The names of other persons, places, or things

    The people clapped for **the program.**
    They clapped for **it.**

Like nouns, pronouns can be singular or plural. Usually, the whole word changes to make different forms.

Singular Pronouns			
Person Speaking:	I	my, mine	me
Person Spoken To:	you	your, yours	you
Other Person, Place, or Thing:	he	his	him
	she	her, hers	her
	it	its	it
Plural Pronouns			
Person Speaking:	we	our, ours	us
Persons Spoken To:	you	your, yours	you
Other Persons, Places, and Things:	they	their, theirs	them

Exercises   Using Pronouns for Nouns

A. Number your paper from 1 to 8. Find the pronoun in each sentence. Write it on your paper.

1. I listened to the music.
2. Diana introduced her cousin.
3. Can you deliver the newspapers?
4. Nora showed us the drawing.
5. Mr. Kent washed his car.
6. Phil gave him the present.
7. Lisa said she was hungry.
8. Are your parents coming?

B. Copy the sentences below. Use pronouns instead of nouns to make the sentences sound better.

1. Mike played Mike's records.
2. Betty ate Betty's lunch.
3. The horse won all the horse's races.
4. The gloves lay where George had dropped the gloves.
5. I asked Tim what Tim was doing.
6. The girl's dog obeyed the girl.
7. Carl took pictures with Carl's camera.
8. Teresa watched Teresa's little sister.

C. Number your paper from 1 to 8. Write the pronoun in each sentence. Then write the noun or nouns that it stands for.

1. Booker flew his kite.
2. Donna, please read your answer.
3. Jerry threw the ball, and Andy caught it.
4. Gail spilled her milk.
5. The girls rode their bikes.
6. Norm and Jan thought they would bake some cookies.
7. Ramiro, will you wait here?
8. Melissa returned her library books.

79

Part 2 Using Pronouns as Subjects

The subject of a sentence tells who or what does something. Find the subject of each of these sentences:

1. I met the new boy next door.
2. He came from Idaho.
3. We are both nine years old.

Did you find that the subjects were these pronouns: *I, He,* and *We?*

We often use these pronouns as subjects.

Pronouns We Often Use as Subjects		
I	he	we
you	she	they
	it	

Usually, we have no trouble using these pronouns as subjects. However, when there are two parts in a subject, we sometimes have trouble.

Read the two sentences below. It may be difficult to tell which one is correct.

Richard and I washed the windows.
Richard and me washed the windows.

To figure out which pronoun to use, try each part separately.

Richard washed.
I washed.

Then put the two parts together, using the same pronoun.

Richard and I washed the windows.

Follow the same plan when there are two pronouns as the subject.

(She, her) and (I, me) went shopping.
She went shopping. I went shopping.
She and I went shopping.

Here are two important rules for you to study about using pronouns:

1. These pronouns may be used as the subject:

   I   we   you   he   she   it   they

2. These pronouns may *not* be used as the subject:

   me   us   him   her   them

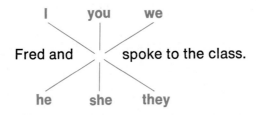

Fred and [I, you, we, he, she, they] spoke to the class.

Using Pronouns as Subjects

A. Number your paper from 1 to 10. Choose the right pronoun. Write it on your paper.

1. Helen and (her, she) tied for first place.
2. (They, Them) are my best friends.
3. Doris and (I, me) made a model airplane.
4. Calvin and (her, she) are the class officers.
5. Mary and (him, he) played in the band.
6. Jerry and (we, us) went to the store.
7. Barbara and (me, I) watched the parade.
8. Ed and (they, them) bought tickets to the game.
9. (He, Him) and Nancy found a quarter.
10. (Us, We) and the Browns are neighbors.

B. Number your paper from 1 to 10. Choose the right pronoun. Write it on your paper.

1. My brother and (I, me) woke up late.
2. Amy and (we, us) went skating.
3. Ron and (me, I) studied together.
4. Carmela and (he, him) like movies about animals.
5. (She, Her) and I came to school early.
6. (They, Them) and their friends enjoyed the play.
7. Randy and (him, he) picked cherries.
8. Ms. Adachi and (us, we) hiked on the trail.
9. Dana and (she, her) grow vegetables.
10. Marvin and (them, they) raced home.

Part 3   Using *Me, Us, Her, Him,* and *Them*

You know that a pronoun may be used as the subject of a sentence. The pronouns *I, we, you, he, she, it,* and *they* may be used as subjects.

If the noun you are replacing is not the subject, you usually use *me, us, her, him,* or *them.*

> Mr. Linden thanked *me.*
> Mr. Linden thanked *us.*
> Mr. Linden thanked *her.*
> Mr. Linden thanked *them.*

You and *it* may be used in any part of the sentence.

> *You* saw me.
> I saw *you.*

If a pronoun is not the subject, you usually use these pronouns:

me   us   her   him   them

Use these pronouns in any part of the sentence:

you   it

Which pronoun should be used in each of these sentences?

> The rain soaked Pat and (I, me) .
> The bus waited for Gene and (she, her) .

How do you choose the correct pronouns? First, find out if the pronouns are the subjects. The subjects of these sentences are *rain* and *bus.* The pronouns you should choose are not the subjects.

You know, then, that both of these sentences follow the rule for *me, us, her, him,* and *them.* Here is the correct way to write the sentences:

The rain soaked Pat and me.
The bus waited for Gene and her.

Using *Me, Us, Her, Him,* and *Them*

A. Number your paper from 1 to 10. Choose the right pronoun. Write it on your paper.

1. Dad bought ice cream cones for the girls and (we, us).
2. The park ranger found Ned and (her, she).
3. Milly was playing with (he, him) and Frances.
4. The crowd cheered for Al and (them, they).
5. Luther met Greg and (I, me) in the gym.
6. The clown made faces at Mom and (us, we).
7. We looked for Mr. Klein and (they, them).
8. The big dog chased Joan and (me, I).
9. We waited for (she, her) and Leonard.
10. Gina talked to Val and (him, he) last night.

B. Follow the directions for Exercise A.

1. The principal gave James and (she, her) the award.
2. Michael invited Christy and (me, I) to his party.
3. Aunt Gloria took Steven and (us, we) to the circus.
4. Harry's dog followed (he, him) and Andrea to school.
5. Have you met Raul and (her, she)?
6. My family will visit my cousins and (them, they) next summer.
7. Doug sent letters to (him, he) and Lorna.
8. Ms. Winter asked Joyce and (I, me) a question.
9. Nicole could not see (they, them) and the bands.
10. Mr. Dudley paid Marla and (us, we) for the work.

Part 4   Using *I* and *Me*, and *We* and *Us*

The pronouns *I* and *me* present special problems. So do the pronouns *we* and *us*.

I and *Me*

Whenever you use *I* or *me* with a noun or another pronoun, use *I* or *me* last.

> Sally and I can play checkers.
> You and I can play checkers.
>
> The dog followed Janet and me.
> The dog followed her and me.

We and *Us*

Read this pair of sentences. Only one is correct.

> We girls learned a new dance.
> Us girls learned a new dance.

When *we* or *us* is used with a noun, try the sentence without the noun.

> We learned a new dance.
> Us learned a new dance.

Now you can see that the pronoun is the subject. As you remember, the pronoun *we* may be used as the subject. The first sentence is correct.

Which sentence is correct in this pair?

> Dad sent we boys on an errand.
> Dad sent us boys on an errand.

Try each sentence without the noun *boys*. It will be clear that the pronoun is not the subject. You know that when the pronoun is not the subject, you use *us*. The second sentence is correct.

Using *I* and *Me*, and *We* and *Us*

A. Number your paper from 1 to 10. Choose the right word or words. Write them on your paper.

1. (Kurt and I, I and Kurt) went skating.
2. (We, Us) girls formed a club.
3. Mr. Granger gave (we, us) winners our prizes.
4. The roof leaked over (Jesse and me, me and Jesse).
5. (We, Us) boys enjoyed the story.
6. (Leslie and I, I and Leslie) decorated the room.
7. (We, Us) gardeners bought our seeds early.
8. Mom bought balloons for (Ann and me, me and Ann).
9. Mrs. Taylor thanked (we, us) hard workers.
10. (We, Us) children planned a picnic.

B. Follow the directions for Exercise A.

1. (Ray and I, I and Ray) sold lemonade.
2. Mrs. Kaplan wished (we, us) players luck.
3. Ms. Johnson chose (Peter and me, me and Peter) for helpers.
4. The police chief talked to (we, us) students about safety.
5. (We, Us) fans cheered our favorite player.
6. (Jane and I, I and Jane) bought tickets for the program.
7. (We, Us) boys collected old newspapers.
8. (We, Us) girls painted those pictures.
9. Mr. Tan waved to (Dom and me, me and Dom).
10. (We, Us) Scouts camped overnight.

The bone is his.

Part 5 Possessive Pronouns

You can make a noun show possession by adding an apostrophe or an apostrophe and *s* to the noun.

Laura—Laura's   singers—singers'

Pronouns change their forms to show possession. The possessive forms of pronouns do not use apostrophes at all.

These are the possessive forms of pronouns:

my, mine   **our, ours**

your, yours   **you, yours**

his, her, hers, its   **their, theirs**

Look at these examples:

This is **my** hamburger. This hamburger is **mine**.
These are **your** French fries. These French fries are **yours**.
Barry has **his** shake. That shake is **his**.
Melina has **her** Coke. That Coke is **hers**.
These are **our** orders. These orders are **ours**.
They have **their** drinks. Those drinks are **theirs**.

Using Possessive Pronouns

A. Copy each sentence. Write a possessive pronoun in the blank. Use the information in red type.

> Example: Tom borrowed _____ pencil. (The pencil belongs to me.)
>
> Tom borrowed my pencil.
>
> That skateboard is _____. (The skateboard belongs to her.)
>
> The skateboard is hers.

1. This bracelet is _____. (The bracelet belongs to her.)
2. Those books are _____. (The books belong to them.)
3. These skates are _____. (The skates belong to us.)
4. This is _____ hat. (The hat belongs to me.)
5. I enjoyed _____ book. (The book belongs to you.)
6. The robin flew to _____ nest. (The nest belongs to the robin.)
7. That puppy is _____. (The puppy belongs to me.)
8. _____ watch stopped. (The watch belongs to her.)

B. Follow the directions for Exercise A.

1. _____ wallet is empty. (The wallet belongs to me.)
2. Please move _____ bike. (The bike belongs to you.)
3. _____ club met yesterday. (The club belongs to us.)
4. The Johnsons painted _____ house. (The house belongs to them.)
5. The best drawing is _____. (The drawing belongs to you.)
6. Tony pulled weeds in _____ garden. (The garden belongs to him.)
7. The dog chased _____ tail. (The tail belongs to the dog.)
8. _____ shoes are new. (The shoes belong to her.)

Sentence Patterns The N V Pattern

Every sentence has a subject and a predicate. The complete subject may have one word or more than one word. If it has more than one word, one is more important than the others. This word is the simple subject. It may be a noun. It may be a pronoun. There may be adjectives in the complete subject. In this chart, N stands for the simple subject. V stands for the verb.

N	V
Susan	called.
He	fell.
The old door	creaked.

The word order in these sentences follows a pattern. That pattern is noun-verb, or N-V. This pattern is called the **N V pattern.**

Exercises The N V Pattern

A. Make a chart like the one above. Label one column N. Label the other V. Write these sentences on the chart.

1. Kittens purr.
2. The plane landed.
3. My T-shirt shrank.
4. The old clock stopped.
5. The brown bear growled.
6. Jill's pet bird talks.

B. Copy this chart. Complete each sentence in the N V Pattern.

N	V
1. _____	shouted.
2. _____	skidded.
3. _____	arrived.
4. _____	waved to us.

More Exercises — Review

Using Pronouns

A. Using Pronouns for Nouns

Number your paper from 1 to 10. Write the pronoun in each sentence. Then write the noun or nouns that it stands for.

1. Dennis ran to his house.
2. Peg saved her allowance.
3. Eric took lessons, and now he can play the trumpet.
4. Alice, can you solve this problem?
5. Brian and Paula wrote their reports.
6. The mouse ate its cheese.
7. Louise ran fast, but she could not catch the bus.
8. Mr. Grant called the students, and they came.
9. John, don't forget your catcher's mitt.
10. Julie dropped the cup, and it broke.

B. Using Pronouns as Subjects

Choose the right pronoun. Write it on your paper.

1. Bill and (she, her) went to the museum.
2. (Him, He) and I set the table.
3. Erma and (we, us) knitted these scarves.
4. Isabel and (I, me) did the experiment together.
5. (She, Her) and her brother own a pet turtle.
6. Aunt Jean and (them, they) listened to the radio.
7. Ruben and (him, he) jumped into the pool.
8. Yuri and (we, us) won prizes at the fair.
9. My friends and (I, me) saw a shooting star.
10. (Them, They) and the twins are in the school play.

C. Using *Me, Us, Her, Him,* and *Them*

Choose the right pronoun. Write it on your paper.

1. Rhoda gave a present to Jason and (I, me).
2. Did Carl take a picture of Ms. Kemper and (us, we)?
3. Sharon picked Ezra and (they, them) for her team.
4. Paco saw Chad and (her, she) in the park.
5. Shawn told the joke to (she, her) and me.
6. Vince walked to school with Wendy and (them, they).
7. Toni looked for Kim and (him, he) all afternoon.
8. Mick left his pets with Phil and (she, her).
9. Judy showed Florence and (I, me) a card trick.
10. The deep snow trapped our neighbors and (us, we).

D. Using Possessive Pronouns

Copy each sentence. Write a possessive pronoun in the blank. Use the information in red type.

1. *Heidi* is _____ favorite book. (The book belongs to me.)
2. Kathy and John are flying _____ kite. (The kite belongs to them.)
3. Doreen kept _____ nametag. (The nametag belongs to Doreen.)
4. Hank chipped _____ front tooth. (The tooth belongs to Hank.)
5. This eraser is _____. (The eraser belongs to him.)
6. The class liked _____ play. (The play belongs to us.)
7. My book is next to _____. (The book belongs to you.)
8. This ball is _____. (The ball belongs to us.)
9. The red coat is _____. (The coat belongs to her.)
10. These magazines are _____. (The magazines belong to them.)

Chapter 8

Using the Exact Word

Do people always understand what you mean? Do you always understand what other people mean?

It is not always easy to say exactly what you mean. Sometimes you are not sure what you want to say. Other times your problem is choosing the right words to express your meaning. This chapter will discuss how important it is to choose your words carefully. You must become more aware of thinking about the exact word. Then you will be able to express yourself more clearly.

Part 1 Synonyms

Synonyms are words that mean the same thing, or almost the same thing. Here are some examples:

picnic, cookout   yell, shout   sport, game

touch, tap, bump, knock, brush, hit, stroke

Usually there is one particular word that most exactly expresses the meaning you have in mind. To find that one best word, you should compare the meanings of several synonyms. The first word you think of may not always be the best for your meaning.

For example, suppose you are describing a chair that is not strong. Here is a list of synonyms for *not strong*.

weak   delicate
shaky   flimsy

Use each synonym in this sentence:

The chair is _____.

Think of how the meaning changes with each word.

A *weak* chair might break if someone sat on it. A *shaky* chair is not steady. A *delicate* chair is made of thin pieces of wood. It would break easily. A *flimsy* chair is poorly made.

To describe a particular chair well, you would have to compare the specific meanings of these synonyms. Then you could choose the one that best describes that chair.

Read this list of synonyms for *big*. Choose the synonym that you think is best for describing an elephant.

huge   thick
broad   tall
spacious   grand

Next, choose the synonym that you would use to describe a dictionary. Did you choose the same word both times? Can you explain why you chose the words you did?

Exercises   **Using Synonyms**

A. Number your paper from 1 to 10. Copy the words in List 1. Next to each word, write its synonym from List 2. Be ready to explain any difference in meaning between the two synonyms.

List 1	List 2
1. run	tardy
2. look	poky
3. hot	race
4. late	powerful
5. strong	hurry
6. touch	infant
7. slow	watch
8. baby	speak
9. rush	tap
10. talk	steaming

95

B. In each of the following sentences, the underlined word must be replaced by one of the synonyms in parentheses. Read the explanation in brackets below each sentence. Then choose the synonym that best expresses the meaning in the explanation.

1. Libby's jacket was <u>old</u>. (ragged, old fashioned)
   [The jacket was out of style.]
2. The wooden box was <u>big</u>. (enormous, large)
   [Three people were needed to move the box.]
3. The police <u>followed</u> the thief. (chased, trailed)
   [The police found clues that the thief had left along his way.]
4. Jeannie <u>moved</u> across the room. (walked, glided)
   [Her movements were extremely smooth.]
5. George answered <u>quickly</u>. (thoughtlessly, rapidly)
   [He did not take time to find out what the question meant.]
6. The fielder <u>grabbed</u> the ball. (snatched, caught)
   [The ball was almost out of reach over the fence.]
7. Tiny is an <u>active</u> puppy. (busy, restless)
   [Tiny never stays in one place for more than a minute.]
8. Ben bought a <u>picture</u> of a boat. (photograph, drawing)
   [The picture was made with a camera.]
9. Ms. Washington <u>directed</u> us to clear our desks. (asked, ordered)
   [She said, "When you have time, put your desks in order."]
10. Is there room in the trunk to <u>fit</u> in one more box? (put, squeeze)
   [The trunk is already crowded with boxes.]

Part 2   Using Words To Express Feelings

In Part 1, you read about synonyms for *weak*. You learned that both a *delicate* chair and a *flimsy* chair could break easily. However, a delicate chair is well made. A flimsy chair is poorly made. Our feelings about these words are different.

Delicate suggests a good feeling. We call it a **positive** word. *Flimsy* suggests an unpleasant feeling. We call it a **negative** word. *Weak* itself does not suggest any particular feeling. We call it a **neutral** word.

Suppose you feel good about something. You will want to use positive words about that thing. Maybe you dislike or feel unhappy about something. You will want to use negative words to tell about it. Your words will do two jobs. They will describe the object. They will also describe your feelings.

Here are three synonyms: *thin, scrawny, slender. Thin* is neutral. *Scrawny* is negative. It suggests too much thinness. *Slender* is positive. It suggests just the right amount of thinness.

The following chart compares negative, neutral, and positive synonyms in sets of three. Read the chart. Can you think of a sentence for each word? Use negative words to tell about things you dislike. Use positive words for things you like.

Negative	Neutral	Positive
dull	uneventful	quiet
picky	careful	accurate
out-of-date	old	antique
noise	sound	music

Worms are slimy.   Worms are juicy.

Using Words To Express Feelings

A. Write a sentence about each of these subjects. Do not say *I like* _____ or *I don't like* _____. Use specific positive or negative words to show your feelings. Then exchange papers with a classmate. The other student should be able to tell which things you like and which you don't like.

> Example: hamburgers
>
>> Mom served thick, juicy hamburgers on warm buns.   like
>>
>> We bit into the dry, thin hamburgers served on stale buns.   dislike

1. butterscotch topping
2. the smell of gasoline
3. the feel of velvet
4. the ticking of a clock
5. the color purple
6. tomatoes
7. hats
8. fairytales
9. detective programs
10. the season of fall

B. Make two columns on your paper. Write *Negative* at the top of the first column, and *Positive* at the top of the second. Write each of these words in the correct column. Then add two of your own words to each column.

1. slimy
2. to hiss
3. sunny
4. a miracle
5. to smile
6. harsh
7. a disaster
8. to snarl
9. friendly
10. to enjoy
11. sloppy
12. tasty

Part 3   Being Alert to How Others Use Words

It is important to know when words are neutral, negative, or positive. Sometimes your listener understands your meaning better because of the feelings a word gives. Sometimes you can make your listener think the same way you do because of those feelings.

The people who write commercials know how powerful words are. They use positive words to make you feel good about their product. They know that if you feel good about the product, you may buy it.

Compare these two sentences.

Have a piece of strawberry cheesecake at Simpson's Restaurant.

Enjoy a mouth-watering piece of Strawberry Dream Cheesecake in Simpson's comfortable dining room.

The first sentence uses neutral words. The second sentence uses positive words. The pie may be the same, but the second sentence makes you hungrier for it.

When you listen to commercials, it is important to notice the positive words. Find out if the commercial gives a strong reason for using the positive words.

Read this sentence from a commercial:

Munchy Snacks are good for you.

Did you notice the positive word *good?* Can you find any reason that backs up the positive word? There is no reason. You should not let the word *good* by itself convince you to buy the snacks.

Now read this sentence:

Munchy Snacks are good for you because they contain three kinds of dried fruit.

In this sentence, there is a reason for the positive word. Fruits are necessary in a balanced diet.

However, the sentence doesn't say whether dried fruit is the major ingredient in Munchy Snacks. It doesn't tell what else is in the Snacks. It doesn't say whether the Snacks taste good. All these things may be important to you. You still don't know whether you agree with the word *good.* However, if you like the fact that Munchy Snacks contain dried fruit, you might decide to look for them at the store to find out more about them. The positive word *good* by itself did not persuade you to buy the snacks.

Every commercial uses positive words. Don't let these words persuade you to buy the product. Try to imagine each commercial in neutral words. You can then make up your own mind about whether you want to try the product.

Better! IMPROVED!
New!

A. Listen carefully to several commercials, or read several ads in the paper or in magazines. List ten positive words used in the commercials.

B. Find one commercial or ad that gives at least one reason for using positive words. Copy the commercial. Underline the positive words and the reason. Be ready to tell whether you think the reason is strong enough to make you buy the product.

C. Make up a TV commercial for Nancy's Candy Bar. Rewrite each of these sentences. Use positive words that will make your listener want to buy a candy bar.

1. Do you want something to eat?
2. There's a new candy bar.
3. It has peanuts and chocolate and raisins.
4. The candy bar is called Nancy's Candy Bar.
5. The candy bar is in a red wrapper.

Chapter 9

Writing Paragraphs

How do you express an idea? In writing, you write a sentence about it. You try to make it a good sentence. You want the sentence to express your idea.

Sometimes, however, one sentence is not enough to explain your idea. You need more sentences. When you write several sentences to explain one idea, you are writing a paragraph.

In this chapter you are going to learn about paragraphs. You will begin by learning what a paragraph is.

Part 1   What Is a Paragraph?

A paragraph is a group of sentences. Here is an example of a paragraph.

> Far to the South, where it is very hot, live the animals that like hot weather. There the lively Monkey hides in the leaves. The shy Zebra gallops over the grass. The fat Hippopotamus rises yawning out of the river. The proud Giraffe peers over the tallest trees. The Ostrich fluffs its fine tail feathers.
>
> —INGRI AND EDGAR PARIN D'AULAIRE

The paragraph has six sentences:

1. Far to the South, where it is very hot, live the animals that like hot weather.
2. There the lively Monkey hides in the leaves.
3. The shy Zebra gallops over the grass.
4. The fat Hippopotamus rises yawning out of the river.
5. The proud Giraffe peers over the tallest trees.
6. The Ostrich fluffs its fine tail feathers.

Here is another paragraph.

> On Saturday, Evan went to the playground. He took his toothbrush glass and a spoon. The paving of the playground was cracked. Grass and weeds grew up through the broken concrete. Evan found a weed that had big, lacy flowers on it. He dug it up with his spoon. He planted it in his toothbrush glass. Then he took it home and put it on the windowsill, in his own corner.
>
> —ELIZABETH STARR HILL

The paragraph has eight sentences. What are they?

Look again at the two paragraphs. The first line of each is **indented.** It does not begin at the left margin. It begins a few spaces to the right. This is one way to signal the beginning of a paragraph.

More About Paragraphs

A paragraph explains one idea. Here are two paragraphs. After each paragraph there is a question. Answer it in your own words.

Paragraph 1

Here is a trick you can teach a goldfish. Each time you feed him, first tickle the top of the water in a corner of the tank. Your finger will make little ripples. The goldfish will feel the ripples with his body. Then feed your fish right away. Soon he will learn that your finger is calling him to dinner. He will swim right up to his dining room. You can say, "Dinnertime!" too. The fish won't understand your words, but your friends will like the trick better.   —SARA BONNETT STEIN

What is the paragraph about?

Paragraph 2

Deep in the forest, there lived a young hunter called Waupee, or White Hawk. He was tall and strong. He walked unafraid through the gloomiest woods. He could follow a track made by any bird or beast. Every day he would return to his lodge with game. He was one of the most skillful hunters of his tribe.   —JOHN BIERHORST

What is the paragraph about?

The main idea of paragraph 1 is how to teach a trick to a goldfish.

The main idea of paragraph 2 is a hunter called White Hawk.

Reading Paragraphs

Here are three paragraphs. Read them. Then answer these questions about each.

1. How many sentences does the paragraph have?
2. What are the sentences?
3. What is the main idea of the paragraph?

Paragraph 1

On the porch steps three small children were sitting in the sunshine. The girl in the middle had lots of freckles. She had two red pigtails that stuck straight out. On her right side sat a blond, curly-haired girl in a blue-checkered dress. On her left side sat a little boy with neatly combed hair. On the shoulder of the redheaded girl sat a monkey. —ASTRID LINDGREN

Paragraph 2

Suddenly the world seemed to stop. A hush settled over the hills. The sky swirled soundlessly round the moon. The river stopped murmuring. The wind stopped whispering. The frogs and the owls and the crickets fell silent. They were all watching and waiting and listening. —EZRA JACK KEATS

Paragraph 3

All around his house Jay could see hills. He could see hills when he stood whittling in the kitchen doorway. He could see hills when he swung on the gate in front of his house. When he climbed into the apple tree beside his house, he could see hills.—REBECCA CAUDILL

Part 2 Studying Paragraphs

The main idea of a paragraph is told in one sentence. This sentence is the **topic sentence.** It is often the first sentence. The rest of the sentences tell more about the main idea.

Telling the Main Idea

Here is a paragraph. Can you tell what the main idea is?

> When I was five years old, I discovered a wonderful creature. It looked like a bird, but it was able to do things that many other birds cannot do. It swam and dove in the lakes. Sometimes it just floated on the water's silver surface. It could also waddle in the tall grass that grew along the edges of the water. The bird was called *méksikatsi*. In the Blackfoot language this means "pink-colored feet." Méksikatsi was the perfect name for the swim-fly bird. It really did have bright pink feet.—JAMAKE HIGHWATER

All of this paragraph is about one bird. The first sentence tells you that it is a "wonderful creature." The first sentence is the topic sentence.

Finding the Topic Sentence

Here are two more paragraphs.

Paragraph 1

> Most plants need three things to live and grow. They need soil. They need water. They also need plenty of sunlight.

What is the main idea of this paragraph?
What is the topic sentence?

Paragraph 2

Everyone knows about Spider. He is a favorite person in the stories of West Africa. He is clever and mischievous. He loves to eat and he hates to work. He plays so many tricks that he gets into a lot of trouble. When he is good, though, he is full of fun.

—JOYCE COOPER ARKHURST

What is the main idea of this paragraph?
What is the topic sentence?

A topic sentence gives the main idea of a paragraph.

Studying Topic Sentences

Here are two paragraphs. Read them. Then answer these questions.

1. What is the main idea in each?
2. What is the topic sentence in each?

Paragraph 1

Arabelle decided to plant a garden. She dug up a bare corner of the backyard. She turned over the dirt with a shovel. She chopped the dirt fine with a hoe. She smoothed it flat and soaked it. Then she planted poppy seeds, pansy seeds, carrot seeds, tomato seeds, some old bush bean seeds, and the watermelon seeds from her lunch.

—BEVERLY KELLER

Paragraph 2

The fisherman had heard many stories about the cougarfish. He had heard that the cougarfish was a wild and savage fish. It had long tentacles like an octopus, armed with sharp, catlike claws. Its giant head was the head of a cougar, with snarling, fanglike teeth. —GEORGE MENDOZA

Adding to the Main Idea

The topic sentence gives the main idea of a paragraph. The rest of the sentences add to, or develop, the main idea.
Read the following paragraph.

1 Chinese cooks use three kinds of soy sauce. 2 The first is light soy. 3 It is named *sang chau.* 4 The second is dark, or black, soy. 5 It is named *see au.* 6 A third kind is thick soy, or bead molasses. 7 Its Chinese name is *jee yau.*

The first sentence is the topic sentence. It tells what the paragraph is about. The paragraph is about three kinds of soy sauce. This is the main idea. The rest of the sentences tell more about this idea.

The second sentence names one kind of soy sauce.
The third sentence tells the Chinese word for it.
The fourth sentence names another kind of soy sauce.
The fifth sentence gives the Chinese word.
The sixth sentence names a third kind of soy sauce.
The seventh sentence gives the Chinese word.

109

Each sentence adds to, or develops, the main idea.

> The sentences in a paragraph develop the main idea of the paragraph.

Exercise **Studying a Paragraph**

Read the following paragraph. Then answer the questions after it.

> [1]Soup is served in many ways. [2]It can be clear and thin. [3]It can be thick with ingredients like meat, vegetables, fish, and even fruit. [4]Some soup is served hot. [5]Some is served cold. [6]Soup can be part of a meal or a whole meal by itself.—HANNAH LYONS JOHNSON

1. What is the topic sentence?
2. What is the main idea of the paragraph?
3. What does the second sentence tell about the main idea?
4. What does the third sentence tell about the main idea?
5. What does the fourth sentence tell about the main idea?
6. What does the fifth sentence tell about the main idea?
7. What does the sixth sentence tell about the main idea?

Part 3   Reviewing Topic Sentences

A topic sentence gives the main idea of a paragraph. It is often the first sentence in a paragraph.

Studying Topic Sentences

In Part 2 you studied topic sentences. Let's take a look at a few more.

Here is a paragraph. It begins with a topic sentence.

> Mexican-American children play this game. Players start with legs apart. They jump and put their right legs in front. They jump back to their starting position. Then they jump again. They put their left legs in front. They chant this rhyme as they jump:
> Elephant, elephant, sitting on a bench,
> Trying to make a dollar out of fifty-five cents,
> He missed, he missed, he missed like this . . .
> A player caught with a leg in front at the end of the rhyme is out. The others go on.—RUBEN SANDOVAL

The topic sentence tells you that the paragraph is about a game. This is the main idea.

Here are two more topic sentences.

1. One night in Uncle Charlie's barn was enough for me.
2. The sounds of summer were all around us.

What will the first paragraph be about? What will the second paragraph be about?

111

A topic sentence gives the main idea of a paragraph.

Here are five topic sentences. They will begin five separate paragraphs. Explain what each paragraph will be about.

1. Ruby is a special rabbit.
2. Our new house is too small.
3. *Elmo the Magnificent* is not a good movie.
4. Yesterday I wrote to the President.
5. I read an exciting book last week.

Identifying the Main Idea

To write a good topic sentence, you must first be able to recognize a main idea.

Here is a paragraph. The topic sentence is not complete. Read the paragraph. Try to decide what it is about.

Olga _____. She is a great bowler. She gets good grades in school. She rollerskates and can ride horseback. She knows the words to all the hit songs. She is also blind.

Here are three choices for topic sentences.

1. Olga has nice parents.
2. Olga has a Seeing Eye dog.
3. Olga is a special person.

Sentence 1 would not make a good topic sentence for this paragraph. The paragraph has nothing to do with Olga's parents.

Sentence 2 would not be a good choice either. The paragraph is not about her Seeing Eye dog.

Sentence 3 is the best choice. Each sentence in the paragraph tells something that makes Olga special. This is the main idea. Sentence 3 states that idea.

In a paragraph, all the sentences tell about the main idea.

Choosing the Main Idea

Here are three paragraphs. Three sentences are listed after each. Choose the one that would make the best topic sentence.

Paragraph 1

_____(topic sentence)_____ On New Year's Eve, everyone stays home. The children go to bed early. The older folks stay up. Some time during the night a man visits each house. He asks parents for a report of their children's behavior. If the report is good, he secretly wishes the children a happy new year. If the report is bad, he makes sure that something bad happens to those children during the coming year.

113

1. The Senecas are a Native American group.
2. The Seneca people have a New Year's tradition.
3. The Senecas belonged to the Iroquois Federation.

Paragraph 2

_____(topic sentence)_____ His coat was matted with rain and mud. He shivered in the chill wind. His large, unhappy eyes pleaded for help.

1. One cold night a sad-looking dog scratched at our door.
2. One dog liked dried food better than canned.
3. Some dogs have long, silky hair.

Paragraph 3

_____(topic sentence)_____ Some of us form teams and play tug-of-war. We have a jacks tournament almost every week. Small groups play hopscotch. Some days everyone joins in a fast game of tag.

1. I like to play games.
2. Games are fun.
3. The children in my class have fun at recess.

Part 4   Pre-Writing: Planning a Paragraph

You have learned what makes a good paragraph. You have learned what makes a good topic sentence. Now you will learn how to write your own paragraph.

Before you write, you must first plan your paragraph.

Choosing a Topic

Think of many topics you might write about. A topic may be something you are interested in. It may be something you like to do. Sometimes your friends can give you good ideas, too. Make a list of all the possible topics.

Now read the list over carefully. Which topic gives you the most ideas of things to say? Choose the topic you can think of many ideas for.

Here is an example of one boy's topics. Robert made this list:

1. My hobby
2. My vegetable garden
3. My vacation last summer
4. Things I see on the way to school

Robert read his list. He thought about the things he could say about each topic. He chose the one for which he had many ideas. He decided to write about his vegetable garden.

Exercise   Choosing a Topic

Write four or five topics for your paragraph. Think about them. Choose the topic you want to write about.

Taking Notes

The next step is to write down several ideas about your topic. These notes will help you choose your main idea.

Here are Robert's ideas about his vegetable garden.

Planning the garden in spring
Tomatoes in rows
Need lots of sunshine
Flowers around the edges

Beans and corn
Picking vegetables
Planting pumpkins
Wear my old clothes

Exercise **Taking Notes**

Write down several ideas about your topic. For now, put down any ideas that you have on this topic.

Choosing a Main Idea

When you wrote your notes, you probably thought of many things to say. Notice that some of your notes fit together. They all tell about one idea. This can be the main idea of your paragraph.

Robert read his list of ideas. He decided that his garden took a lot of work. That would be the main idea of his paragraph. At the bottom of his list he wrote his main idea:

The work I put into my garden.

Exercise **Choosing a Main Idea**

Read your list of ideas. Decide on the main idea for your paragraph. Write it below your list.

Making a Plan

Now you can plan your paragraph. Read your list of ideas again. You may find ideas that do not fit together with the rest. Cross them out. You will not include them in your paragraph. You may think of new ideas. Add them to your list.

Exercise   Making Your Plan

Read your list of ideas. Cross out ideas that do not belong there. Add new ideas if you think of them.

Part 5   Writing a Paragraph

Now you are ready to write your paragraph. Read over the main idea you wrote below your list of ideas. Write a full sentence that tells the main idea. That is your topic sentence.

Reread your list of ideas about the topic. Write at least one full sentence about each idea. Make each sentence tell more about the main idea.

You may think of more things to say. Add the new ideas to your list. Write sentences about those ideas in your paragraph.

Robert wrote this topic sentence.

I work hard on my vegetable garden.

Then he added sentences about the other ideas on his list.

Exercise

Write your paragraph. First write a topic sentence. Then write sentences for each of your ideas.

Part 6   Revising a Paragraph

Now you have written your paragraph. However, you may want to make changes on your paragraph. These changes will make your paragraph better. Making these changes is called revising, or editing, a paragraph.

Revising for Ideas

The first step in revising is to reread your paragraph. As you read, ask yourself the following questions.

Guides for Revising

1. Is the paragraph easy to understand?
2. Is every group of words a sentence?
3. Do all the sentences tell about the same thing? Should any sentence be taken out?
4. Does the paragraph need more sentences? Do any sentences need more words?

There are **symbols,** or marks with special meanings, that you can use for marking your changes. You will find the symbols on page 119.

Proofreading

The next step in revising your paragraph is to **proofread.** When you proofread, you read the paragraph carefully. Look for mistakes in your use of capital letters and punctuation marks. Check your spelling. Look for words used in the wrong way.

As you go through your paragraph, you will find some mistakes. Use the symbols in the following chart to mark your corrections. You can use the symbols in both revising and proofreading.

Symbols for Revising and Proofreading

Symbol	Example	Meaning	Correction
≡	a	Capitalize a letter.	A
/	ᗷ	Change a capital letter to a lowercase letter.	b
∧	libary	Add letters or words.	library
—	too	Leave something out.	to
⊙	Mr.	Add a period.	Mr.
∿	aks	Trade places.	ask

Here is part of Robert's revised paragraph. Notice how he marked his changes.

I work hard on my vegetable garden. In Spring I decide ^what~ to plant. I plant the peas and radishes first, and later I plant corn, tomatoes, and pumkins^p. ~I don't like radishes but my mother asks for them.~ My favorites ^vegetables~ are the pumkins^p.

Robert noticed that he had three ideas in one group of words. He inserted periods to separate the ideas into three sentences. He decided that the sentence about not liking radishes didn't fit his main idea. He drew a line through it, to show he wished to leave it out. Then he realized he had forgotten a word in the second sentence, and so he added it. He moved, dropped, and added other words to make the sentences clearer.

Then he checked capital letters, punctuation marks, and spelling, and marked several more corrections.

Exercise   Revising a Paragraph

Reread your paragraph carefully. Ask yourself the questions in the Guides for Revising and the Guides for Proofreading. Mark any changes you want to make.

Making a Clean Copy

Now you will make the final copy of your paragraph. Write it in your best handwriting. Look at the marks you made when you revised your paragraph. Make the changes you have marked.

Here is Robert's finished paragraph.

I work hard on my vegetable garden. In spring I decide what to plant. I plant the peas and radishes first. Later I plant tomatoes, corn, and pumpkins. My favorite vegetables are the pumpkins. I plant them in little mounds. I weed my garden every day. When the vegetables are ripe, we pick and eat them. Then I don't mind the work.

Exercise Making a Clean Copy

Write your paragraph on a clean sheet of paper. Make all the changes you marked on your first copy. Use your best handwriting. Your paper should be clear and readable. Make it easy for anyone to read and enjoy.

Chapter 10

Improving Your Speaking and Listening Skills

Sometimes you need to exchange information with someone. Suppose your mother receives an important telephone call. Do you know how to take a message?

If you make an announcement, do you get the facts right?

How well do you give directions?

Good speaking and listening take practice. Let's begin with telephone skills.

Part 1 Using the Telephone

Suppose you want to get a message to one of your parents at work. You will probably have to leave the message with someone else. Know what you are going to say before you call. Then speak clearly. Here is what Sara says to the secretary at her mother's office.

VOICE: Good morning. Taylor and Company. Ms. Berman speaking.

SARA: Hello. My name is Sara Baker. I would like to leave a message for my mother, Mrs. Baker.

VOICE: Yes, Sara. What is your message?

SARA: I did not go to my piano lesson today. My teacher is sick. I came home instead. Please tell my mother.

VOICE: All right, Sara. I will tell your mother that you are at home. Your piano lesson was cancelled.

SARA: Thank you, Ms. Berman.

VOICE: You're welcome. Goodbye, Sara.

SARA: Goodbye.

Sara gave her name and her mother's name. Then she gave Ms. Berman her message. She listened while Ms. Berman repeated the message. She remembered to thank Ms. Berman.

Why didn't Sara talk longer? Do you think she should have told Ms. Berman about her day at school?

Sometimes you will be the one to take a message. Try to remember these things:

1. Keep pencil and paper near the phone.
2. Write down messages.
3. Be sure to get the facts right.
4. Ask for the name and phone number of the person calling.

The example below shows how Meiko takes a message.

MEIKO: Hello. This is Meiko speaking.

VOICE: Hi, Meiko. This is Al Stern. Is your dad there?

MEIKO: No, Mr. Stern. He'll be home at five. May I take a message?

VOICE: Yes, you may. Please tell him that our hiking club will meet Monday night at eight o'clock.

MEIKO: I'll tell him that Mr. Stern called. The hiking club will meet at eight next Monday night.

VOICE: That's right. Thanks, Meiko.

MEIKO: You're welcome, Mr. Stern. Goodbye.

VOICE: Goodbye, Meiko.

Meiko says his name when he answers the phone. He offers to take a message. He writes down what Mr. Stern says. Then he reads the message back.

Why do you think Meiko repeats the message?

Here are some guides. They will help you remember your telephone skills.

Guides for Using the Telephone

1. Speak politely. Say your name.
2. Know what you want to say before calling someone.
3. If someone gives you a message, write it down.
4. Read back the message. Check the facts.
5. Don't waste the other person's time.
6. Say goodbye politely.

A. Work in pairs. Act out one of these telephone calls. One person should make the call. The other should receive the call. Follow the Guides for Using the Telephone.

1. Donna calls her father at his plant. She wants to tell him that she forgot her housekey, and that no one else is home. The switchboard operator answers the call. Donna leaves a message.

2. Mark calls his friend Ralph. He wants Ralph to meet him at the gym after school. Ralph's sister Sharon takes the message.

3. Mr. Lane calls your mother. His car is in the repair shop. He would like to ride to work with your mother tomorrow. You take the message.

B. Read the telephone call below.

PEGGY: Hello.

VOICE: Hello. Who is speaking, please?

PEGGY: Peggy. Who are you?

VOICE: This is Ms. Simmons. May I please speak to your mother?

PEGGY: She's not here.

VOICE: Please ask her to call me. Here is my new phone number: 863–5481.

PEGGY: Okay. I hope I can remember it. Goodbye.

(She hangs up.)   **127**

Peggy has made many mistakes. What are they? Discuss her mistakes in class. Try to correct them.

Part 2 Making Announcements

Making announcements requires careful preparations.
First you must gather the facts. Then you must arrange them.
Practice making your announcement several times.
Check yourself. Are you speaking clearly? Can people hear
you? Are the details in your announcement correct?

Let's look at a sample announcement. Here is what Diego
tells the other classes in his school.

Next Tuesday is Arbor Day. Mr. Wong's class will
have a tree-planting ceremony. Some people will read
poems. Others will sing. Three of us will help plant
the tree. The ceremony will be at three o'clock in front
of the school. We hope you will come.

Now study these guides.

Guides for Making Announcements

1. Speak clearly. Your voice should be loud enough to be heard.

2. Look at the people listening to you.

3. Include all the important facts.

4. Be sure your information is correct.

Exercises   Making Announcements

A. Read the information below. Copy the important items about the Drama Club. Then write an announcement about the Drama Club meeting. Include the items you copied.

1. The Drama Club will meet next Monday.
2. Next Monday is St. Patrick's Day.
3. All interested students should come to the meeting.
4. We will see a movie called *Putting on a Play*.
5. The meeting will be in Mr. Hope's room.
6. The Safety Patrol will have a picnic on Monday.
7. The Drama Club meeting will begin at 3:00.

B. Make up an announcement for a coming event. Then pair off. Practice giving your announcement to your partner. Follow the Guides for Making Announcements. After the practice, take turns making your announcements in class.

Part 3   Giving Directions

It is important to explain carefully when you give directions. Otherwise people will be confused. You must tell exactly what to do, step by step.

In the example below, Karen tells her class how to make a bird feeder. Here is what she says.

You will need four things. They are a pine cone, a piece of string, some beef suet, and some bird seed. Beef suet is the fat from beef. You can get it at your grocery store.

Mix the bird seed with the suet. Fill the layers of the pine cone with the mixture. Tie the string to the end of the pine cone. Then hang the pine cone on a tall bush or a tree branch.

Do you have any questions?

Now let's look at some guides.

Guides for Giving Directions

1. Speak clearly.

2. Choose words that give exact information.

3. Don't leave out any steps. Give the steps in the correct order.

4. Invite your listeners to ask questions.

Exercises   **Giving Directions**

A. Read the directions below. What is wrong? Rewrite the directions. Give exact information. Put the steps in the right order.

MAKING A CHICKEN SANDWICH

Spread the bread with butter or mayonnaise. You will need two slices of bread. You will also need butter or mayonnaise and several slices of chicken. Some people like lettuce on the sandwich. You may want to have some lettuce. Lay the chicken on the bread. Wash the lettuce. Put it on, too. Cut the sandwich in half. Eat it.

B. Draw a simple design, using your choice of circles, squares, triangles, and lines. Write a set of directions for drawing your design. Then pair off. Do not show your design to your partner. Practice giving your directions to your partner.

See how well your partner can draw your design following your directions, without seeing your paper. Have you followed the Guides for Giving Directions?

Now say your directions for the class. Discuss them with each other.

Part 4   Listening To Learn

When you read, your eyes help you learn. You can also learn with your ears. When you think about what you hear, you are listening.

Daydreaming

We don't always listen well. Sometimes we daydream when others talk. Let's look at an example.

> Cliff opened his reader. He listened. Several students read aloud. Then Cliff began to daydream. He gazed out the window and thought about his tree house. He had worked on it all weekend.
> "Cliff, please read next," the teacher said.
> Her voice startled Cliff. He had lost the place. He didn't know where to begin reading.

Cliff had stopped listening. For the last few minutes, he had not learned. Cliff would have extra work to do after school.

Asking People To Repeat

Sometimes we don't hear well. Perhaps people are speaking softly. Perhaps the room is noisy. If you don't hear, ask people to repeat. They seldom mind doing so. Here is an example.

> When Kate met Janet, she didn't hear Janet's name. At first Kate didn't want to ask Janet to repeat her name. Finally, she asked her. Now Kate feels at ease with Janet. It helps to call her new friend by name.

Asking Questions

To learn, you must understand what you hear. Sometimes things are not clear. Don't stay confused. Ask questions. Be sure you have the facts straight. Let's look at Milo's problem.

> Milo's teacher said, "Ponce de Leon discovered Florida in 1513." Milo was confused. He knew America was discovered in 1492. Florida is part of America. Milo asked his teacher to explain. He learned because he was not afraid to ask a question.

The guides below will help you remember how to listen.

Guides for Listening To Learn

1. Pay attention.
2. If you don't hear something, ask someone to repeat it.
3. If you are confused, ask questions.

Exercises   Listening To Learn

A. Close your eyes for twenty seconds. Listen. Then open your eyes. Write down everything you heard. Talk about those things in class. Did everyone hear the same things?

B. Listen as your teacher reads to you. Answer these questions.

1. What was the main idea of the paragraph?
2. Name three objects mentioned in the paragraph.
3. Write a question about the paragraph.

133

C. Form groups of three or four. With your group, make a poster. Show times when listening is important. You may draw pictures, use magazine photographs, or make a comic strip.

Chapter 11

Talking in Groups

By talking with others, you can make plans. You can solve problems. You can also learn more about something you have studied.

Talking in groups lets you share ideas. When you share ideas, you can understand things better. You won't always agree with everyone in your group. When you disagree, it is important to speak politely.

Part 1 Sharing Ideas

To share ideas, you must think clearly. You must also keep the discussion moving.

In the example below, the group is talking about their social studies lesson. Read what they say. Then answer the questions.

MARY:	In France most people buy their bread at a bakery. It is always fresh.
TOM:	Doesn't the bread come in long, skinny loaves?
JUAN:	Yes. The baker doesn't slice it.
ELLEN:	People buy the bread whole. They break off pieces to eat.
JUAN:	Do the bakeries ever close?
MARY:	I think most of them close on Wednesdays.
ELLEN:	My mom bakes bread. She puts sour milk in it.
TOM:	That sounds awful. Is the bread sour?
ELLEN:	Not really. The sour milk makes the bread soft.
JUAN:	We're getting off the subject. What happens in France when the bakeries close?
MARY:	One bakery in each neighborhood stays open on Wednesday. Each week a different baker keeps his shop open on Wednesday.
TOM:	Let's see if we can get someone to talk to our class about customs in France.
JUAN:	Good idea. I'll ask Ms. Booth. She may know a speaker who can come.

The discussion began very well. Each person who spoke added an idea. Then the group got off the subject. Where did that happen? How did they get back on the subject again?

Now answer these questions in class.

1. What questions did people in the group ask?
2. How did the questions help the discussion move ahead?
3. How did the group bring the discussion to a close?

The guides below will help you learn to share ideas when you talk in groups.

Guides for Sharing Ideas

1. Stay on the subject.
2. Add new ideas to the discussion.
3. Ask questions.
4. Help bring the discussion to a close.

Exercises Sharing Ideas

A. Form groups of four or five. Decide on a topic for discussion. Talk together for ten minutes. Follow the Guides for Sharing Ideas.

Here are some ideas for discussion topics.

1. A program or play that you saw with your class
2. Problems in taking care of pets
3. Plans for a field trip or class party
4. A subject that you have studied in school.

B. When your discussion ends, answer these questions on your paper.

1. What did your group talk about?
2. What ideas did you add to the discussion?
3. Did you ask a question? If so, what was it?
4. How did your group bring the discussion to a close?

Part 2   Disagreeing Politely

When you talk with others, you should say what you think. Sometimes you will disagree with someone else. At such times, it is hard to be both truthful and polite. What should you do?

Here are some ways to handle disagreements.

Listening to Others

The first step is to try to understand the problem. Listen carefully. Ask questions. Learn what other people think.

Now let's look at an example.

Nan and Paula share a bedroom. Nan has put her doll collection under Paula's bed. Paula gets angry. Finally, they talk about their problem. Paula finds out that their parents have stored old clothes under Nan's bed. There is no room for Nan's dolls. Paula is glad she listened to Nan. Now she can understand Nan's problem. The girls decide to talk to their parents. Perhaps the clothes can be moved.

Avoiding Hurt Feelings

You should be honest, even when you disagree with someone else. However, you should try not to hurt anyone's feelings. Let's look at some problems others have had.

1. Pedro is having corn for dinner. He doesn't like corn. It would be rude to say, "I hate corn." What could he say?

2. Suppose your mother is wearing a new dress. You think it is not in style. She asks you, "Do you like my new dress?" You don't want to hurt her feelings. However, you want to be honest. What could you say?

Admitting Mistakes

Disagreements can be upsetting when people are stubborn. Try to keep an open mind. If you are wrong, say so. Otherwise, you may end up like George. See the example below.

George didn't like snow. He refused to play outdoors in winter. His friends tried to get him to go sledding. He wouldn't even try. Finally, his friends gave up. Every afternoon they took their sleds to the slopes. George went home alone. He wished he had gone sledding. George couldn't admit he had been wrong.

When you must disagree with others in your group, try to follow the guides on the next page. Remember that it is normal for friends to have different opinions on some things.

Exercises   Disagreeing Politely

A. Think about these two problems. Write your answers on your paper. Then discuss your answers in class.

1. Your parents expect you to wash dishes, make your bed, and take out the trash. They want you to do these chores in the morning. Today your duties made you late for school. After dinner, you want to talk over the problem. How do you begin?

2. Your family wants to get a dog. You want to pick out a dog from the animal shelter. Your sister Molly wants to buy a dog at the pet shop. You don't like her attitude. You think Molly is silly and snobbish. What would you say to her?

B. Mr. Kaplan's students are planning a program on China. They are discussing what to do. Here is what they say.

MARK: Let's invite Mr. Yang to talk to us.

SUSAN: That's no fun. I think we should put on a play.

CARLA: We could use our puppets.

MARK: I still think we could invite Mr. Yang.

BILL: Let's do both. Mr. Yang could talk to us about his village. Then we could do a puppet show.

SUSAN: Speeches are boring.

MARK: Cut it out, Susan. You just want to show off. I think puppet shows are dumb.

141

What is wrong here? Discuss your answers in class. Suggest changes. Be sure to follow the Guides for Disagreeing Politely.

Chapter 12

Using the Dictionary

Why do some people know more words than other people know? How can you learn more words? How can you learn more about the words you already know?

A dictionary is a helper. It can teach you many things about words. Many times you will read a new word. You may not know what it means. You may have trouble sounding it out. A dictionary can help you. It can make the word clear to you, and easy to use.

However, before a dictionary can help you, you must learn how to use it. This chapter will show you how.

Part 1 Entry Words

A dictionary is really a very long word list. In this word list, you can find most of the words in the English language. Each word that is listed in the dictionary is called an **entry word.** The dictionary explains the meaning of each entry word. Look at the sample dictionary page on page 145. You will find two columns of entry words on the page.

Look at the sample dictionary page on page 145.

Exercises **Entry Words**

A. Make a list of any ten entry words that you find on the sample dictionary page.

B. Make a list of six entry words from the sample dictionary page that begin with capital letters. These words are written with capital letters because they are names of particular people, places, or things.

Part 2 Finding the Word You Want

Every dictionary lists thousands of words. How do you find the one word you are looking for? To begin, you must understand how the words are put in order.

Using Alphabetical Order

The entry words in a dictionary are in alphabetical order. This makes it easy for you to find the word you are looking for. Words that start with A are in the first part of the dictionary. The words that start with B come next. The words that start with C come next, and so on. All the words that start with the same letter are put together.

i·so·la·tion·ist (ī'sə lā'shən ist), *n.* a person who believes his country should not take part in international affairs. —**i'so·la'tion·ism,** *n.*

i·sos·ce·les triangle (ī säs'ə lēz), a triangle that has two equal sides.

i·so·therm (ī'sə thûrm), *n.* a line on a map connecting places where the average temperature is the same.

i·so·tope (ī'sə tōp), *n.* any of two or more forms of a chemical element having the same atomic number but different atomic weights.

isosceles triangle

Is·ra·el (iz'ri əl), *n.* **1.** a country at the eastern end of the Mediterranean. **2.** an ancient Hebrew kingdom in Palestine. **3.** in the Bible, the name given to Jacob after he wrestled with the angel. **4.** the Jewish people, as descendants of Jacob.

Is·rae·li (iz rā'lē), *adj.* of modern Israel or its people. —*n.* a person born or living in modern Israel.

Is·ra·el·ite (iz'ri əl īt'), *n.* any of the people of ancient Israel; also, any Jew.

is·su·ance (ish'ōō əns), *n.* the act of issuing.

is·sue (ish'ōō), *n.* **1.** a sending out or giving out [the army *issue* of clothing to the soldiers]. **2.** a thing or group of things sent or given out [the July *issue* of a magazine]. **3.** a problem to be talked over [New paving is an *issue* in our town.] **4.** a flowing out; outflow [*issue* of water from a pipe]. **5.** a result; outcome [The *issue* of the battle was in doubt.] **6.** a child or children; offspring [Elizabeth I died without *issue*.] —*v.* **1.** to put forth or send out [The city *issues* bonds. The general *issued* an order.] **2.** to give or deal out; distribute [The teacher *issued* new books.] **3.** to go forth or flow out [Blood *issued* from the wound.] **4.** to come about as a result [Victory *issued* from our efforts.] —**at issue,** to be decided. —**take issue,** to disagree. —**is'sued,** *p.t. & p.p.*; **is'su·ing,** *pr.p.*

-ist (ist), a suffix meaning: **1.** a person who [A *moralist* is one who moralizes.] **2.** a person who is skilled in or who works at [An *artist* is one skilled in art.] **3.** a person who believes in [A *socialist* is one who believes in socialism.]

Is·tan·bul (is'tän bōōl'), *n.* a city in the European part of Turkey: see **Constantinople.**

isth·mus (is'məs), *n.* a narrow strip of land with water on each side, that joins two larger bodies of land [the *Isthmus* of Panama].

it (it), *pron.* the animal or thing being talked about [I read that book and liked *it*.] *It* is also used as: **1.** the subject of a clause to refer to another clause that comes later [*It* is settled that he will go.] **2.** a word referring to the condition of the weather or to things in general [*It* is snowing. *It's* all right; no harm was done.] —*n.* in some children's games, such as tag, the player who must try to catch another. —**they,** *pl.*

i/t/a or **I.T.A.,** abbreviation for **Initial Teaching Alphabet,** an alphabet of 44 letters, each having a single sound: it is used for teaching beginning students to read English.

I·tal·ian (i tal'yən), *adj.* of Italy, its people, etc. —*n.* **1.** a person born or living in Italy. **2.** the language of Italy.

i·tal·ic (i tal'ik), *adj.* describing printing type in which the letters slant upward to the right: it is used to call attention to words [*This is italic type*.] —*n.* **italics,** *pl.* italic type: sometimes used with a singular verb.

i·tal·i·cize (i tal'ə sīz), *v.* **1.** to print in italic type. **2.** to underline something written, to show that it is to be printed in italics. —**i·tal'·i·cized,** *p.t. & p.p.*; **i·tal'i·ciz·ing,** *pr.p.*

It·a·ly (it'ə lē), *n.* a country in southern Europe, including the islands of Sicily and Sardinia.

itch (ich), *v.* **1.** to have a tickling feeling on the skin, that makes one want to scratch. **2.** to have a restless desire [He's *itching* to leave.] —*n.* **1.** an itching feeling on the skin. **2.** a skin disease in which this feeling is very strong. **3.** a restless desire [an *itch* to buy a car]. —**itch'y,** *adj.*

-ite (īt), a suffix meaning: **1.** a person born in [A *Canaanite* was one born in Canaan.] **2.** a person who believes in or supports [A *laborite* is a supporter of a labor party.]

i·tem (ī'təm), *n.* **1.** a separate thing; one of a group of things; unit [Check each *item* on this list.] **2.** a piece of news or information.

i·tem·ize (ī'təm īz), *v.* to list the items of, one by one [Please *itemize* my purchases.] —**i'tem·ized,** *p.t. & p.p.*; **i'tem·iz·ing,** *pr.p.*

it·er·ate (it'ə rāt), *v.* to say or do over again; repeat. —**it'er·at·ed,** *p.t. & p.p.*; **it'er·at·ing,** *pr.p.* —**it'er·a'tion,** *n.*

Ith·a·ca (ith'ə kə), *n.* an island off the west coast of Greece: said to be the home of Odysseus.

i·tin·er·ant (ī tin'ər ənt), *adj.* traveling from place to place [an *itinerant* preacher]. —*n.* a person who travels from place to place, especially in connection with his work [Farm work in some parts of the country is done by *itinerants*.]

i·tin·er·ar·y (ī tin'ə rer'ē), *n.* **1.** the route that one travels or plans to travel on a journey. **2.** a record of a journey. —**i·tin'er·ar'ies,** *pl.*

it'll (it'l), **1.** it will. **2.** it shall.

its (its), *pron.* of it or done by it: the possessive form of *it*, thought of as an adjective [Give the cat *its* dinner. The frost had done *its* damage.]

it's (its), **1.** it is. **2.** it has.

it·self (it self'), *pron.* its own self: the form of *it* that makes the subject also the object of the verb [The dog scratched *itself*.] *Itself* is also used to give force to a noun [Life *itself* was not dearer to him than freedom.]

-i·ty (ə tē), a suffix meaning "condition" or "quality" [*Acidity* is the condition or quality of being acid.]

I've (īv), I have.

Of course, many words will have the same first letter. When that happens, they are listed in alphabetical order by the second letter. For example, *me* is listed before *my*. *Bat* is listed before *boat*. What happens when both the first and second letters are the same? Those words are listed by the third letter. For example, *their* comes before *them*.

Here are some words listed in alphabetical order:

By first letter	By second letter	By third letter
ape	race	spark
bear	ready	special
cat	rider	splash
dog	rules	spot

Exercise   Using Alphabetical Order

Here are six groups of words. Put each group of words into alphabetical order.

1	2	3
brother	Amy	match
cousin	Steve	move
aunt	Debbie	drive
sister	Bill	do
father	Peter	mail
uncle	Mary	deal

4	5	6
spider	peanut	Josephine
squash	plant	John
swim	pet	Joe
summer	pepper	Joan
sled	plum	Joy
snow	pest	Jody

Opening a Dictionary at the Right Place

Look at the picture of an open dictionary. It has been opened at about the middle. The first half is on the left side. The second half is on the right side. Words starting with A through L are in the first half. Words starting with M through Z are in the second half.

A–L   M–Z

Open your dictionary about in half. What letters do you see? You should see words starting with L or M. These letters are in the middle of the alphabet.

Let's say that you want to find a word that starts with a letter from A through L. Look for your word in the first half of the dictionary. The first half is on the left. Let's say that you want to find a word that starts with a letter from M through Z. Then look in the second half of the dictionary.

Practice opening your dictionary to different letters. This will help you to find words quickly.

Exercises   Opening a Dictionary at the Right Place

A. Choose a partner. Ask your partner to say a letter. Then try to open your dictionary as close as you can to that letter. Then let your partner have a turn. Practice until both of you can open to nearly the right place most of the time.

B. Copy the following words. Decide in which half of the dictionary you would find each word. Write *A-L* or *M-Z* beside each word.

moon	beach	piano	planet	sand
star	wave	drum	space	ocean

Using Guide Words

Many dictionaries have **guide words** at the top corners of each page. The guide words are in heavy, black type. They guide you to the word you want. The guide word at the left is the first entry word on that page. The guide word at the right is the last entry word on that page. All the entry words on the page are in alphabetical order. In alphabetical order, they come *between* the two guide words on the page.

Look again at the sample dictionary page on page 145. Can you find the guide words? They are *isolationist* and *I've*. Look quickly at all the other words on these pages. They are in alphabetical order. They come between *isolationist* and *I've*.

Learn to watch for guide words as you use a dictionary. Watch for guide words that start with the same letter as the word you want. Then watch for the same second and third letters. Look for guide words that come before and after your word.

Exercises   **Using Guide Words**

A. On the left are eight sets of guide words. On the right is a list of entry words. Copy the sets of guide words. Find an entry word that would come on the *same* page as each set of guide words. Write the entry word next to the set of guide words.

	Guide Words	Entry Words
1.	corner—correct	order
2.	orchid—organic	thrill
3.	reed—refit	corral
4.	thought—throb	refill
5.	spire—split	slice
6.	bank—barbecue	bone
7.	sleeve—slip	banker
8.	boiler—boot	splash

B. In the following list there are sets of guide words from a dictionary. After each set of guide words is an entry word. Is that entry on a page *before* the guide words? Is it on a page *with* the guide words? Is it on a page *after* the guide words?

Number your paper from 1 to 10. For each item on your paper, write *before*, *with*, or *after* to tell where the entry word is.

Example: **Guide Words**   **Entry Word**

ham—hat   has

Has comes between *ham* and *hat* in the alphabet. Therefore, you would find *has* on the page *with* the guide words *ham* and *hat*. *With* is the right answer.

Example: **Guide Words**   **Entry Word**

tooth—trap   trip

Trip comes after *trap* in the alphabet. Therefore, you would find *trip* on a page *after* the page with the guide words *tooth* and *trap*. *After* is the right answer.

Guide Words	Entry Word
1. bakery—banana	balloon
2. Hank—heavy	hide
3. rubber—rust	rose
4. melt—mill	mighty
5. base—bear	beam
6. rainy—ranch	ram
7. link—listen	lion
8. decided—declare	deeply

C. Look up each of these words in your dictionary. Copy the guide words from the page where you find each one.

149

1. houseboat   4. North Pole   7. grasshopper
2. sailboat   5. equator   8. locust
3. rowboat   6. South Pole   9. cricket

Part 3   Finding the Pronunciation

The first thing a dictionary tells about an entry word is its pronunciation. The **pronunciation** is the right way to say the word.

Finding the Respelling

In most dictionaries, the entry word is printed in dark black letters. After the entry word come some strange-looking letters in parentheses. These letters are the **respelling.** The respelling is different from the usual spelling. It uses special letters and marks that show the pronunciation of the word.

Look at the sample dictionary page on page 145. Find the respelling of several words.

Using the Pronunciation Key

Every dictionary has a **pronunciation key.** The pronunciation key explains the special letters and marks used in the respellings of entry words. The key tells what sounds these letters and marks stand for.

On the sample dictionary page, the pronunciation key is at the bottom. Turn to that page. Find the pronunciation key.

Understanding the Respelling

How can the respelling help you? Let's say that you wanted to know how to pronounce *isthmus*. Find *isthmus* on page 145. The entry word and respelling look like this:

isth·mus (is′ məs)

Do you see the symbol ə (called *schwa*) in the respelling of *isthmus*? Find ə in the pronunciation key. The key shows that the ə sound is like the *a* sound in *ago*.

There is another special mark in the respelling of each entry word. Find the entry word *item* on page 145. Look at the respelling. It looks like this:

i·tem (i′ tem)

In the respelling, the word is broken into parts. Each part is called a **syllable.** The slanted line between syllables is called an **accent mark.** Accent marks tell you which part, or syllable, of a word is said in a strong voice. The dictionary has placed an accent mark after the first part of the word *item*. When you say the word *item*, you say this:

Item

You say the first syllable of the word more strongly than you say the second syllable.

Just to hear the difference, say the word *item* incorrectly. Say this:

iTEM

Doesn't the word sound strange? The accent marks help you to say new words correctly.

rough (ruf)

women (wim´ in)

nation (nā´ shən)

GHOTI TANK

Exercises **Finding the Pronunciation**

A. Here are six sets of words and their respellings. In each set, two of the three words rhyme, or have the same ending sound. Number your paper from 1 to 6. For each set, write the words that rhyme.

1. tough (tuf)   through (thro͞o)   rough (ruf)
2. weight (wāt)   fight (fīt)   height (hīt)
3. dough (dō)   though (thō)   cough (kôf)
4. seek (sēk)   beak (bēk)   break (brāk)
5. rind (rīnd)   reigned (rānd)   signed (sīnd)
6. ounce (ouns)   once (wuns)   dunce (duns)

B. Here are eight words and their respellings. Find the accent mark in each respelling. Number your paper from 1 to 8. Write which syllable has the accent—first, second, or third.

Example: tomato (tə mā´ tō)
         second syllable

1. kitten (kit´ n)   5. afraid (ə frād´)
2. peanut (pē´ nut)   6. stranger (strān´ jər)
3. hello (he lō´)   7. diabetic (dī ə bet´ ik)
4. entertainment   8. imagine (i maj´ in)
   (en tər tān´ mənt)

Part 4   Finding the Meaning

Definitions are the largest part of each dictionary entry. The definition tells what the entry word means. Find the entry word *italic* on page 145. Read the definition. Now you know that *italic* means "slanted type."

Sometimes definitions may sound a little strange. They aren't full sentences. Sometimes the words in the definitions are hard to understand. You'll get used to reading definitions. It takes practice.

Many definitions are followed by a sample sentence. The sentence shows one meaning of the word. For example, look at the entry for *itch*. Definition 2 has this sentence:

He's *itching* to leave.

Many words have more than one meaning. A dictionary gives all the meanings of each entry word. Each definition is numbered. You may have to choose from more than one meaning of a word. You need to be able to find the one that fits best. Look at this sentence:

The newscaster read an item about the zoo.

What does *item* mean? Read the entry for *item* on page 145. *Item* has more than one meaning. Which one fits the sentence?

Try each definition in the sentence. Would a newscaster read "a separate thing" about the zoo? No, that meaning of *item* does not fit this sentence. Try the other definition of *item*.

Would a newscaster read "a piece of news or information" about the zoo? Yes, that makes sense. Definition 2 gives the correct meaning.

Always be careful to choose the definition that fits the meaning of the sentence.

entry word   meaning

gale (gāl)   a strong wind

pronunciation

Exercises   **Finding the Meaning**

A. Number your paper from 1 to 6. Look at the entry for *issue* on the sample dictionary page. There are six definitions for *issue* used as a noun. There are four definitions for *issue* used as a verb. Choose the best definition for *issue* in each of the following sentences. Write the definition beside each number.

1. At our class meeting, we discussed the issue of our field trip.
2. Water issued from the broken dam.
3. Mom bought the latest issue of *Good Housekeeping*.
4. The general was not worried about the issue of the battle.
5. The theater will issue free tickets for this program.
6. The principal issued an order against skating on the playground.

B. Read the sentences below. Each one has an underlined word. Look up the definition of each underlined word in your dictionary. Write the meaning that best fits the sentence.

1. My hamster is a <u>voracious</u> eater.
2. The <u>legend</u> on the map explained its different marks.
3. <u>Sloth</u> keeps me from cleaning my room.
4. The hungry children <u>bolted</u> their food.
5. They used a <u>machete</u> to make a jungle path.
6. The dictionary is a <u>mine</u> of information.
7. In sports <u>jargon</u>, a *goose egg* means a zero.
8. The boy in this story sailed on a <u>clipper</u>.

154

More Exercises — Review

Using the Dictionary

A. Finding the Word You Want

Look up each of these words in your dictionary. Copy the guide words from the page where you find each one.

1. arrow
2. diamond
3. heart
4. vanilla
5. chocolate
6. strawberry
7. milk
8. fruit
9. meat

B. Finding the Pronunciation

Here are six sets of words and their respellings. In each set, two of the three words rhyme. Number your paper from 1 to 6. Write the words that rhyme in each set.

1. aisle (īl)   paisley (pāz′ lē)   file (fīl)
2. caught (kôt)   drought (drout)   thought (thôt)
3. rake (rāk)   arch (ärch)   ache (āk)
4. debt (det)   ticket (tik′ it)   met (met)
5. noise (noiz)   fuse (fyo͞oz)   bruise (bro͞oz)
6. gnaw (nô)   awe (ô)   ewe (yo͞o)

C. Finding the Meaning

Read the sentences below. Each one has an underlined word. Look up the definition of each underlined word in your dictionary. Write the meaning that best fits the sentence.

1. The rancher wore new chaps.
2. It's a mean trick to put a kiwi in a tree.
3. Don't strew popcorn at the theater.
4. Does it irk you to forget your lunch money?
5. What is the girth of that giant tree?
6. Gail packed her winter clothes in a trunk.

155

Chapter 13

Using Verbs

Part 1 Verbs That Tell About Action

What can you do in a baseball game?

You <u>throw</u> a baseball.
You <u>hit</u> the ball.
You <u>play</u> in the outfield.

The underlined words tell what you can do. They tell about action. Words that tell about action are **verbs.** Can you think of other verbs that tell about actions in a baseball game?

Many verbs tell about actions you can see. For example, you can see someone *throw*, *hit*, and *play*. Other verbs tell about actions you cannot see. The underlined words in these sentences tell about actions you cannot see:

Jerry <u>likes</u> hot weather.
Sarah <u>thought</u> about vacation.
Ted <u>knew</u> many Cherokee legends.

157

A. Copy these sentences. Underline the verb in each sentence.

1. Thunder scares my dog.
2. Eric combed his hair.
3. The frog jumped into the pond.
4. Elena painted a picture.
5. Pioneers built log cabins.
6. The children hoped for snow.
7. Melissa plays the organ.
8. Adam wished on a falling star.
9. My sister Joy marched in a parade.
10. Eddie returned his books.

B. Think of a verb that will complete each sentence. Copy each sentence. Fill in the blank with your verb. There are many different correct answers for each sentence.

Example: Jeannie _____ a peach.

Some Possible Answers:

       Jeannie wanted a peach.
       Jeannie ate a peach.
       Jeannie picked a peach.

1. Jeff _____ the rose.
2. My cat _____ over the fence.
3. Dana _____ to the game.
4. The police _____ the robbers.
5. April _____ a new sweater.
6. Randy _____ the window.
7. I _____ the movie.
8. Joanna _____ the Frisbee.
9. The pirates _____ the treasure.
10. Paco _____ the song.

Part 2 Verbs That Say That Something Is

Many verbs tell about action. However, there is another kind of verb. This other kind says that something is. Here are some examples:

> Peggy <u>is</u> my friend.
> Boats <u>are</u> on sale now.
> I <u>am</u> here.

Here are some verbs that say that something is:

am   is   are   was   were

Jana **jumps** higher than anyone else.

Ira **is** on the bench.

> **Verbs** are words that tell about action or say that something is.

Exercises   Finding the Verb

A. Copy these sentences. Some of the sentences have verbs that tell about action. Others have verbs that say that something is. Underline the verb in each sentence.

1. Darren lost a nickel.
2. The truck stopped suddenly.
3. I am nine years old.
4. Kevin and Chip study together.
5. A squirrel was on the windowsill.
6. My jeans are in my closet.
7. Marta skates very well.
8. Polly is early.
9. David poured a glass of milk.
10. The floor was dirty.

B. Number your paper from 1 to 10. Find the verb in each sentence. Write it down. Be ready to tell whether it tells action or states that something is.

1. Our class enjoyed the play.
2. German shepherds are smart dogs.
3. Chuck slipped on the ice.
4. Luci likes peppermint ice cream.
5. The cars were in the parking lot.
6. George Washington was our first president.
7. Erica laughed at Tom's joke.
8. Lauren is the pitcher on our team.
9. The sun is a star.
10. Carrie followed the trail.

Part 3   Main Verbs and Helping Verbs

Some verbs are only one word.

Kathy <u>talked</u>. Bob <u>listened</u>.

Many other verbs are more than one word. Notice the verbs in these sentences. The verbs are underlined.

Kathy <u>was talking</u>.
Bob <u>should have listened</u>.

When a verb is more than one word, the last word is the **main verb.** The parts of the verb that come before the main verb are the **helping verbs.** Here are some examples:

	Helping Verbs	Main Verb
My watch has stopped.	has	stopped
Nora will close the window.	will	close
Larry has been studying hard.	has been	studying

The main verb often ends in *-ing* or *-ed*.

Here are some verbs that are often used as helping verbs:

am   is   are   was   were   have   has   had
                                    do   does   did

These verbs are always used as helping verbs:

can   will   shall   may
could   would   should   might

> A verb may be a single word or group of words. A verb with more than one word is made of a **main verb** and one or more **helping verbs.**

Exercises Finding Main Verbs and Helping Verbs

A. Copy each sentence. Underline the main verb and the helping verb or helping verbs.

1. You should brush your dog's coat.
2. My parents might buy a new car.
3. Cheryl may stay for dinner.
4. The people were waiting for the bus.
5. Birds can fly.
6. Frank was finishing his report.
7. Lisa can stand on her head.
8. Our team has won the game.
9. Barry will keep his promise.
10. The snow is falling.

B. Number your paper from 1 to 10. Make two columns. Head the first column *Helping Verbs*. (Some sentences have only one helping verb.) Head the second *Main Verb*. Write the verbs for each of these sentences in the correct column.

Example: The dragon would have eaten the princess.

Helping Verbs	Main Verb
would have	eaten

1. I am wrapping the present.
2. Phil would have played with me.
3. Tanya will be visiting her aunt.
4. Mr. Garcia was driving the school bus.
5. You may play outside.
6. We should have worn boots.
7. Lupe has been swimming.
8. The monster might be hiding in the woods.
9. The flowers will bloom in the spring.
10. The door should have been open.

Part 4 Using Helping Verbs

Can you tell what is missing in each of these sentences?

Jack gone to the beach.
Pearl delivering papers.

In each sentence, the verb is not complete. The sentences do have verbs. However, they need helping verbs also. Here are some guidelines for using helping verbs.

Always use helping verbs with these four verbs:

> **been   done**
> **seen   gone**

Verbs that end in -en must be used with helping verbs.

Here are some examples of verbs that end in -en:

> fallen   eaten
> broken   risen

Verbs that end in -ing must be used with helping verbs.

Here are some examples of verbs that end in -ing:

> being   doing   falling   eating
> seeing   going   breaking   rising

Use the right helping verb.

The fish **has** eaten.   The fish **was** eaten.

A. Number your paper from 1 to 10. Read each sentence. If the sentence is correct, write *Correct*. If the verb needs a helping verb, write a helping verb and the main verb. There may be more than one correct helping verb.

Example: James calling his cousin Alicia.

Some Possible Answers:

> is calling
>
> was calling

1. Peter done his work.
2. The wind was blowing hard.
3. Ken broken his glasses.
4. Loretta playing shortstop.
5. Vincent seen the elephants at the zoo.
6. The leaves are falling.
7. Brian chosen a partner.
8. Rabbits like carrots.
9. Angela and Tina gone on a picnic.
10. The clothes are spinning in the dryer.

B. Follow the directions for Exercise A.

1. Terence was listening to the radio.
2. Risa should have hurried.
3. Raymond and Max gone to the park.
4. My basket bursting with apples.
5. Chad might be moving to a new home.
6. The lights blinking.
7. The class elected Beth president.
8. I been hoping for a sunny day.
9. Al coming to the party.
10. The logs were burning.

Lightning **does** not often **strike** twice in the same place.

Part 5   Separated Parts of Verbs

Sometimes a helping verb does not come right before the main verb. Here are some examples.

José **had** never **ridden** a motorcycle.
Mona **will** always **remember** this adventure.
Humpty Dumpty **should** not **have been sitting** on a wall.
Ms. Lester **has**n't **come** for her package.

Notice that *not* and *n't* are not verbs.

Questions often begin with a helping verb. Then other parts of the sentence come between the helping verb and the main verb.

Did you **hear** a siren?
Doesn't the movie **begin** at two o'clock?

Exercises Finding Separated Parts of the Verb

A. Number your paper from 1 to 10. Make two columns. Head the first column *Helping Verb*. Head the second *Main Verb*. Write the verbs for each of these sentences in the correct columns.

Example: Did Theresa bring her lunch?

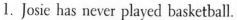

Helping Verb	Main Verb
did	bring

1. Josie has never played basketball.
2. Would you like a doughnut?
3. Michael is usually called Mike.
4. My father doesn't enjoy disco music.
5. The horse could not jump over the fence.
6. Mano's dog has always barked at cars.
7. Alison hasn't eaten dinner yet.
8. Albert did not follow the map.
9. Is Micky taking a picture of us?
10. The baby is still sleeping.

B. Follow the directions for Exercise A.

1. Nicole has not missed a day of school.
2. Dan could barely lift the weights.
3. Did you water the plants?
4. Flo will never forget this party.
5. I have always wanted his autograph.
6. May I eat a snack now?
7. This corn is really growing tall.
8. You should not pet strange dogs.
9. My friend from Mexico had never seen snow before.
10. Fish can't live outside of water.

Part 6   Using the Right Form of *Be*

The verb *be* has many forms:

is	was	be
are	were	being
am		been

Here are five important rules to remember in using the forms of the verb *be*:

1. Use a helping verb before the forms *be, being,* and *been.* Do not use one of these forms alone or as the only helping verb before a main verb.

> Dad *will be coming* soon.
> The boys *are being driven* to the airport.
> Nita *has been cleaning* the garage.
> We *have been* here for an hour.

2. If the subject names one person, place, or thing, use the form *is* or *was.*

> Billy *is* a good runner. He *is running*
>   in the junior marathon.
> Rachel *was* best in basketball. She
>   *was practicing* all the time.

3. If the subject names more than one person, place, or thing, use the form *are* or *were.*

> The twins *are* good runners. They
>   *are running* in the junior marathon.
> Rachel and Jean *were* best in basketball.
>   They *were practicing* all the time.

4. When the subject is *you,* use the form *are* or *were.*

You *are* the winner. You *are getting* first prize.
You girls *were* helpful. You *were working* hard.

5. When the subject is *I,* use the form *am* or *was.*

I *am* the winner. I *am getting* first prize.
I *was* helpful. I *was working* hard.

Exercises Using the Right Form of *Be*

A. Number your paper from 1 to 10. Choose the right form. Write it on your paper.

1. Kristen (was, were) buying a poster.
2. You (is, are) my friend.
3. Scott (was, been) saving his money.
4. I (am, is) learning a magic trick.
5. We (be, are) collecting old newspapers.
6. The children (were, was) hiking in the park.
7. My sister (is, am) moving to Chicago.
8. You boys (is, are) good singers.
9. I (been, was) watching the parade.
10. You (were, was) standing on thin ice.

B. Follow the directions for Exercise A.

1. Dwayne and Sharon (be, are) selling lemonade.
2. We (was, were) watching the fireworks.
3. The traffic light (is, are) red.
4. You girls (have been, was) decorating the room.
5. Robert (being, is) a good dancer.
6. We (are, is) excited about vacation.
7. The Franklins (be, have been) visiting us.
8. Amanda (was, been) shoveling snow.
9. You (are, is) wearing a pretty ring.
10. I (was, be) late for school.

Part 7   Using Contractions

Sometimes a verb is combined with another word to make a
new word. The new word that is made in this way is called a
contraction. Read this list of contractions.

I am	I'm	is not	isn't
I will	I'll	are not	aren't
I had,		was not	wasn't
I would	I'd	were not	weren't
I have	I've	has not	hasn't
he had,		have not	haven't
he would	he'd	can not	can't
he will	he'll	will not	won't
she is,		does not	doesn't
she has	she's	do not	don't
it is,		did not	didn't
it has	it's	would not	wouldn't
we will	we'll	here is	here's
you are	you're	there is,	
they are	they're	there has	there's
they have	they've	where is	where's

In contractions, one or more letters are dropped in making
the new word. For example, *she* and *is* are combined to make
she's. *Was* and *not* are combined to make *wasn't*.

169

Whenever we write a contraction, we use an **apostrophe
(')** to show where letters are left out. Look at the list of
contractions again. Notice where letters are dropped.

Exercises Making Contractions

A. Copy the contractions. Place the apostrophe where it belongs.

1. couldnt
2. hasnt
3. theyll
4. its
5. doesnt
6. Im
7. shouldnt
8. theyre
9. hes
10. werent
11. theyd
12. isnt

B. Copy the contractions. After each contraction, write the two words it is made from.

1. I'll
2. don't
3. here's
4. wouldn't
5. they've
6. won't
7. aren't
8. he'll
9. wasn't
10. you're
11. I've
12. didn't

C. Copy each sentence. Make a contraction of the underlined words.

1. <u>She is</u> the best runner in the class.
2. Kirk <u>could not</u> reach the top shelf.
3. I <u>have not</u> seen that program.
4. <u>They have</u> raked the leaves.
5. The TV set <u>is not</u> working.
6. Penguins <u>can not</u> fly.
7. <u>There is</u> enough food for everybody.
8. <u>You are</u> welcome.
9. Martin <u>did not</u> expect the party.
10. <u>I will</u> never tell our secret.

Part 8   Using Negatives Correctly

Some contractions are made by joining *not* with certain verbs, like this: are + not = aren't.

The apostrophe (') takes the place of the *o* in *not*. Words made in this way are called *not*-words.

have + not = haven't   is + not = isn't
were + not = weren't   do + not = don't
would + not = wouldn't   could + not = couldn't

There are some other words called *no*-words. You can see *no* in all but one:

no   nobody   none   never
no one   nothing   nowhere

The *not*-words and the *no*-words are called **negatives.** Two negatives used together are called a **double negative.** Avoid double negatives.

Wrong: That car isn't going nowhere.

This sentence is wrong because it uses a *not*-word, *isn't*, with a *no*-word, *nowhere*.

The sentences below show the right way to use *no*-words and *not*-words. Read them aloud. Then study the rule.

1. That car isn't going anywhere.
   That car is going nowhere.
2. Donald didn't tell anybody.
   Donald told nobody.
3. Norita hasn't any paper.
   Norita has no paper.
4. I won't ever tease you.
   I will never tease you.

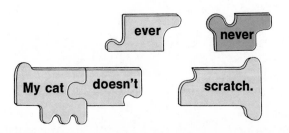

Do not use a *no*-word and a *not*-word together.

Exercises Using Negatives Correctly

A. Number your paper from 1 to 10. Choose the right word from the parentheses. Write it on your paper.

1. I don't want (any, no) more soup.
2. Ray (won't, will) never be late again.
3. There wasn't (no one, anyone) on the playground.
4. Don't (never, ever) cross the street without looking.
5. Connie didn't want (anybody, nobody) to help her.
6. I don't know (nothing, anything) about the accident.
7. The plane can't fly (nowhere, anywhere) in this fog.
8. Luis didn't hit (any, no) home runs today.
9. The baby hasn't (no, any) teeth.
10. There (aren't, are) no chips left.

B. Follow the directions for Exercise A.

1. Denise won't go (nowhere, anywhere) without Lillian.
2. I (wouldn't, would) never lie to you.
3. Gail hasn't painted (nothing, anything) today.
4. Paul can't reach (no, any) higher.
5. There (wasn't, was) nobody home.
6. We haven't left (anyone, no one) out of our club.
7. Willy didn't find (nothing, anything) .
8. Pam got three Valentines, but I didn't get (any, none) .
9. There (wasn't, was) no mail delivery today.
10. Stan (won't, will) never skip dessert.

Sentence Patterns The N V Pattern

The complete predicate of a sentence may have one word or more than one word. If it has more than one word, one part is more important than the rest. This is the simple predicate, or the verb. Usually, the verb tells of an action. In this chart, N stands for the noun in the subject. V stands for the verb in the predicate.

N	V
Susan	called again.
The tree	fell suddenly.
The old door	creaked mysteriously.

The word order in these sentences follows a pattern. That pattern is noun-verb, or N-V. These sentences are in the N V pattern.

Exercises The N V Pattern

A. Make a chart like the one above. Label one column *N.* Label the other *V.* Write these sentences on the chart.

1. Ed walked slowly.
2. The bus stops here.
3. Gina came later.
4. Two birds sang together.
5. My watch is running fast.
6. Dad should wait for me.

B. Copy this chart. Complete each sentence in the N V Pattern.

N	V
1. Doreen	_____.
2. A green car	_____.
3. Three children	_____.
4. The hungry tiger	_____.

More Exercises — Review

Using Verbs

A. Using Verbs That Tell About Action

Copy each sentence. Underline the action verb.

1. Ellen saved ninety cents.
2. Sally raises hamsters.
3. Marvin caught three fish.
4. John yelled to his friend.
5. Mom cooked hamburgers for lunch.
6. The ship sailed across the ocean.
7. Cindy broke a glass.
8. The horse galloped home.
9. George fixed his bike.
10. The school bell rings at nine o'clock.

B. Finding the Verb

Copy these sentences. Some have verbs that tell about action. Others have verbs that say that something is. Underline the verb in each sentence.

1. Barbara is ten years old.
2. Norman dropped his books.
3. Matthew ate two sandwiches.
4. Your team was lucky.
5. Lemons are sour.
6. Debra mailed a letter.
7. Ted's father drives a truck.
8. The class was quiet.
9. Elaine flew in an airplane.
10. The price is too high.

C. Finding Main Verbs and Helping Verbs

Copy each sentence. Underline the main verb and the helping verb or helping verbs.

1. The dragon was breathing fire.
2. Greg is typing his report.
3. Pat has been thinking about spring.
4. Cindy had been waiting.
5. The house was burning.
6. Leonard's ice cream had melted.
7. My father has been jogging every day.
8. Juan would have gone to the zoo.
9. Marsha should cut the grass.
10. The bells were ringing loudly.

D. Using Helping Verbs

Number your paper from 1 to 10. Read each sentence. If the sentence is correct, write *Correct.* If the verb needs a helping verb, write a helping verb and the main verb. There may be more than one correct helping verb.

1. Jimmy written me two letters.
2. Some sharks have huge jaws.
3. Cliff wearing his gloves.
4. Penny been downtown with her mother.
5. Alaska is the biggest state.
6. The weather has been cold.
7. Rosa arranging the flowers.
8. Nick eaten most of the cake.
9. Susan was feeding the goldfish.
10. Mark done the work in the yard.

175

E. Finding Separated Parts of the Verb

Number your paper from 1 to 10. Make two columns. Head the first column *Helping Verb*. Head the second *Main Verb*. Write the verbs for each of these sentences in the correct columns.

1. Has Diane found her book?
2. Sandy has never come to school late.
3. Sam has always been my friend.
4. R2D2 couldn't talk.
5. I have never visited the museum.
6. Walter would usually drink chocolate milk.
7. Will you come with me?
8. Franklin hasn't heard the news.
9. We must not talk during the movie.
10. Janet would often talk about her cat.

F. Using the Right Form of *Be*

Number your paper from 1 to 10. Choose the right form. Write it on your paper.

1. The leaf (be, is) floating on the water.
2. Terry (was, were) sweeping the floor.
3. You (is, are) writing an interesting story.
4. We (were, been) waiting for a bus.
5. I (be, am) angry.
6. You boys (are, is) honest.
7. Marco and Tina (is, are) good runners.
8. Cathy (be, is) acting in the school play.
9. Bernie (was, were) in the kitchen.
10. Emily and I (being, are) working together.

G. Using Contractions

Copy each sentence. Make a contraction of the underlined words.

1. The plumber has not come.
2. I will wear my new jacket.
3. She has won the race.
4. That house is not haunted.
5. I have been stung by a bee.
6. It is raining.
7. We could not hear the thunder.
8. Skip did not listen to the news.
9. He is the Lone Ranger.
10. They are my sister's records.

H. Using Negatives Correctly

Number your paper from 1 to 10. Choose the correct word from the parentheses. Write it on your paper.

1. I don't go to (any, no) scary movies.
2. Ron hasn't (never, ever) skated.
3. Karen (would, wouldn't) never forget my birthday.
4. You shouldn't go (nowhere, anywhere) with that cold.
5. There isn't (anybody, nobody) in the gym.
6. Tracy hasn't wasted (any, none) of her time.
7. Rosita didn't buy (anything, nothing) at the fair.
8. Chico won't allow (no one, anyone) on his bike.
9. Vicky hasn't (no, any) homework tonight.
10. We couldn't travel (nowhere, anywhere) during the blizzard.

Chapter 14

Using Verbs Correctly

Verbs are important words. You use them all the time. You always use a verb when you say or write a sentence. Verbs make your thoughts complete. They help people understand what you are saying.

You have learned that verbs tell about action. You know that some verbs are more than one word. In this chapter you will learn how verbs tell the time of an action. You will also learn more about how to use helping verbs.

Part 1 Verbs That Tell About Present Time

Read these two sentences. How are their meanings different?

Fred plays in the band.
Fred played in the band.

Did you say that the action happens at different times? When we say *Fred plays*, we mean he is playing now. We call this action in the **present** time. When we say *Fred played*, we mean that he did it before, and he is finished now. We call this action in the **past.**

Verbs have two forms to show action in the present. One form can be called the basic form. It is the verb by itself, such as *play, run,* or *cook.* The other form is the *-s* form. It is the basic form with an *s* added, as in *plays, runs,* and *cooks.* The form we use in a sentence depends on the subject of the sentence.

If the subject is singular, use the -s form.

Lisa *trains* dogs.
She *likes* animals.

**If the subject is plural, use the basic form.
Also, use the basic form if the subject
is the pronoun *I* or the pronoun *you.***

Lisa and Michael *train* dogs.
They *like* animals.
I *enjoy* sports.
You *swim* well.

Some verbs add *-es* instead of *-s* to the basic form. Add *-es* to verbs that end in *s, x, z, ch,* or *sh*.

she *tosses*   he *boxes*

If a verb ends in *y* following a consonant, change the *y* to *i*, and add *-es*.

carry—carries   hurry—hurries

-s -es -ies

Exercises   **Using Verbs That Tell About the Present**

A. Copy each of the following basic verbs. Then write the verb with *-s* or *-es* added.

1. sleep	5. catch	9. worry
2. want	6. answer	10. take
3. crash	7. fly	11. sell
4. marry	8. push	12. munch

B. Number your paper from 1 to 10. Choose the correct verb form from the parentheses. Write it on your paper.

1. Peter (study, studies) hard.
2. Every Thursday, Lily (watch, watches) her favorite TV show.
3. You (bake, bakes) tasty cookies.
4. I (drink, drinks) a glass of milk every day.
5. Brad and Craig (walk, walks) to school together.
6. My dog (bark, barks) at strangers.
7. In fables, animals (talk, talks).
8. Jenny (finish, finishes) her work quickly.
9. Every night, Holly (wish, wishes) on a star.
10. You always (speak, speaks) clearly.

181

Part 2   Verbs That Tell About the Past

Most verbs have two ways to tell about actions that happened in the past.

Using the *-ed* Ending

To make most verbs tell about the past, you can add *-ed* to the basic form.

     play—played   look—looked   talk—talked

You use the *-ed* form of a verb with both singular and plural subjects.

Some verbs need spelling changes when they are changed to the *-ed* past form. Watch for verbs of one syllable that have a single vowel followed by a single consonant. Double the final consonant of each of these verbs before adding *-ed*.

     tag—tagged   stop—stopped

If the verb ends in a silent *e*, drop the final *e* before adding *-ed*.

     paste-pasted   tame—tamed

If a verb ends in *y* following a consonant, change the *y* to *i* before adding *-ed*.

     carry—carried   hurry—hurried

Exercise   **Forming Verbs with the *-ed* Ending**

Copy the following verbs. After each verb, write its *-ed* form. Follow the rules about spelling changes.

1. jump
2. smile
3. rub
4. crack
5. fry
6. arrive
7. tap
8. reply
9. raise
10. melt
11. bury
12. slap

Using Helping Verbs

Another way to tell about the past is to use helping verbs. Usually, you use the helping verbs *has, have,* and *had* with the *-ed* form of the verb.

> Karen *has voted* for class president.
> The boys *have voted.*
> They *had voted* before Karen.

As the examples show, you use the helping word *has* with a singular subject. You use *have* with a plural subject, or with the pronouns *I* and *you.* You may use *had* with either a singular or a plural subject.

Exercises **Using Verbs That Tell About the Past**

A. Copy the following verbs. Then write the past form using a helping word and the *-ed* ending. Use *has* or *have* or *had.*

1. laugh	4. deny	7. close	10. paint
2. clap	5. waste	8. wrap	11. stir
3. wait	6. apply	9. worry	12. slice

B. Number your paper from 1 to 10. Write the subject from each of the following sentences. Then write the correct verb from the parentheses.

> Example: Andy and Nina (has climbed, have climbed) the rope.
> Andy and Nina have climbed

1. Monica and Tammy (has joined, have joined) the softball team.
2. Wally (has planned, have planned) a picnic.
3. Frank (has dried, have dried) the dishes.
4. The baby chicks (has hatched, have hatched).

183

5. Carmen (has returned, have returned) her library books.
6. I (has used, have used) my new hammer.
7. Penny (has stubbed, have stubbed) her toe.
8. Mitch and Susan (has made, have made) a snowman.
9. You (has missed, have missed) a good movie.
10. Luis (has practiced, have practiced) his piano lesson.

Part 3 Irregular Verbs

Some verbs do not show past time in the usual ways. Instead of adding the *-ed* ending to the basic form, these verbs change their entire form. Here are some examples:

lose—lost   make—made
find—found   bring—brought

Some verbs change their forms two times. They change to show the past. Then they change again to tell about the past with a helping verb. Notice how these verbs change:

come   came   have come
do   did   have done
go   went   have gone
see   saw   have seen

Verbs that show past time in the usual ways are called **regular verbs.** The verbs that show past time in different ways are called **irregular verbs.**

184

There are about sixty irregular verbs. Many of the verbs we use every day are in this group. It is important to know which verbs are irregular. You must know the different forms of the irregular verbs and which forms are used with helping verbs.

Irregular Verbs

Present	Past Alone	Past with Helping Verb
bring	brought	brought
come	came	come
do	did	done
eat	ate	eaten
give	gave	given
go	went	gone
run	ran	run
see	saw	seen
take	took	taken
throw	threw	thrown

Exercise Using Irregular Verbs

Number your paper from 1 to 10. Choose the correct verb form from the parentheses. Write it on your paper.

1. The mailcarrier (brung, brought) three letters.
2. I have (came, come) for a sausage pizza.
3. What have you (done, did) with your Scout troop?
4. The rabbit (ate, eaten) all my lettuce plants.
5. The salesperson has (gave, given) two free samples to me.
6. The children (went, gone) to the pool today.
7. The water has (ran, run) out of the cracked vase.
8. Everyone (saw, seen) a bright flash of lightning.
9. The lost child had (took, taken) the wrong path.
10. After the picnic, we (threw, thrown) our litter into a bag.

Chapter 15

Telling Stories

Everybody likes stories. When you were little, you probably asked someone to read a story to you. A story can take you to a different place. It can take you to a different time.

As you grew older, you began to tell stories yourself. You listened to friends as they told stories. You probably noticed that some people tell stories in an especially good way. A story is particularly interesting, or funny, or exciting when they tell it.

This chapter will help you tell stories well, too. It will show you how to prepare for storytelling. Knowing how to tell stories well makes storytelling more fun for you and for your listeners.

Part 1 Finding the Shape of a Story

A story tells what happened. It has a beginning, a middle, and an end. The high point of the story usually comes in the middle. Most stories are shaped like this:

Beginning   Middle   End

The **beginning** sets the scene. The action starts.

The **middle** contains the high point of the action. The high point is the most exciting moment in the story.

The **end** tells what happens after the high point.

Here is a sample story. It is not true, of course.

KERRY'S BUBBLE GUM RIDE

Kerry was chewing bubble gum. He began to blow a bubble. It got bigger and bigger. He kept blowing. The bubble got so big it began to lift him off the ground. Over the trees his bubble carried him. The clouds raced by above him.

"I'm flying! I'm flying!" Kerry cried to the wind.

Just then, Kerry began to drop. Air was leaking out of the bubble. Kerry could see the ground now. He got closer and closer. He was beginning to be afraid. He closed his eyes. Suddenly his feet landed on the little hill next to his house.

Kerry's bubble flopped down around his ears. It fell down to his shoes. He was covered with thick, gooey, pink gum. What on earth would he tell his mother?

188 Discuss the shape of "Kerry's Bubble Gum Ride" story in class. Where is the high point?

Remember the guides on the next page when you find the shape of your own story.

Exercises Shaping a Story

A. Read the following sentences. They tell a story. However, the events are out of order. On your paper, write the sentences in the proper order.

1. John got on his bicycle early one morning.
2. He landed on his side.
3. He biked down the dirt road behind his house.
4. John flew off the seat of his bike.
5. Suddenly, his bike hit a rock.
6. John was okay, but his bike would need a new tire.
7. He watched the bike crash to the ground.
8. He got up and brushed off the dirt.

B. Find a short story that you like. Write it in your own words, in the order it happened. Use less than ten sentences. Then underline the sentence that tells the high point.

Part 2   Getting People To Listen

Think about storytellers you have liked. How do they make their stories exciting?

Here are a few suggestions. They will help you become a good storyteller. To begin with, choose a story you like. Then let your voice and body show your excitement.

Speak slowly. Try to create suspense. You can create suspense by leading your listeners. Take them, one step at a time, toward the high point of your story. Tell events in the right order.

After you have reached the peak of your story, head toward the ending. Again, tell one step at a time in the right order. Be sure you know the last sentence of your story. The last sentence should let your listeners know that the story has ended.

When you finish, pause for a moment. Don't rush away. Let your listeners feel the effect of your story.

These guides will help you remember how to tell stories.

Guides for Getting People To Listen
1. Look directly at your listeners.
2. Speak clearly.
3. Create suspense.
4. Show your feelings.
5. Know the last sentence of your story.
6. Pause when your story is finished.

Exercise   **Getting People To Listen**

Work in groups of three or four. Take turns telling the stories you wrote in Part 1. Follow the guides above. After you have told your story, ask the others to tell you how well you told it.

Part 3   Telling a Story

There are many different kinds of stories. However, most stories belong to these two kinds: "what" stories and "why" stories. Here are some ideas about telling these two kinds of stories.

Telling a "What" Story

A "what" story has fast action. It is usually short. Often it contains a surprise. The surprise tells "what" happened.

Do you remember the nursery rhyme about Little Miss Muffet? It is a good example of a "what" story.

Little Miss Muffet
Sat on a tuffet
Eating her curds and whey.
Along came a spider
Who sat down beside her
And frightened Miss Muffet away.

Miss Muffet sat, eating peacefully. All of a sudden, a spider appeared. It frightened Miss Muffet, and she ran away.

Now let's see how the story unfolds.

1. The author sets the scene. The action begins.
   (Miss Muffet sits and eats.)

2. Something unexpected happens.
   It is the high point of the story.
   (The spider comes.)

3. The action changes.
   (Miss Muffet runs away.)

191

Telling a "Why" Story

A "Why" story explains something in nature. It tells how something came to be. Here are some sample titles of "Why" stories.

> Why the Oak Tree Loses Its Leaves
> Why the Stars Come Out at Night

"Why" stories are made-up stories. They are not true.

Now read the story below. It is an example of a "Why" story.

WHY THE BEAR HAS A STUMPY TAIL

One winter day the bear met the fox, who came slinking along. The fox carried a string of fish he had stolen.

"Where did you get those fish?" asked the bear.

"Oh, Mr. Bear, I've been out fishing and caught them," said the fox. The bear thought he would like to learn to fish, too. He asked the fox to tell him how to go about it.

"It's easy," said the fox. "You just go out on the ice and cut a hole. Then you stick your tail into the hole. You must hold your tail there as long as you can. You must not mind if your tail hurts a little. That's when the fish bite. The longer you sit with your tail in the hole, the more fish you'll get. Then, all at once, pull your tail out. Give it a cross pull sideways, and a strong pull, too."

The bear did what the fox had told him to do. He held his tail down in the hole a long, long time. Finally it was frozen fast. Then he pulled it out with a strong cross pull. It snapped off.

That's why the bear has such a short tail.

In this tale the high point comes almost at the end of the story. Can you find it?

Exercises   Telling a Story

A. For this exercise, work with a partner. Find a "what" or a "why" story that you like. Your teacher or librarian will help you. Read your story out loud to your partner. Together, answer these questions.

1. Where is the high point of the story? Copy it on your paper.

2. Why do you like the story? Write your answer on your paper.

193

B. Tell your story to the class. Follow the Guides for Getting People To Listen, on page 190.

Chapter 16

Writing About Things That Happened

Think about the many things that have happened to you. You have started school. You have made friends. You have won and lost games. Maybe you have moved. Maybe you have shared a sad time with your family.

Think about the things that you have imagined or daydreamed. Maybe you have imagined traveling to another planet. Maybe you have dreamed of running away to the circus. Maybe you have thought about the feelings of a captured bird.

In this chapter you will learn to write about things that have happened. You will learn to write about make-believe happenings, too.

Part 1 Pre-Writing: Choosing a Topic

Before you can write, you must know what you want to write about. You can write about something that happened to you. You can write about something that happened to someone else.

Telling What Happened to You

Writers often write about things that have happened to themselves. They retell their own experiences.

The writer of this paragraph describes what happened at the beach.

> I once spent a day at the beach. In the morning I watched wave after wave roll into shore and pull out again. I collected white clam shells and blue mussel shells. I found a hermit crab inside a snail shell. At noon I ate peanut butter and banana sandwiches and drank lemonade. I built a sand castle and watched the tide fill the low spots. Late in the afternoon I gave up my part of the beach to the tide and left for home. I had enjoyed a wonderful day.

The word *I* tells you something. It tells you that the writer is describing something that happened to her. She tells it in the order that it happened.

The writer includes details. She describes the waves. She tells how she collected "white clam shells and blue mussel shells." She found "a hermit crab inside a snail shell." She "ate peanut butter and banana sandwiches" and "drank lemonade." She built a "sand castle." In her paragraph, she makes that day come alive for the reader.

Writers often tell what happened to themselves. They use details to make their experiences seem real to the reader.

Telling What Happened to Others

Here are two paragraphs. Each one tells about something that happened. The first one tells about a happening in real life. The second tells about a made-up happening.

Paragraph 1

One day a terrible thing happened to the bears of Koala Park. It was early morning. Suddenly a green cloud appeared. It was a thick cloud, full of tiny eyes, wings, and legs. The thick cloud was made up of grasshoppers. They swooped in over the gum trees where the bears lived. There was a noise like a thousand babies shaking rattles. Then, as quickly as they had come, the grasshoppers left. The bears opened their eyes and looked around them. All their food was gone. The grasshoppers had eaten every leaf off every gum tree. —WILLIAM PÈNE DU BOIS

The paragraph begins with a topic sentence. It tells you what the paragraph is about. It is about something that happened to the bears. The rest of the paragraph describes what happened.

Paragraph 2

Once upon a time, there were two good friends, a frog and a toad. Frog was not feeling well. He asked his friend Toad to tell him a story. Toad could not think of a story. He walked up and down on the porch, but he could not think of a story. He stood on his head, but he could not think of a story. He poured water over his head, but he could not think of a story. He banged his head against the wall, but he still could not think of a story. Suddenly Toad did not feel very well, but Frog was feeling better. Then Toad went to bed and Frog got up and told him a story.—ARNOLD LOBEL

The paragraph tells what happened to a frog and a toad. The events are described in the order that they happened.

> Some paragraphs tell about things that happened to others. The writers tell what happened in the order that it happened.

Exercise   Choosing a Topic

Think of several topics you can write a paragraph about. Write them in a list. If you can't think of anything, here are some questions. They will help you get started.

1. Think of things that happened to you.
   Have you done any interesting school projects?
   Have you taught your pet any special tricks?
   Have you ever won or lost an important game?
   What is your favorite holiday? How have you celebrated it?
   Have you ever spent the night in a tent?

2. Think of things that happened to other people.
   Has anyone in your family done something funny?
   Did you hear about someone who did a brave deed?
   Did someone you know get on the TV or in the newspaper?
   How could a man from Mars get to Earth?

198   Study your list. Remember that when you write your paragraph, you will have to tell about several events that happened. Choose the topic that you have something to say about. Circle it.

Part 2 Pre-Writing: Making Your Plan

Think about the topic you chose. Make a list of all your ideas about the topic. If you are writing about something that really happened, use your memory. If you are writing about a made-up topic, use your imagination.

Usually when you think of a story, you get many ideas at once. Write them quickly, before you forget them. It doesn't matter if they are out of order or if they don't all fit together.

After you list the ideas, put them in order. Try to remember the order of the events that happened to you or someone else. If you are writing about made-up events, put them into a logical order. Cross out any ideas that don't fit with the rest of the story.

Peter decided to write about his special chair, Fred. Here are the ideas Peter listed about his topic:

Called the chair Fred Where Fred is now
How Fred looked Fred's color
When Fred broke When I got Fred
Fred's size When I used Fred

Next, Peter put the events in order. He wrote a numeral 1 in front of the first thing that happened. He wrote a numeral 2 in front of the second thing, and so on. He added some ideas and crossed out ideas that he didn't want to use.

Exercise Making a Plan

List all the ideas you have about your topic. Next, put the ideas or events in order. You may want to cross out some ideas or add new ones.

Part 3 Writing

You are now ready to write a paragraph about what happened. First, write a good topic sentence. It should tell what your paragraph will be about. It should tell whether the paragraph is about you or another person or a thing. It may also tell where the event happened. The topic sentence gives the main idea.

The rest of the sentences should tell more about the main idea of the paragraph. Write a complete sentence about each idea on your list, or put two ideas that go together in a sentence. The sentences should follow the same order as the ideas on the list.

This is Peter's topic sentence.

When I was very young, I had a special chair.

Steps for Writing About What Happened

Pre-Writing

1. Choose your topic.
2. Make a plan. Put the events in the order that they happened.

Writing

1. Write a good topic sentence that tells the main idea.
2. Write other sentences that tell about what happened in the order in which the events happened.

200

Exercise **Writing a Paragraph About What Happened**

Write a paragraph about something that happened. Write a topic sentence. Write other sentences that tell about what happened in the order the events happened.

Part 4 Revising

After you have written your paragraph, you will probably think of several ways to make it better. You might remember another event. You might want to tell more about an event. Now is the time to revise, or edit, your paragraph.

Guides for Revising

1. Is the paragraph easy to understand? Are the sentences in an order that makes sense?

2. Is the paragraph interesting? Does it need more sentences? Does any sentence need more words?

3. Do all the sentences tell about the main idea? Should any sentence be taken out?

4. Is every group of words a sentence?

When you find something you want to change, mark the change on your paragraph. The paragraph will begin to look messy, but this is normal. You must expect to make a clean copy later. To mark your changes, you can use the symbols in the chart on page 202.

Proofreading

After revising your paragraph to make its ideas clearer, you must then proofread the paragraph. When you proofread, you look for mistakes. The mistakes may be in capitalization, punctuation, spelling, or the right use of words. The following questions will help you.

Guides for Proofreading

Form

1. Is the first line indented? (See page 105.)

Grammar

2. Is every verb form correct? (Pages 167 to 168, 180 to 185)
3. Is every pronoun used correctly? (Pages 77 to 87)

Capital Letters

4. Does every sentence begin with a capital letter? (Page 340)
5. Does every proper noun begin with a capital letter? (Pages 336 to 339)

Punctuation

6. Does every sentence have the correct end mark? (Pages 347 to 351)
7. If your paragraph includes the exact words someone said, did you use quotation marks correctly? (Pages 360 to 361)

Spelling

8. Is every word spelled correctly? (Pages 367 to 374)

Here is part of Peter's paragraph marked for changes.

∧ Add a word.　　／ Make lowercase.　　— Leave out.

When I was very young, I had a special chair. It was sort of small
bright
and green and close to the ground. I loved fred. I named it fred.
the chair

≡ Capitalize　　∩ Trade places.　　⊙ Add a period.

Making a Clean Copy

Now you are ready to write the final copy of your paragraph. Use your best handwriting. Be sure to make all the changes that you marked when you revised and proofread.

When Peter was finished revising his paragraph, this is what it said:

> When I was very young. I had a special chair. It was small and bright green and close to the ground. I named the chair Fred. I loved Fred. I took him everywhere with me. After a while, Fred's straight back began to hit me in a funny place. It wasn't high enough anymore. His legs weren't long enough either. Even so, I just couldn't give Fred to someone else. One day I sat down on Fred and his legs flew in all directions. Fred was beyond repair. He could never belong to anyone else. Now he sits all day long in a corner of my room. He is still my very own chair.

Exercises   Revising Your Paragraph

A. Revise your paragraph. Follow the Guides for Revising and the Guides for Proofreading.

B. Now you have planned, written, revised, and proofread a paragraph that tells about things that happened. The last step is to share your paragraph with others. Write your final copy neatly on a clean sheet of paper. Remember to make all the changes you have marked on your first copy. Make it easy for others to read. Use your best handwriting.

Chapter 17

Taking Tests

You have already taken many tests at school. Learning how to take a test will help you do better on tests in the future. Here are some steps to follow when you take a test:

1. **Be prepared.** Be sure you get enough sleep the night before. Eat a good breakfast on the day of the test.

   Bring the materials that your teacher tells you to bring. Often you will need a few sharpened pencils with good erasers. You may also need paper or a ruler.

2. **Be sure you understand the directions.** Listen carefully to your teacher. Read the directions. Then read them again. If there is a direction you do not understand, ask your teacher to explain it before the test begins.

3. **Think about what each question is asking.** Then choose your answer and mark it the way the directions tell you.

205

This chapter will help you become familiar with the form of a test. Then, when you take a test, you can concentrate on the questions.

Part 1   Giving Information about Yourself

The first questions on a test will be about you. You will be asked to give information about yourself, such as your name, your grade, and whether you are a girl or a boy. On many tests, you will be writing this information in a row of little boxes called a **grid.**

Look at the following grid. A girl named Jennifer Pasquale has filled it out.

Name

P	A	S	Q	U	A	L	E		J	E	N	N	I	F	

Notice how Jennifer followed these rules when she filled out the grid.

1. Use a pencil, not a pen.
2. Always print neatly. Do not write in cursive.
3. Always start in the first box.
4. Fill in your last name first. Print your complete last name.
5. Skip a space between words.
6. Fill in as much of your first name as you can. Do not try to squeeze the letters in at the end of the grid.

This is how Jennifer filled in the name of her school.

School

P	A	U	L		R	E	V	E	R	E		S	C	H

Jennifer skipped spaces between words. Also, she left out some letters in the word *school* because they did not fit.

Now we are going to look at a different way of giving information. Study these examples.

0 Boy ● Girl   Grade 0 3 ● 4 0 5

Jennifer has filled in the circle before *girl*. She has also filled in the circle before *4* to show what grade she is in. This kind of marking is often used in the test questions, too. Sometimes, instead of circles, you will see tiny rectangles that you must fill in.

Exercise   Giving Information About Yourself

Here is the first part of a test. Read over the rules on page 206. Examine this sample. Then answer the questions below the sample.

Name

W	A	S	H	I	N	G	T	O	N		J	A	S	ON

School

M	A	Y	F	I	E	L	D	S	C	H	O	O	L	

● Boy 0 Girl   Grade 0 3 0 ④ 0 5

Look at how Jason gave information and answered questions. If there is something wrong with the line, write what he did wrong. If there is nothing wrong, write **Correct.** Be prepared to discuss your answers with your teacher.

1. The student's name
2. The student's school
3. Whether the student is a boy or girl
4. The student's grade

Part 2 Marking Your Answers

The directions on a test will tell you how to mark your answers. Sometimes you will mark them on your test paper. Other times you will mark them on a different answer sheet. Look at these two questions and answers.

Test Paper

Directions: Choose the antonym, that is, the word that means the opposite, of the word in heavy type. Fill in the circle for the correct answer on the answer sheet. Do not write on the test paper.

1. happy
   A. sad   B. cheerful   C. late

2. easy
   A. nice   B. hard   C. free

Answer Sheet

1. A B C
   ● 0 0

2. A B C
   0 ● 0

This example shows you some important points to remember when you are answering test questions.

1. Use a pencil, not a pen.
2. Mark your answers exactly the way the directions tell you to.
3. Mark only one answer for each question.
4. If you are marking your answers on a special answer sheet, be sure to match the number of the question with the number on the answer sheet.
5. If you are marking your answers in circles, be sure to darken the circles completely and neatly. Do not write in the circles.

6. Think before you mark an answer. If you change your mind, or you mark the wrong answer, erase your mark completely and carefully. Do not tear the paper.

Marking Answers

Examine these samples from a test and its answer sheet. Read over the guides on page 208. Then answer the questions below the test.

Test Paper

Directions: Choose the word that correctly completes each sentence. Fill in the correct answer on the answer sheet. Do not write on the test paper.

1. Another word for *afraid is* _____.
   A. awful   B. fearful   C. wonder

2. Another word for *little* is _____.
   A. tiny   B. big   C. great

3. The opposite of *sick* is _____.
   A. well   B. ill   C. tired

4. The opposite of *loud* is *soft*.
   A. noisy   B. sound   C. soft

Answer Sheet

	A	B	C
1.	0	X	0
2.	0	0	0
3.	●	0	●
4.	0	0	0

Look at the way the student marked each question. If the student made a mistake, write what he or she did wrong. If there is nothing wrong, write **Correct.** Be prepared to discuss your answers.

1. Test question number 1   3. Test question number 3
2. Test question number 2   4. Test question number 4

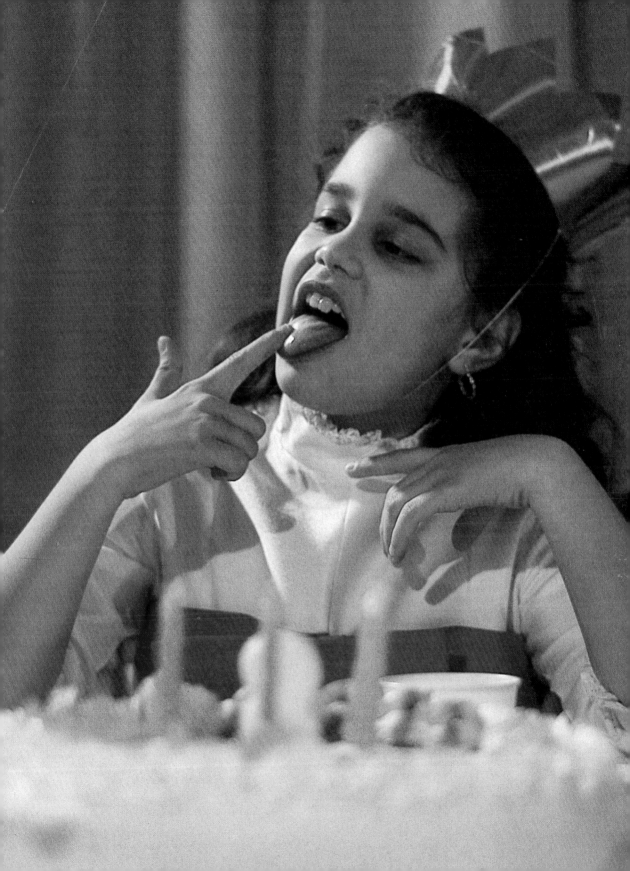

Chapter 18

Using Adjectives

Part 1   What Are Adjectives?

Read this riddle. Can you answer it?

> I am a vegetable that grows underground. I am *orange*. I am *long*, like a pencil. I am *fat* at the top and *thin* at the bottom. What am I?

The words *orange, long, fat,* and *thin* are clues. They *describe* the vegetable. They give you an idea of what the vegetable looks like. They probably let you know that the answer is a carrot.

Can you answer a second riddle?

> I am a vegetable that grows underground. I am *red* and *white*. I am *round* and *small*. I have a sharp taste. What am I?

The words *red, white, round, small,* and *sharp* describe the vegetable. They tell you some differences between the first vegetable and this vegetable. They probably give you enough clues to guess that the answer is a radish.

The clue words in these riddles are **adjectives.** *Orange* and *long* are adjectives that describe *vegetable. Red* and *round* are adjectives that describe *vegetable.* The different adjectives make you think of different vegetables. The adjectives change, or *modify,* the meaning of the word *vegetable.* For this reason, adjectives are called **modifiers.**

The following sentence was in the second riddle. Find the adjective. Then find the word that the adjective modifies.

> I have a sharp taste.

The adjective is *sharp.* It modifies *taste,* a noun. *Sharp* comes before the word it modifies.

Find the adjective in this sentence from the first riddle. Then find the word it modifies.

> I am orange.

The adjective is *orange.* It modifies *I,* a pronoun. *Orange* comes after the word it modifies.

212

> An **adjective** is a word that modifies a noun or a pronoun. An adjective may come before or after the word it describes.

Usually, when we use two or more adjectives together, we separate them with commas. Adjectives telling *how many* do not follow this rule.

Six large, raw carrots were on the tray.
Several small, red radishes lay next to them.

Exercises **Finding Adjectives**

A. Number your paper from 1 to 10. In each pair of sentences below, only the adjectives have been changed. Write the noun that is modified. Then, write the adjectives that modify it.

Example: Rabbits love juicy strawberries.
Rabbits love ripe strawberries.

strawberries—juicy, ripe

1. My jeans are blue.
   My jeans are dirty.
2. Maggie is tired.
   Maggie is sleepy.
3. My cat has thick fur.
   My cat has soft fur.
4. Jean drank cold milk.
   Jean drank fresh milk.
5. Steve's dog is friendly.
   Steve's dog is little.
6. Sandpaper feels rough.
   Sandpaper feels scratchy.
7. Mark bought crisp apples.
   Mark bought juicy apples.
8. Several people waited.
   Angry people waited.
9. Two shy ponies ran away.
   Four wild ponies ran away.
10. Carl wears warm scarves.
    Carl wears woolen scarves.

B. Fold a paper into four squares. Number the squares from 1 to 4. Follow the directions below. Draw a different picture in each square. Then compare your paper with your classmates' papers. Which pictures were the most alike? Why?

1. Draw a face in the first square.
2. Draw a large face in the second square.
3. Draw a large, square face in the third square.
4. Draw a large, square, happy face in the fourth square.

213

Part 2   Three Kinds of Adjectives

Almost every adjective can be placed in one of three groups.

Adjectives That Tell *What Kind*

Most of the adjectives used so far have been adjectives that
tell *what kind*. Here are some adjectives in this group.

orange	long	fat	funny	dangerous
red	small	thin	silly	helpful
white	round	bitter	washable	careless

Adjectives That Tell *How Many*

Some adjectives tell exactly *how many*.

    seven   two

Other adjectives give a general amount.

some	many
few	several

Adjectives That Tell *Which Ones*

A few adjectives tell *which one* or *which ones*. Here are four
of this group that are used often:

    this   that   these   those

These adjectives always come before the words they modify.

this pin	these pins
that nail	those nails

Exercises   Using Adjectives

A. Number your paper from 1 to 10. Make three columns. Head one column *What Kind.* Head the second *How Many.* Head the third *Which Ones.* Find the adjectives in each sentence. Write them in the right columns.

1. Many people like hot popcorn.
2. Ms. Walsh asked some hard questions.
3. Jody and Ramon are close neighbors.
4. This magician performs difficult tricks.
5. Neil told several funny stories.
6. Wear this warm jacket.
7. Fresh strawberries are good.
8. This flag is red, white, and blue.
9. Louisa carried that heavy box.
10. Those two knives are sharp.

B. Add an adjective of any kind to each sentence below. Write your new sentence. Draw a line under the new adjective.

Example: Ants carried the crumbs.

Some Possible Answers:

Many ants carried the crumbs.
Those ants carried the crumbs.
Ants carried the stale crumbs.

1. The girl ran to the store.
2. Roses have thorns.
3. I saw squirrels in the tree.
4. Dogs bark at noises.
5. Boats sailed on the lake.
6. The student heard a siren.
7. Nurses help people.
8. My brother owns a bike.
9. The children rode the bus.
10. The robot carried a message.

Part 3 Using *A, An,* and *The*

The words *a, an,* and *the* make a special group of adjectives. *The* may be used before singular or plural nouns that begin with any letter.

the Earth the planets

A and *an* are used only before singular nouns.

Use *a* before words beginning with consonant sounds:

a lion a police officer
a truck a blue umbrella

Use *an* before words beginning with vowel sounds:

an officer an angry lion
an umbrella an empty truck

Some words begin with a silent *h*. That means you do not say the *h* sound. You begin the word with the vowel sound after the *h*. Therefore, you use *an* with silent *h* words.

216

an hour an honest person

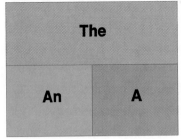

The

An | A

Before singular nouns

The

Before plural nouns

Using *A*, *An*, and *The*

A. Copy the following sentences. Fill in the blanks with *a* or *an*.

1. Joe entered _____ contest.
2. Dawn wants to be _____ astronaut.
3. The pony ate _____ apple.
4. Mei Ping sang _____ pretty song.
5. The library is _____ old building.
6. My father bought _____ new hammer.
7. The class won _____ honor.
8. Richard dropped _____ ice cream cone.
9. Mars is _____ planet.
10. Linda pitched _____ strike.

B. Copy the following sentences. Fill in the blanks with *a, an,* or *the*. For some sentences, there are two correct answers.

1. Maureen cooked _____ hamburgers.
2. My dog has _____ collar.
3. Alice has _____ uncle in Hong Kong.
4. John called _____ fire department.
5. Anna watched TV for _____ hour.
6. Carlos is slicing _____ onion.
7. Pat counted _____ pencils.
8. Lottie drew _____ picture of the sea.
9. The horses pulled _____ wagon.
10. Abraham Lincoln was _____ lawyer.

217

Part 4 Using Adjectives To Compare People or Things

We often **compare** people or things. That means we look at two or more people or things to see how they are alike and how they are different. We can use adjectives to tell about what we find.

Comparing Two People or Things

A mouse is *small*.
A mouse is *smaller* than a cat.

If we talk about a mouse by itself, we simply call it *small*. However, we can compare the mouse with a cat. Then we add the *-er* ending to *small*. We use *smaller* to compare two things, the mouse and the cat.

When you compare two people, places, or things, you usually add *-er* to the adjective.

darker   stronger
brighter   louder

Notice how the spelling of these adjectives changes when *-er* is added:

big + er = bigger   wide + er = wider
silly + er = sillier

218

Follow these spelling rules before adding *-er:*

1. If a word ends in a single consonant following a single vowel, double the final consonant before adding the ending.

big + er = bi**gg**er

2. If a word ends in a silent *e*, drop the final *e* before adding the ending.

wi**de** + er = wi**d**er

3. If a word ends in *y* following a consonant, change the *y* to *i* before adding the ending.

sill**y** + er = sill**i**er

Comparing Three or More People or Things

A mouse is *smaller* than a cat.
It is *smaller* than a dog.
A mouse is the *smallest* of the three animals.

In the third sentence, three animals are compared. A mouse is compared with both a cat and a dog. Notice how the ending *-est* is added to the word *small* to make the word *smallest*. We use *smallest* to compare three or more things.

When you compare three or more people, places, or things, you usually add *-est* to the adjective.

darkest   strongest
brightest   loudest

When you add *-est*, follow the same spelling rules as when you add *-er*.

Copy each adjective. Then write the two forms it uses in comparisons. Follow the spelling rules on page 219.

Example: lazy

lazy, lazier, laziest

1. loud	4. hot	7. young	10. easy
2. scary	5. large	8. nice	11. rich
3. tight	6. red	9. brave	12. hungry

Using *More* and *Most*

We do not always add *-er* or *-est* when we compare people or things. We would not add *-er* or *-est* to adjectives such as *dangerous*, *helpful*, or *careless*. Usually, when we make comparisons with long adjectives, we use *more* and *most*.

The wind made the fire *more dangerous*.
Tumi was the *most helpful* student in the class.

There are three rules to remember about *more* and *most*.

1. Use *more* when you compare two people, places, or things.

more dangerous   more helpful   more careless

2. Use *most* when you compare three or more people, places, or things.

most dangerous   most helpful   most careless

3. When you compare people, places, or things, use only one way at a time.

220

If you use *-er* or *-est*, do not use *more* or *most* at the same time. You would not say "The elephant is the most biggest animal in the zoo."

The Forms of *Good* and *Bad*

A few adjectives change to completely new words when they are used to compare things. Two of these adjectives are the words *good* and *bad.*

good I have a *good* set of tools.
better This hammer is *better* than that one.
best This hammer is the *best* tool for the job.

bad Chan has a *bad* cold.
worse He is in *worse* shape now than yesterday.
worst We are having the *worst* weather of the year.

Exercises **Comparing People or Things**

A. Some of the following adjectives add *-er* and *-est* when they are used to compare things. Others are used with *more* and *most.* Number your paper from 1 to 12. Copy each adjective. Then write the two forms it uses in comparing things.

Examples: sharp
               sharp, sharper, sharpest
          terrible
               terrible, more terrible, most terrible

1. colorful   4. graceful   7. funny   10. neat
2. rough   5. difficult   8. simple   11. light
3. serious   6. unusual   9. tame   12. pretty

B. Read each sentence. Choose the correct form from the two in parentheses. Write the correct form.

1. Of the two days, yesterday was the (colder, coldest).
2. This tree is (larger, more larger) than that one.
3. Which of these five dresses is the (newer, newest)?
4. This test was (harder, more harder) than the last one.
5. That was the (goodest, best) movie I have ever seen.

Sentence Patterns **The N LV Adj Pattern**

Sentences in the N LV Adj pattern have three parts. The N stands for the noun in the subject. The *Adj* stands for an adjective in the predicate. The *LV* stands for the linking verb connecting the noun and adjective. A **linking verb** is a verb that says that something is.

The sentences in this chart are in the **N LV Adj pattern.**

N	LV	Adj
The sky	is	cloudy.
Tuesday	will be	sunny.
Eileen	was	late.
These ripe cherries	are	sweet.

Exercises   The N LV Adj Pattern

A. Make a chart like the one above. Label the three columns N, LV, and *Adj*. Write these sentences on the chart.

1. Phyllis is happy.
2. This hall is huge.
3. Steve was early.
4. The sea was calm.
5. Bea's pies are delicious.
6. The movie was funny.
7. The bus will be late.
8. All of us were sleepy.

B. Make a chart like the one below. Complete each sentence in the N LV Adj pattern.

N	LV	Adj
1. _____	is	fuzzy.
2. Pickles	are	_____.
3. Glue	is	_____.
4. Janet	_____	awake.
5. _____	was	_____.

222

More Exercises — Review

Using Adjectives

A. Finding Adjectives

Number your paper from 1 to 10. In each pair of sentences, only the adjectives have been changed. Write the noun that is modified. Then write the adjectives that modify it.

Example: Use sharp pencils.
Use red pencils.

pencils—sharp, red

1. Mary Ann collects old stamps.
   Mary Ann collects rare stamps.
2. Camels are strong animals.
   Camels are unusual animals.
3. Robin Hood thought of bold plans.
   Robin Hood thought of daring plans.
4. Tammy picked pretty flowers.
   Tammy picked many flowers.
5. Sam bought two notebooks.
   Sam bought red notebooks.
6. We drove down wide streets.
   We drove down busy streets.
7. Ellen enjoys cold lemonade.
   Ellen enjoys pink lemonade.
8. King Henry wore shiny crowns.
   King Henry wore golden crowns.
9. Sandy climbs high mountains.
   Sandy climbs rocky mountains.
10. Dan likes hot soup.
    Dan likes tomato soup.

B. Using Adjectives

Number your paper from 1 to 10. Make three columns. Head one column *What Kind*. Head the second *How Many*. Head the third *Which Ones*. Find the adjectives in each sentence. Write them in the right columns. (A sentence may have two or three adjectives.)

1. Those children are brave.
2. That bakery sells many delicious doughnuts.
3. This camera is expensive.
4. Huge dinosaurs lived here.
5. Several girls planted these vegetables.
6. This black cat has four kittens.
7. Strong workers carried those heavy boxes.
8. That actor has been in several good movies.
9. Many bright stars shine at night.
10. There are fifty states in this country.

C. Using *A, An,* and *The*

Copy the following sentences. Fill in the blanks with *a, an,* or *the.* For some sentences there are two correct answers.

1. Brian lives in _____ apartment.
2. Cheryl pulled _____ weeds in her garden.
3. George has _____ turtle.
4. Melvin heard _____ strange noise.
5. Rick pulled _____ huge dandelion root.
6. Ms. Wong is _____ police officer.
7. The kitten chased _____ butterflies.
8. Anita peeled _____ orange.
9. Pedro stapled _____ papers together.
10. Karen ate _____ egg for breakfast.

D. Comparing People or Things

Read each sentence. Choose the correct form from the two in parentheses. Write the correct form.

1. Of the three snowmen, mine is the (fatter, fattest).
2. Wilbur is the (larger, largest) of my three hamsters.
3. Brand X keeps my clothes (cleaner, more cleaner) than Brand Y.
4. Among all these jackets, the green one is the (warmer, warmest).
5. Betsy is the (better, best) basketball player in the class.
6. Which of these two apples is (riper, ripest)?
7. This is the (more useful, most useful) book in the library.
8. The weather is (worser, worse) than usual this winter.
9. Between our two trips, the trip to the zoo was the (more pleasant, most pleasant).
10. The mummy is the (most scariest, scariest) monster of all.

Chapter 19

Using Adverbs

Part 1   What Are Adverbs?

Read the three sentences below. Only one word changes.
Notice how the meaning changes.

> Dina draws pictures quickly.
> Dina draws pictures everywhere.
> Dina draws pictures constantly.

Only the last word is different in each sentence. These three
words give us different ideas.

Quickly tells **how** Dina draws.
Everywhere tells **where** she draws.
Constantly tells **when** she draws.

These three words are **adverbs.** They modify the verb *draw.* They can modify other verbs, too. Adverbs tell *how, where,* and *when.*

Like adjectives, adverbs make the meaning of the sentence clearer. If you change the adverb, you will change the meaning of the sentence. Read these sentences several times. Use a different word from the parentheses each time.

How   Louis reads books (quickly, slowly, carefully).
Where   He reads (here, there, inside, outdoors).
When   He was reading (early, late, yesterday).

Many adverbs are formed by adding *-ly* to adjectives.

Adjective + ly = Adverb

complete + ly = completely
quiet   + ly = quietly
wild   + ly = wildly
loud   + ly = loudly

Some Words Used Frequently as Adverbs

How	Where	When
well	inside	now
badly	outside	then
carefully	up	early
carelessly	down	often
politely	here	today
rudely	there	yesterday
fast	everywhere	tomorrow
easily	nowhere	soon
quickly	far	never
slowly	near	sometimes

An **adverb** is a word that modifies a verb
or an adjective. It tells *how, where,* or *when.*
Many adverbs end in *-ly.*

Exercises   Using Adverbs

A. Copy each sentence. Underline the adverb.

1. The stars shone brightly.
2. The robot moved noisily.
3. Carlos answered immediately.
4. Francine is waiting outside.
5. The raft floated downstream.
6. Marilyn petted the dog gently.
7. Don, come here.
8. Barb won the race today.
9. Martin looked at the cake hungrily.
10. Suddenly, lightning flashed.

B. Number your paper from 1 to 10. Write the adverb in each sentence.

    1. The car ran smoothly.
    2. Snow was falling everywhere.
    3. Our guests came late.
    4. The crowd shouted loudly.
    5. Yesterday Mary found a wallet.
    6. Tony was hiding there.
    7. The cat crept silently.
    8. Laura hurried upstairs.
    9. The dogs barked noisily.
  10. The students worked hard.

C. Add an adverb of any kind to each sentence below. Write your new sentence. Draw a line under the adverb.

    Example: Petey ate his dinner.
    Some Possible Answers
            Petey ate his dinner *happily*.
            Petey ate his dinner *outside*.
            Petey ate his dinner *early*.

    1. Gilberto ran.
    2. Helen threw the ball.
    3. John and Marcie played the game.
    4. Ellie sang a song.
    5. The bird flew.
    6. My mother went shopping.
    7. The children worked.
    8. Hal poured the juice.
    9. The baby cried.
  10. Glen painted the fence.

Part 2 Making Comparisons with Adverbs

You learned in Chapter 17 how adjectives can be used to **compare** people and things. Adverbs, too, can be used to make **comparisons.**

Harriet swam *faster* than the other girls.

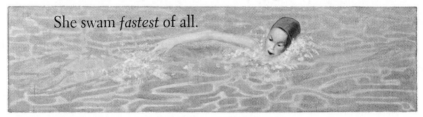

She swam *fastest* of all.

There are three ways adverbs are changed to show comparisons.

1. Some short adverbs add *-er* when two people or things are being compared. They add *-est* when three or more are compared.

fast	faster	fastest
hard	harder	hardest

2. Most adverbs that end in *-ly* use the word *more* in comparing two people or things. They use *most* in comparing three or more.

brightly	more brightly	most brightly
carefully	more carefully	most carefully
happily	more happily	most happily

3. Some adverbs change their forms completely when they are used in comparisons.

well	better	best
badly	worse	worst

Our team pulled harder.

Exercises   Using Adverbs To Make Comparisons

A. Copy each adverb. Then write the two forms it uses in comparisons.

1. slowly
2. politely
3. quietly
4. gently
5. quickly
6. late
7. joyfully
8. well
9. softly
10. foolishly
11. rapidly
12. carelessly

B. Read each sentence. Choose the correct adverb form from the two in parentheses. Write the correct form.

1. Clem spoke (softly, more softly) than George.
2. Lila worked (more carefully, most carefully) than Ann.
3. Patrick arrived (more late, later) than Ed.
4. Sue sings (better, gooder) than I can.
5. Andrew spoke (louder, more louder) than usual.
6. Of all the dancers, Sara danced (more gracefully, most gracefully).
7. Since it was repaired, this sewing machine has run (more smoothly, most smoothly).
8. Between the two days, it rained (more heavily, most heavily) today.
9. Of all the runners, Fran moved (faster, fastest).
10. The movie started (earlier, more earlier) than we had expected.

More Exercises — Review

Using Adverbs

A. Using Adverbs

Copy each sentence. Underline the adverb.

1. Maria whispered quietly.
2. The package came late.
3. Come in for a snack.
4. Alan waited patiently.
5. Vivian rode her bike here.
6. Then Ms. Willis went shopping.
7. Rose talks clearly.
8. The lion roared loudly.
9. Mr. Chun shook my hand firmly.
10. Ray walked outside.

B. Making Comparisons with Adverbs

Read each sentence. Choose the correct adverb form from the two in parentheses. Write the correct form.

1. Pearl swam (faster, fastest) than Marlene.
2. Ron worked (more eagerly, most eagerly) of all.
3. Between Chuck and Jerry, Chuck tried (harder, hardest).
4. Clint finished his work the (more cheerfully, most cheerfully) of all the boys.
5. Of all the students, Grace listened to the speaker the (more politely, most politely).
6. My bicycle squeaks (more noisily, more noisier) than ever before.
7. Of the two sisters, Rita cooks (better, best).
8. Who ran (slowest, slower), the turtle or the hare?

233

Chapter 20

Writing Descriptions

Paragraphs can be about any topic. They can explain how to make something. They can tell about an experience. They can give reasons for doing something.

Some paragraphs tell what something or someone looks like. When you see something exciting, you want to describe it to someone. You like to read stories that describe people, or places, or things. Describing things helps other people to see what you have seen.

These paragraphs are **descriptions.** In this chapter, you are going to study and write descriptions.

Part 1   Studying Descriptions

Here is a description.

> Annie's Navajo world was good. It was a world of rippling sand. There were high, copper-red bluffs in the distance. There was a mesa near her own snug hogan. The pumpkins were yellow in the cornfield. The tassels on the corn were turning brown.   —MISKA MILES

The paragraph begins with a topic sentence. It tells you that the paragraph is about Annie's world. The rest of the sentences **describe** her world. They tell what it looked like. Here is another description.

> The King sent for the Royal Wizard. He was a little, thin man with a long face. He wore a high, red, peaked hat covered with silver stars. He wore a long blue robe covered with golden owls. His face was very pale.
>
> —JAMES THURBER

The paragraph describes the Royal Wizard. It paints a picture of the Wizard with words. As you read, you "see" the Wizard in your mind. The next description is a little longer. It describes a town square. It, too, paints a picture with words.

> The town square was filled with people busily working. They were bringing great trays of cakes, pies, and cookies. They were sawing and hammering wood into little stands where drinks and tasty food would be sold. They were building booths for games, too, with prizes if you were lucky. The children were all helping, too. They were running errands, carrying things, and joking with one another.—REMY CHARLIP

236

> A description paints a picture with words.

Exercise   Forming a Picture in Your Mind

Here is a description. Read the paragraph. Then draw and color a picture of a mountain troll.

> Marty stared at the mountain troll. It was huge and covered with brown, shaggy hair. Flies and dead leaves clung to its body. The troll had three heads. Dirty clumps of lighter brown hair stuck out from each head. It had three long, thin noses with warts on the ends. Weeds grew from its noses and ears. It had three large upper teeth. They hung over its three lower lips. The troll's tail was thin and curved like a pig's tail. It was tied into two knots.

Now check your picture. Ask yourself these questions:

1. Is the troll huge and covered with brown, shaggy hair?
2. Are there flies and dead leaves on its body?
3. Does it have three heads?
4. Does it have clumps of lighter brown hair sticking out from each head?
5. Does it have long, thin noses?
6. Do the noses have warts on the ends?
7. Are weeds growing from its noses and ears?
8. Does it have three teeth? Do they hang over the lower lips?
9. Does it have a tail like a pig?
10. Does the tail have two knots?

237

Did you answer *yes* to all the questions? If so, you have formed a good picture in your mind. You have put your picture on paper.

Part 2   Pre-Writing: Choosing a Topic

The first step in writing anything is choosing a topic. When you write a description, the topic may be a place. Annie's Navajo world and the town square were topics of descriptions. The topic of a description may be a person. The paragraph about the Royal Wizard is an example. The topic of a description may be anything you can see or touch, taste or smell, hear or imagine.

Begin now to think of possible topics for a description. Make a list of things or people you know well. It helps if you can look at the topic of your description as you write about it. If you want to describe something imaginary, draw a picture. Use the picture as a guide.

Next, think about each possible topic. Do you want to describe only how it looks? The descriptions of Annie's world and the Royal Wizard tell how these things look. These descriptions tell about size, as in "high, copper-red bluffs" and "long blue robe." They tell about shape, as in "peaked hat." They tell about colors, as in these phrases: "pumpkins were yellow," "tassels were turning brown," "blue robe covered with golden owls."

Do you want to describe how the topic sounds? Imagine that you are describing a house that people say is haunted. Sounds might be very important in that description.

Do you want to describe how the topic feels? How would you describe the feel of clay or of spaghetti or of fur?

Do you want to describe how the topic tastes or smells? Sometimes you can compare new tastes or smells with tastes or smells that everyone knows about, such as those of chocolate or onions.

Here are other questions you should think about: Do you want to describe your topic standing still. Or do you want to tell about how it moves? The writer of the town square description wants the reader to see how busy the square was. He uses many action words, such as *sawing, hammering, building, running, joking.* He did not use many size, shape, or color words.

As you think about each possible topic on your list, make some notes. Write down the important **details** about that topic. Details are the small parts of a thing. They are the shapes and colors and sounds and smells. They are the actions that are special to that thing.

When you are finished, look at your lists of possible topics and their details. Some topics have more details than others. One topic may have many details about sight. Another topic may have details about sight and sound and action. Choose one topic. Decide whether you will answer one or more than one of these questions:

How does the topic look?
How does it sound?
How does it feel?
How does it taste?
How does it smell?
How does it move?

Then add more details to your list for that topic.

Exercise Choosing a Topic

Choose a topic for description. Follow the steps you have have learned in this part:

1. List possible topics.
2. Note details about each topic.
3. Choose the topic. Decide what you want to tell about it.   **239**

If you think of more details, add them to the list. Save your list of details for the topic you have chosen.

Part 3 Pre-Writing: Arranging Details

Here is a description. It is filled with details. Something is wrong with it, though. Can you figure out what?

1 The Zebra butterfly gets its name from its striped markings. 2 This butterfly has a long, narrow body. 3 The wings are dark brown. 4 Across each wing are three bands of yellow. 5 Attached to the butterfly's head are delicate feelers. 6 The body is nearly black in color and has yellow markings. 7 The feelers are almost as long as the body. 8 The butterfly has a wide wing span. 9 The front wings are almost half again as large as the back wings.

The description gives details about the body, feelers, and wings of the butterfly. However, the sentences are all mixed up. Sentence 1 is the topic sentence, sentence 2 gives a detail about the body. Sentences 3 and 4 give details about the wings. Sentence 5 gives a detail about the feelers. Then sentence 6 talks about the body once more. What does each of the other sentences tell about?

The description can be improved. First, the sentences need to be grouped according to what they describe. Sentences 2 and 6 tell about the body. Sentences 5 and 7 tell about the feelers. Sentences 3, 4, 8, and 9 tell about the wings.

Here is the rewritten paragraph. The details are in a better order. The description is now much easier to follow.

The Zebra butterfly gets its name from its striped markings. This butterfly has a long, narrow body. It is nearly black in color and has yellow markings. Attached to the butterfly's head are delicate feelers. They are almost as long as the body. The butterfly has a wide wing span. The front wings are almost half again as large as the back wings. The wings are dark brown. Across each wing are three bands of yellow.

What order is followed in this description?

> Big Bird is a large and famous bird. His body is almost completely covered with soft, yellow feathers. He has round, close-together eyes with pink and blue lids. Because he's so big, he must look down most of the time. Therefore, his eyelids are nearly always half-closed. Big Bird's long beak is yellow. His hands are yellow, too. His stick-like legs are orange. They have purple bands that end just above his orange, three-toed feet.

The writer first tells about Big Bird's large size and yellow feathers. This is what you would probably notice first. She then describes Big Bird's eyes, beak, hands, legs, and feet. She moves from top to bottom.

> The details in a description must follow some order.

Exercises Arranging Details

A. Think about what you look like. What is your size and shape? What color hair do you have? How would you describe your eyes, nose, and mouth? Is anything unusual about you?

Make a list of details that describe how you look. The details should be in top-to-bottom order.

Your teacher will collect the lists of details. She will mix up the lists. She will then give a list to each person in the class. That person should be able to recognize the person described.

B. Take out the list of details that you wrote for Part 2. Read over the list, and then arrange the details. Put them in a natural order that fits your topic. It may be top to bottom, front to back, inside to outside, or some other arrangement. Add any new details that you have thought of. Save your paper.

Natural Order

The description of the Zebra butterfly moves from body, to feelers, to wings. The description is in a **natural order.** The order is called *natural* because it is the way you would probably look at these things without even thinking.

There are many natural orders. Tall things, such as trees and buildings, are often described from bottom to top. People are often described from top to bottom.

Exercise **Putting Details in Order**

This description gives details about the stem, leaves, and flower of a plant. The details are mixed up. Rewrite the description so that the sentences are in some order.

The Spinner is an unusual plant. Its long straight stem is silvery. The plant has two sharply pointed leaves. The flower of the Spinner is a cluster of a hundred petals. During the day the stem sparkles in the sun. The flower catches every breeze and spins into a whirl of color. The silvery leaves grow halfway up the stem. At night the stem shines in the moonlight. Each petal is red, orange, or yellow.

Part 4 Writing: Using Details

The two paragraphs below describe the same subject. They both tell about the passengers on an elevator. They follow the same order. However, the second paragraph is much more interesting. It paints a much clearer picture than the first one. Read the two paragraphs and notice how important details are in a description.

Paragraph 1

The elevator had three passengers. One was a woman in a fur coat. She wore a hat and glasses. She held a dog. Another passenger was a man. He wore a coat and hat. He stood in the back of the elevator. The third passenger was a boy. He carried a box.

Paragraph 2

The elevator had three passengers. One was a tall, dignified woman in a mink coat. She wore a brown felt hat and round, green-framed sunglasses. She clutched a tiny, dark gray poodle wearing a red sweater. Another passenger was a crossing guard. He wore a bright yellow raincoat and a floppy hat. He stood in the back of the elevator with a happy smile on his face. The third passenger was a short, chubby delivery boy. He carried a large box of groceries marked JUDSON'S FINER FOODS.

Paragraph 2 gives you a much better idea of what the passengers look like. You can "see" them in your mind. They become interesting people.

Details help to paint a picture with words.

Ways of Using Details

The writer of Paragraph 2 used details well in her description. She followed these three guides.

1. Use adjectives to modify the nouns.

In Paragraph 1 the writer used many nouns. In Paragraph 2 adjectives describe some of these nouns.

Paragraph 1	Paragraph 2
woman	tall, dignified woman
hat	brown felt hat
glasses	round, green-framed sunglasses

2. Use exact words.

Words from Paragraph 1, such as *dog* and *man*, are **general words.** They fit many different mental pictures. Words from Paragraph 2, such as *poodle* and *crossing guard*, are **specific words.** They help you to form an exact picture.

Paragraph 1		Paragraph 2	
fur	dog	mink	poodle
glasses	man	sunglasses	crossing guard
held	coat	clutched	raincoat

3. Use phrases that add details.

Paragraph 2 added phrases to three of the sentences in Paragraph 1.

1. The *poodle* became *the poodle wearing a red sweater.*
2. The *crossing guard* became the *crossing guard with a happy smile on his face.*
3. The *box* became *a box of groceries marked JUDSON'S FINER FOODS.*

Exercises   Working with Details

A. In Column 1 are ten words and phrases. They have few details. In Column 2 details have been added to them. Answer these three questions about each phrase in Column 2.

1. What adjectives have been added?
2. Have any words been changed? What are the changes?
3. Have any phrases been added? If so, what are they?

Column 1	Column 2
the sky	the inky black sky
a bucket	a green plastic bucket with a hole in it
eyes	round eyes with thick lashes
teeth	sound white teeth
a horse	a gray pony with a white mark on its nose
toast	golden brown raisin toast
a tent	a green canvas tent
some people	a long line of teen-aged fans in blue jeans
a car	a shiny, red Mustang
a pickle	a fat, green dill pickle

B. Write a sentence about each of the following words. Add as many details as you can. You can add adjectives, change words, or add phrases.

1. shoes
2. boy
3. tool
4. street
5. animal
6. sandwich
7. toy
8. game
9. house
10. girl

C. Using the list of details you arranged in Part 3, write a description. First write a good topic sentence that tells the topic. Then write sentences that give details about the topic. Follow the natural order you chose in Part 3.

245

Part 5   Revising: Making Sure That Details Are Used Well

When you write a description, you cannot write everything you know about the subject. You must concentrate on those details that are important enough to include. Sometimes you may not put enough details into your description. Sometimes you may put in too many details. Until you finish writing and reread your work, you cannot tell whether your description has done the job you want it to do. To make sure that your description is the best you can write, you must revise it.

After you have written a description, put it aside for a while. It helps just to think about something else for a few minutes. Then when you reread your work, you can see it as if it were new to you. Try to picture in your mind what the paragraph is describing. Do the words paint a clear picture?

If there are not enough details, add some. Write the new details on your paper, between the lines. Use this symbol, $\wedge$, to show where a detail belongs. Add details in the three ways discussed in Part 4:

1. Add adjectives.
2. Change words to more exact, or specific, words.
3. Add phrases with details.

If your description has too many details, it can become confusing or boring. Choose the most important details. These give the reader something definite to remember about the subject. Cross out the less important details.

246   Check the order of your details, also. Perhaps your description would be clearer if you rearranged the details you have used.

Here is part of one girl's description. She has revised it, using a red pencil. Notice the changes.

> We have an ~~old~~ ^antique^ chest ^in our living room^. It is made of ~~wood~~ ^mahogany.^ ~~and~~ It is about three feet tall, ~~and~~ three feet wide, and two feet deep. There are claw feet on the ~~thin, curved~~ ^legs^ of the chest. ~~The legs are thin.~~

Add, take out, or rearrange details in your description. Then proofread it. Look for mistakes in grammar, capitalization, punctuation, and spelling. Mark the corrections on your paper.

Last, make a clean copy of your description. Use your best handwriting. When your paper looks clean and attractive, it shows how much work and care you have put into your writing.

Exercise   Revising a Description

Reread the description you wrote for Part 4. Can you add more details to make it clearer? Or should you take out or rearrange some details? Revise your description. Use the Guides for Revising on page 118 and the symbols for revising and proofreading on page 119. Then proofread your paragraph. Use the Guides for Proofreading on page 119. Complete the process of writing a description by making a final, clean copy.

Chapter 21

Writing Paragraphs That Explain Why

Why is the boy in the picture looking through a microscope? You probably can't explain why, but the boy can. When you ask someone why he or she is doing something, you are asking for an explanation.

You have studied paragraphs that paint pictures with words. You have studied paragraphs that tell what happened. In this chapter you will learn about another kind of paragraph. You will study paragraphs that explain why.

Part 1   Understanding Fact and Opinion

Many topic sentences for "why" paragraphs give opinions. An **opinion** is one person's idea about someone or something. Here are two opinions:

> That house is beautiful.
> That house is ugly.

These opinions are opposites. They express two different ideas. Opinions are neither right nor wrong. However, a person must explain his or her opinion. Then the reader can understand why the person thinks that way.

One way to understand an opinion is to compare it with a fact. A **fact** is true. It doesn't have to be explained. It can be proved. Here are two facts:

> That house is red.
> That house is made of bricks.

You can prove that these statements are true by looking at the house.

Study the difference between these pairs of facts and opinions. Each fact is true. It can be proved. Each opinion is one person's own idea. It cannot be proved. The person would need to explain his or her own reasons for thinking that way.

Fact	Opinion
1. Stick-All is a brand of glue.	1. Stick-All is poor glue.
2. Krispy Krunch is a cereal.	2. Krispy Krunch is a delicious cereal.
3. It is 50° and raining.	3. It is a miserable day.
4. The painting shows dandelions.	4. The painting is interesting.

An **opinion** is one person's idea about someone or something.

A **fact** is true. It can be proved.

Exercises   **Understanding Fact and Opinion**

A. Three of the following sentences are facts. Three are opinions. Divide a sheet of paper into two columns. Write the opinions in the first column. Write the facts in the second column.

1. Winter vacations are more fun than summer vacations.
2. Our nation's flag is red, white, and blue.
3. Roller skating is both an indoor and an outdoor sport.
4. Everyone should collect stamps.
5. Toasted cheese sandwiches are delicious.
6. The English language is different from the Russian language.

B. Choose two subjects. Write a one-sentence opinion about each.

1. A dessert
2. A television program
3. An animal that is a good pet
4. A person you know
5. A day of the week

Part 2 Giving Reasons

A "why" paragraph usually begins with an opinion. The opinion is the topic sentence. The rest of the paragraph explains the opinion. It gives reasons why the writer thinks that way. Here is an example.

> Roberto Clemente was a great person. He worked hard to become the best baseball player in the National League. Even when he was lonely and treated unfairly, he didn't give up. After he had become famous, Clemente helped many people. He gave time and money to people in Puerto Rico and other places, too. In fact, he died trying to help earthquake victims in Nicaragua.

The writer gives an opinion:

> Roberto Clemente was a great person.

This is the topic sentence. The writer then gives three reasons for thinking the way he does.

1. Roberto Clemente worked hard.
2. He didn't give up.
3. He helped many people.

Selecting Reasons

Choose a person whom you admire. It can be someone famous or someone who is not well known at all. Copy this topic sentence, filling in the blank.

_____ is a person who is easy to admire.

List at least three reasons for admiring the person. Write your reasons in complete sentences.

Leontyne Price

Jacques Cousteau

Pearl Bailey

Georgia O'Keeffe

Bjorn Borg

Arranging Reasons

The reasons given in a "why" paragraph should be in order. They should go from the least important to the most important.

Let us say you are going to write your opinion about a brand of toothpaste. You might begin with this topic sentence.

Brush-Brite is the best toothpaste.

You would next think about why you like Brush-Brite. You might list reasons such as these:

1. Brush-Brite is a powerful tooth cleaner.
2. Brush-Brite is a beautiful clear red.
3. Brush-Brite tastes like a cherry popsicle.

You would then arrange the reasons. There are different ways of arranging them. Here is one good way.

You would put the least important reason first. You would put the most important reason last. Your final list would probably look like this:

1. Brush-Brite is a beautiful clear red.
2. Brush-Brite tastes like a cherry popsicle.
3. Brush-Brite is a powerful tooth cleaner.

Finally, you would write your paragraph.

Brush-Brite is the best toothpaste. It is a beautiful clear red. It tastes like a cherry popsicle. Most important, Brush-Brite is a powerful tooth cleaner.

Reasons should be arranged from the least important to the most important.

A. Below are three sentences. They are opinions. Pretend that they are your opinions. For each, write three reasons for thinking the way you do. Put the least important reason first. Put the most important reason last.

1. Baseball is a good sport.
   a. _____(reason 1)_____
   b. _____(reason 2)_____
   c. _____(reason 3)_____

2. It is better to make a present than to buy one.
   a. _____(reason 1)_____
   b. _____(reason 2)_____
   c. _____(reason 3)_____

3. High Fliers are the best gym shoes.
   a. _____(reason 1)_____
   b. _____(reason 2)_____
   c. _____(reason 3)_____

B. Here is a list of topic sentences. They name make-believe products. Choose one. Give at least three reasons to explain the opinion given. Arrange the reasons from the least important to the most important. Then write the paragraph.

1. Tuffies are the best blue jeans.
2. Scrub-a-Dub is the best soap for dirty hands.
3. Snap is my favorite bubble gum.
4. Scramble is fun to play.
5. Every bike should have a Reflecto.

C. Read to a friend the paragraph that you wrote for Exercise B. Find out which reason he or she thinks is most important and which is least important. Then revise your paragraph as needed, proofread it, and make a clean copy.

Chapter 22

Writing a Story

What are your favorite stories? Are they animal tales? Are they cowboy adventures? Are they set in the past, in the present, or in the future? Are they about life on a farm? in a city? on another planet? Are they stories about boys and girls like you?

A story can be about anything. All stories, though, are alike in some ways.

A story is made up of several paragraphs.
A story tells about something that happened.
A story is made up by the writer.

Part 1 Studying an Example

Here is a story.

KING ASOKA

About 2,000 years ago, King Asoka was the ruler of India. He decided to declare war on Kalinga, a small country next to India. Asoka led his army into battle. The army fought for many days. It reached the capital of Kalinga and captured the enemy king.

As Asoka rode home from Kalinga, he saw thousands of dead soldiers on the battlefield. He heard wounded soldiers moaning, and women and children crying. His heart felt pain for those who had died and those who were suffering.

Asoka summoned his royal court. He sat on his magnificent throne, took out his sword, and broke it in two. "This sword will kill no more. There will be no more wars in my empire," he declared. "I will rule with love."

From that time on, Asoka was a different person. His heart had been changed. —ASHOK DAVAR

The story is about King Asoka. He is the main character. The story tells what happened to him.

1. He declared war on Kalinga.
2. He led his army into battle.
3. His army defeated Kalinga.
4. He saw the suffering he had caused.
5. He broke his sword and promised to rule with love.

What happened is described in the order that it happened.

The story takes place in India and Kalinga. These places are the **setting** of the story. The setting is where a story happens.

Exercise   **Studying a Story**

Here is another story. Read it. Then answer the questions.

OGRE PIZZA-OLA

Not too long ago, in a place not too far away, there
lived a good person who was as ugly as an ogre. For that
he was called Ogre. Ogre loved to make delicious pizza
pies, and for that he was called Ogre Pizza-Ola.

The pizzeria where Ogre worked was the most
popular place in town. Ogre made his pizzas just right.
He used lots of cheese, anchovies, mushrooms,
peppers, sausage, and gobs of rich tomato sauce.
Pizza lovers would travel for miles just for a slice.
After school, crowds of happy children filled the
pizzeria. None of them ever got a chance to meet
Ogre, though. He was so ugly that he had to stay
hidden away in the rear of the kitchen.

One day, Mrs. Worthington Flaunt, the
well known hostess, insisted on meeting the
chef. Before anyone could stop her, she was
in the kitchen. She came out screaming,
"There's an ogre in the kitchen!"

The secret was out. Parents panicked. They
clutched their children and whisked them away.
After that, no one came to the pizzeria again.
Ogre had to leave town in search of
a new job.

—BILL BASSO

259

1. The story has how many paragraphs?
2. Who is the main character?
3. Are there other characters?
4. What happens to the main character?
5. Where does the story take place? Does the story give this information?
6. When does the story take place? Is it in the past, present, or future?

Part 2   Writing a Story

You are ready to think about writing a story of your own. To write a story that other people will enjoy, follow the steps of pre-writing, writing, and revising.

Pre-Writing: Planning Your Story

In planning your story, you must think of three things: the characters, the setting, and the events.

You are ready to think about writing a story of your own. First you decide whom you are going to write about. You can write about an animal that acts like a human. You can write about a small child or about an older person. You can write about someone just like you. You can write about anyone or anything, real or imaginary.

Next, decide where your story will take place. It can take place in the present, the past, or the future. For some stories, setting is important. For others, it is not important at all.

Then plan the events in the story. List everything that will happen. Put the events in the order in which they happen.

Writing Your Story

When your plans are ready, write your story. Follow your plan. Include details that will make the story interesting.

Revising Your Story

Read over your story. Can you make it more interesting? Should you tell more? Should you add details?

Then proofread the story. Look for mistakes in grammar, capitalization, punctuation, spelling, or the form of the paragraphs.

Seven Steps To Help You Write a Story

Pre-Writing
1. Decide whom you are going to write about.
2. Decide where your story will take place.
3. List all the things that will happen. Put them in the order in which they will happen.

Writing
4. Write the story, following your plan.

Revising
5. Reread your story and revise it to make it more interesting.
6. Proofread your story. Correct any mistakes.
7. Make a clean copy.

Exercises Writing a Story

A. Superkid is a special ten-year-old. She can fly. She can see tiny things that are far away. She is very strong.

Write a three- or four-paragraph story. Use Superkid as your main character. Step 1 above has been done for you. Follow the other steps.

B. Write your own story. Follow the seven steps above.

Chapter 23

Using the Library

A library is like a treasure chest. A treasure chest is filled with money and jewels. A library has a different kind of riches. It is filled with materials that inform or entertain you. It has records, filmstrips, movies, and magazines. The most important things in it are its interesting books. It has books on just about anything you can think of.

The treasures of the library are yours. All you need are the keys. These keys are library skills. In this chapter you will learn these important skills:

1. How different kinds of books are arranged
2. How to find books
3. How to write a book report
4. How to find information in non-fiction books
5. How to find information in an encyclopedia.

Part 1   How Books Are Arranged

The library has two kinds of books. They are fiction and nonfiction.

Fiction Books

Fiction books are stories. They are made up by a writer. The writer of a book is called the **author.**

In the library, all fiction books are in one place. They are in alphabetical order. They are arranged according to the first letter of the author's last name. For example, a story by Lucille Clifton is put with the C's. A story by Crescent Dragonwagon is put with the D's.

Suppose that two authors' names have the same first letter. Then they are alphabetized by the second letter. Suppose the second letters are the same. Then they are alphabetized by the third letter. The following sets of words are in alphabetical order.

able	knock	send
about	knot	senior
above	know	sense

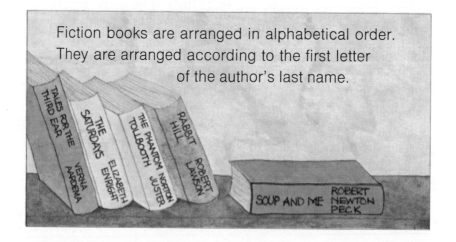

Fiction books are arranged in alphabetical order. They are arranged according to the first letter of the author's last name.

Arranging Fiction Books

A. Copy this list of authors. Underline the first letter of each author's last name. Then write the names in alphabetical order.

Taro Yashima	Elizabeth Coatsworth
Rodney Peppé	Kristin Hunter
Symeon Shimin	Ellen Raskin
Ezra Jack Keats	A. A. Milne
Ludwig Bemelmans	Alice Dalgliesh

B. Here are two groups of authors' names. The last names within each group begin with the same letter. Write the names in alphabetical order.

1. Leo Lionni	2. Roger Duvoisin
Arnold Lobel	Tomie de Paola
Hugh Lofting	James Daugherty
Joan M. Lexau	Bruce Degen
Astrid Lindgren	Glen Dines

C. Here is another list of authors. Write the last names in alphabetical order.

Albert Lamorisse	Mercer Mayer
Eros Keith	Kenneth Grahame
Maurice Sendak	Charlotte Zolotow
George Mendoza	Yoshiko Uchida

Nonfiction Books

Nonfiction books are about real persons, places, and things. They are arranged according to what they are about. They are arranged by their **subjects.** All books about the same subject are grouped together. For example, all books about history are together. All books about science are together.

265

Numbering Nonfiction Books

Every nonfiction book has a number. Many libraries use the same system for giving numbers. It is called the **Dewey Decimal System.**

The Dewey Decimal System has ten categories, or divisions. Each category includes books on certain subjects. Each category has a special set of numbers.

This chart shows the ten categories of the Dewey Decimal System. It shows the subjects in each category. It shows the special numbers given to each category.

Dewey Decimal System

Categories	Subjects	Numbers
General Works	(encyclopedias, almanacs)	000–099
Philosophy	(conduct, psychology)	100–199
Religion	(the Bible, religion)	200–299
Social Science	(law, education, folklore, government)	300–399
Language	(languages, dictionaries)	400–499
Science	(mathematics, chemistry, animals, plants, astronomy)	500–599
Useful Arts	(gardening, cooking, cars, crafts, television)	600–699
Fine Arts	(music, drawing, acting, games, sports)	700–799
Literature	(poetry, plays, short stories)	800–899
History	(biography, travel, geography)	900–999

Using the Chart

Let us look closely at the chart.

Books about television are in the category of Useful Arts. Find this category. It is given the numbers 600–699. Therefore, a book about television would have a number between 600 and 699. This is the **call number** of the book.

Books about sports are under Fine Arts. This category has the numbers 700–799. Therefore, a book about how to play basketball would have a call number between 700 and 799.

Under what category are books about education? What numbers are given to books in this category?

Under what category are books on cooking? What numbers are given to books in this category?

Under what category are books of poetry? What numbers are given to books in this category?

Fiction

Nonfiction

Using Call Numbers

Nonfiction books are placed on the shelves according to their call numbers. They are arranged in order from 000 to 999.

Fiction books are arranged in alphabetical order.
Nonfiction books are arranged in numerical order.

Exercises Arranging Nonfiction Books

A. Here is a list of books. Each book falls into one category of the Dewey Decimal System. Name the category. Tell what numbers are given to books in the category.

1. *How Did We Find Out About Outer Space?*   Isaac Asimov
2. *Stories from the Bible*   Walter de la Mare
3. *World Book Encyclopedia*
4. *Monster Poems*   Daisy Wallace
5. *How We Choose a President*   Lee Learner Gray
6. *Kids Camping*   Aileen Paul
7. *Sequoya, The Cherokee Who Captured Words*   Lilli Patterson
8. *Ice Hockey Rules*   Robert Scharf
9. *You Can Write Chinese*   Kurt Wiese
10. *Slapdash Cooking*   Carol Barkin and Elizabeth James

B. Go to your school, neighborhood, or city library. Draw a floor plan of the young people's section. Show where these books are shelved:

1. Fiction books
2. Nonfiction books
3. Encyclopedias

Part 2 Finding Books

Sometimes you go to the library to find an interesting book. You look over the shelves of fiction and nonfiction. You look through several books. Then you make a choice.

Other times you go to the library to get special books for a report. How do you find the exact books that you want?

If a book is fiction and you know the author's name, finding it is easy. You go to the fiction section. You look under the first letter of the author's last name.

What happens, though, when you know only the title of a book? What if you want many books on one subject? Then you must use the **card catalog.** The card catalog is an important key to the library's treasure of information.

The Card Catalog

The card catalog has information on every book in the library. The information is on cards. The cards are in alphabetical order. They are stored in long drawers. Each drawer is marked with a letter or letters of the alphabet. Cards for these letters are in that drawer.

The card catalog has three cards for each book on the shelves. One card is the **author card.** One is the **title card.** One is the **subject card.** Each card has the same basic information. Each gives the title of the book, the author, and the call number. However, the information is arranged in different ways.

The Author Card

On the author card, the name of the author is on the top line. The last name is first. The card is filed according to the first letter of the last name.

Here is an example of an author card. It is for the book *Beyond the High Hills, a Book of Eskimo Poems.* The letters *coll.* appear after the author's name. This means that he collected the poems.

author
808.1   **Rasmussen, Knud,** coll.

call number
            Beyond the high hills; a book of Eskimo
    title   poems. Photographs by Guy Mary
            Rousseliere. New York, World.   [1961]

O

The Title Card

On the title card, the title of the book is on the top line. The card is filed according to the first important word of the title. The words *a*, *an*, and *the* are not important words.

Here is the title card for the same book of Eskimo poems.

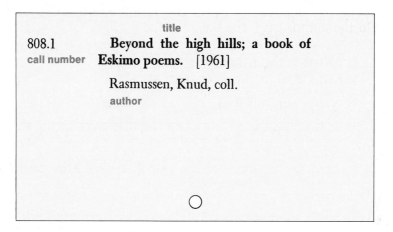

title
808.1   **Beyond the high hills; a book of**
call number   **Eskimo poems.**   [1961]

Rasmussen, Knud, coll.
author

The Subject Card

You will probably use subject cards most often. You will use them when you need information on a topic. You will use them when you want to look at many books on a subject.

On the subject card, the name of the subject is on the top line. The card is filed according to the subject name.

Here is the subject card for the book of Eskimo poems.

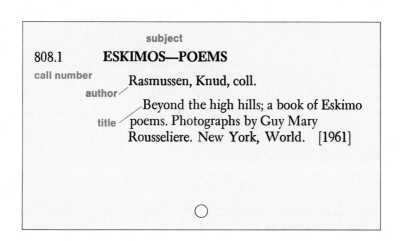

subject
808.1   **ESKIMOS—POEMS**
call number   Rasmussen, Knud, coll.
     author
       Beyond the high hills; a book of Eskimo
    title   poems. Photographs by Guy Mary
       Rousseliere. New York, World. [1961]

A. Here are two sample cards. Answer all of these questions about each of them.

1. What is the title of the book?
2. Who is the author of the book?
3. What is the call number of the book?
4. Is the card the author card, the title card, or the subject card?
5. Under what letter of the alphabet would the card be filed?

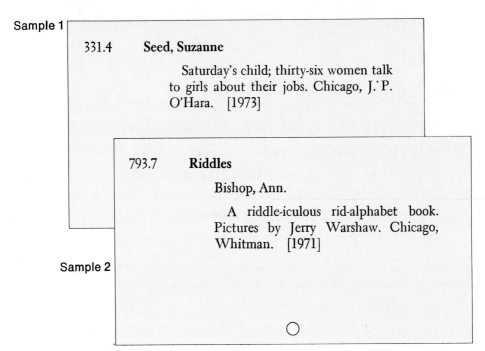

Sample 1

| 331.4 | **Seed, Suzanne** |

Saturday's child; thirty-six women talk to girls about their jobs. Chicago, J. P. O'Hara. [1973]

793.7 **Riddles**

Bishop, Ann.

A riddle-iculous rid-alphabet book. Pictures by Jerry Warshaw. Chicago, Whitman. [1971]

Sample 2

B. Choose three of these subjects. Use the card catalog to find one book on each subject. List the titles, authors, and call numbers of the books.

1. Birds   4. Black history   7. Curie, Marie
2. Weather   5. Thanksgiving   8. Photography
3. Cookery   6. Dinosaurs   9. Gymnastics

Part 3 Appreciating Books

You read books for many different reasons. Sometimes you read them just for fun. Sometimes you read them to find information. In this section you are going to learn some tips on how to get more out of the books you read. In this way, you will appreciate your books even more.

Reading for Enjoyment

Did you ever see a movie that you thought was exciting? You probably wanted to tell all your friends about it. Maybe they would want to see the movie, too. It is fun to share your experiences with others.

Just as you want to share a movie that you enjoyed, you may want to share a book that you enjoy. One way to share is to talk about the book. Another way is to write a **book report.**

In a book report, you should answer four important questions about the book:

1. What is the title?
2. Who is the author?
3. What is the book about?
4. Why do you like the book?

When you tell what the book is about, other people may become interested in it. If you give a good reason for liking the book, your friends will want to read it, too. If your report tells the title and author of the book, the people who are reading the report know exactly what book you are writing about. This makes it easy for them to find the book and read it.

273

You should put your ideas about your book in order before you write your report. In that way, you will be sure to tell all four things about your book.

You can write a book report about a fiction or a nonfiction book. If you make a report on a fiction book, your answer to question 3 should include the following information:

1. who is in the story
2. an important adventure or problem in the story

For some stories, it is also helpful to tell where and when the story takes place.

Here is an example of a book report. Read it and look for the four important things that a book report should tell.

> *Half Magic,* by Edward Eager, is about four children who find a magic coin. There is a problem with the coin, though. The coin grants only half of every wish. I liked this book because the children have lots of adventures, and the book is funny.

Exercises **Reading for Enjoyment**

A. Read the book report below and answer these four questions:

1. What is the title?
2. Who is the author?
3. Which sentences tell what the book is about?
4. Which sentence tells why the writer of the report liked the book?

> *Houses from the Sea,* by Alice E. Goudey, is a very interesting book. It tells about finding seashells. It describes seashells so you can tell what kind they are. I liked this book because it helped me identify the shells that I found last summer.

274

B. Choose a book that looks interesting to you. Read it. Write a report on it.

Reading for Information

Sometimes you need information about a subject. Books can give you the information you need. What is the best way to find that information?

Let us say you are looking for information about Morgan horses. You have found a book about horses by looking in the card catalog. How do you find out if the book has information about the Morgan horse?

First, look at the **table of contents** at the front of the book. Almost all nonfiction books and many fiction books have tables of contents. The table of contents lists every chapter in the book. It lists the page on which the chapter begins. By reading the table of contents, you can find out if there is a whole chapter on Morgan horses.

If your book does not have a whole chapter on your topic, where else can you look? The **index** may help you. An index is found at the back of almost every nonfiction book. It is a list of topics that are discussed in the book, arranged in alphabetical order. Each topic, or entry, is followed by the numbers of the pages on which that topic is discussed. Look at this example:

Morgan horse, 80–85
   characteristics, 82–84
   first Morgan horse, 80–81
   uses, 85
mules, 125
mustang, 48, 101

The second and third entries, *mules* and *mustangs,* simply show where those topics are discussed. The first entry is shown in more detail. The topic of Morgan horses can be found on six pages, 80 through 85. There are three subheadings that show where to find some specific information within those six pages. That way if you want to know how the Morgan horse is used, you can turn to page 85 immediately.

Imagine that, as you are reading, you come across this sentence: "Morgan horses stand about 15 hands high." You have never seen the word *hand* used in this way. How do you find out what it means? One way is to look in the **glossary.** The glossary is usually found at the back of the book before the index. It is a list of the difficult words from the book with definitions. Words used in a special way, such as *hand*, are also included. The words are listed in alphabetical order.

The glossary for a book about horses will tell you that *hand* means "A unit of measurement which is equal to four inches."

Not all books have glossaries. If you find a word that you do not understand, and your book does not have a glossary, you should look up the word in a dictionary.

Exercises   **Reading for Information**

A. Look at the table of contents of this book. Find Chapters 4, 7, and 12. Write on your paper the names of the chapters and the pages on which they begin.

B. Look at this sample index.

film, 96–101	indoor lighting, 228
focusing, 107–112	landscapes, 124, 198–207
framing, 247	lenses, 82–92
group pictures, 172	loading camera, 22

Look for each of the following topics in the sample index. If it is listed, write the topic and the page number or numbers on which it is found. If it is not in the index, write NO.

1. framing   3. lenses   5. filter   7. landscapes
2. flash   4. focusing   6. light   8. film

C. Find a book that has a glossary. Choose three entries defining words that are new to you. Copy the words and their definitions on your paper.

Part 4 Using an Encyclopedia

Encyclopedias are **reference books.** They stay in the library at all times. They have information on many different subjects.

An encyclopedia such as *World Book* or *Britannica Junior* has thousands of articles. The articles are in alphabetical order. Some are about subjects. They are arranged according to the first letter of the subject name. For example, the article "Snakes" is with the S's. The article "Glass" is with the G's.

Other articles are about people. They are alphabetized according to the person's last name. For example, the article on George Washington is alphabetized with the W's. The article on Susan B. Anthony is with the A's.

The title of every article is printed in dark type. The dark type helps you to find articles. It also helps you to know where articles begin and end. Here is an example:

LAKELAND TERRIER is one of the bravest dogs that ever dug a fox out of the ground. It comes from the Lake District of northern England. It was first raised to hunt marauding foxes and to protect sheep. It has a narrow body and a long head, with a beard around its chin. It may be black or blue with tan markings, red, or mustard color. The lakeland terrier weighs from 15 to 17 pounds (7 to 8 kilograms).

JOSEPHINE Z. RINE

The Lakeland Terrier Comes from Northern England.

Each book in a set of encyclopedias is called a **volume.** On the back of each volume are letters or words. They tell what part of the alphabet is covered in that volume.

Here are ten topics. Choose a set of encyclopedias. On your paper, write the name of the encyclopedia. Then number your paper from 1 to 10. Find the volume that has the article on each topic. Write the letter, letters, or words that are on the backs of the volumes.

1. Skiing
2. Rubber
3. Tortilla
4. Geronimo
5. Loch Ness monster

6. Brazil
7. Firefly
8. Eleanor Roosevelt
9. Lion
10. Martin Luther King

Finding Information

You can find information on a topic in two ways. You can go right to the article on the topic and read it. You can also look in the **Index.**

Using the Index

The Index is a separate volume. It lists all the subjects covered in the encyclopedia. They are in alphabetical order. It lists the articles that have information on each subject. It gives the volume and page numbers of each article.

Here are two samples from the Index of the *World Book Encyclopedia.*

Sample 1

Turtle [animal] T:426 *with pictures*
   Reptile R:230
   Terrapin T:138 *with picture*
   Tortoise T:267 *with picture*

Sample 2

Honey butter
  Honey (The Honey Industry) H:282-283

Studying Sample 1

The topic is turtles. You can read about them in the article **Turtle.** It is in volume **T,** on page 426. You can also read about turtles in the article **Reptile.** It is in volume **R,** on page 230. You can find more information in the article **Terrapin.** In what volume is this article? On what page is it? Where else can you read about turtles?

Studying Sample 2

The topic is honey butter. There is no article by this name. However, you can read about honey butter in the article **Honey.** It is in volume **H,** on pages 282 and 283.

When you use an Index, make a list of articles on your subject. Then read the articles.

Exercise   Using an Index

Here are ten subjects. Choose three of them. Look them up in the Index of one encyclopedia. List the articles that have information on each subject. Write the volume and page numbers of the articles.

1. Frederick Douglass
2. Wax museum
3. Grizzly bear
4. Robin Hood
5. Jackie Robinson
6. Bird-of-paradise flower
7. Mars
8. Tennis
9. Trumpet
10. Barbara Jordan

Chapter 24

Enjoying Poetry

Poems are more than words on a page.
Poems are alive. Poems talk.
They tell us about feelings and ideas.
They stretch our imaginations.
Poems show us our world.

You can write a poem about something beautiful. You can write a poem about something sad. You can write a poem about something funny. Let's look at some of the things that make poems work.

Part 1 Getting To Know the Speaker in Poems

One person usually does most of the talking in a poem. That person is called the **speaker.**

The speaker does different things in different poems. In some poems the speaker tells us a story. In other poems the speaker is like a character in a play. He or she talks to someone else in the poem.

To find out about the speaker in a poem, ask these questions:

1. Who is speaking?
2. To whom is the speaker talking?
3. What are the speaker's feelings?

Here is a poem that is like a lullaby. It contains two people. The people are a speaker and a little child. The speaker is talking, or maybe singing, to the child. Listen while your teacher reads the poem to you.

YOU HAVE ME

Sleep, my little one,
sleep and smile,
for the night-watch of stars
rocks you awhile.

Drink in the light,
and happy be,
All good you have
in having me.

Sleep, my little one,
sleep and smile,
for the earth in love
rocks you awhile.

Look at the bright rose,
red as can be.
Reach out to the world
as you reach out to me.

Sleep, my little one,
sleep and smile,
For God in the shade
rocks you awhile.

—GABRIELA MISTRAL
Translated by Langston Hughes

The speaker in "You Have Me" is probably a mother. However, it could be a father, or an older brother or sister. The speaker is talking to a child. He or she is rocking the child to sleep. What feelings does the speaker show?

This poem is gentle. The speaker wants to make the child feel calm. Parents can soothe little children by saying the same words over and over, very softly. Suppose a child is upset. A mother might pat the child and say, "There, there."

In "You Have Me," the speaker says this over and over:

> Sleep, my little one,
> sleep and smile,

In a poem or a song, a set of lines repeated several times is called a **refrain.** The refrain in this poem helps us feel the speaker's tenderness.

Can you think of other poems or songs that have refrains?

Guides for Getting To Know the Speaker in Poems

Find out these things about the people in the poem.

1. Who is speaking?
2. To whom is the speaker talking?
3. What are the speaker's feelings?

Exercises   **Getting To Know the Speaker in Poems**

A. Take turns reading "You Have Me" aloud.

1. Think about the speaker's feelings. Let your voice show those feelings.

2. Pay attention to the refrain. Make it sound soothing. Imagine you are rocking a child to sleep.

B. Find another poem that has a speaker in it.

    1. On your paper, tell who the speaker is.

    2. Practice reading the poem out loud.

    3. Then read the poem to your class.

    4. Ask the class to tell you what your reading showed about the speaker of the poem.

C. In the poem "You Have Me," the lines that are repeated are called a *refrain.* Write a short poem of your own that has a refrain. Use the same line at least twice.

Part 2   Seeing the Pictures in Poetry

Some poets are like painters. Instead of a brush, a poet uses words. Look at the pictures in the poems below.

A Still Picture

The following poem is called a **haiku** (hī′ kōo). A haiku is a short poem. It has only three lines. It describes a scene. The details are very clear. Listen while your teacher reads this haiku.

ON A SANDY BEACH

On a sandy beach
glassy chips sparkle
in the spring sunshine
      —MASAOKA SHIKI, *Translated by Makota Ueda*

Now pretend you are a painter. You are going to paint a picture of this poem. What things would you put into your picture?

Does the poem remind you of anything you have seen? How does the poem make you feel?

Now let's look at another haiku. This one compares things.

LIKE A DIAMOND

Like a diamond
a drop of dew, all alone
on a stone

—KAWABATA BŌSHA, *Translated by Makota Ueda*

First picture a diamond. Now picture a drop of dew. In what way are they alike?

The drop of dew is all by itself on a stone. It is beautiful. It is also alone. What time of day do you think it is?

Pretend you are taking a walk. Suddenly, you see the scene the poet describes. How would it make you feel?

A Moving Picture

The poem below pictures a girl playing dress-up. The girl moves. This poem is more like a moving picture than a still painting.

I LOOK PRETTY

Mama's shiny purple coat
Giant-sized shoulder bag to tote
Tall, tall shoes and pantyhose
Big straw hat with shiny bows
I look pretty
I float
I smile
I pose

—ELOISE GREENFIELD

The poem shows a picture of a child playing dress-up. First we see the coat. Then we see the shoulder bag. Next the poem shows a picture of her shoes and stockings. Then the poem shows a picture of the hat.

The last four lines are different. The poem shows the child's face. The poem also shows her moving. Is she having fun? How can you tell? Do you think she might be looking into a mirror?

Guides for Seeing Pictures in Poetry

Find out these things about the poem.

1. What things does the poet put into the picture?
2. Does the picture show you the time of day?
3. Does the picture look like a painting?
4. Does the picture move?
5. Does the picture remind you of anything you have seen?
6. How does the picture make you feel?

Exercises   **Seeing the Pictures in Poetry**

A. Write a poem that is like a haiku. Describe something you have special feelings about. Your poem should be three lines long. It should paint a picture. The details should be clear.

B. Write a poem that is like a moving picture. Your poem should describe a person doing something. Keep your poem short. It does not have to rhyme.

You may choose your own subject. If you have trouble, here are a few suggestions.

1. Running in a field	4. Splashing in the water
2. Climbing a tree	5. Planting a garden
3. Walking in the snow	6. Riding in a car

Part 3 Hearing the Sound Patterns in Poetry

One sound pattern that poets often use is **rhyme.**

Rhyme

Many words in our language have the same ending sound. When words have the same ending sound, they **rhyme.** For example, *cat* rhymes with *rat*. *Rabbit* rhymes with *habit*.

Here is a poem that rhymes.

A MODERN DRAGON

A train is a dragon that roars through the dark.
He wriggles his tail as he sends up a spark.
He pierces the night with his one yellow eye,
And all the earth trembles when he rushes by.

—ROWENA BASTIN BENNETT

The rhyming words are *dark* and *spark*, and *eye* and *by*. The rhymes form a pattern. The last words in the first and second lines rhyme. The last words in the third and fourth lines rhyme.

Exercises Working with Rhyme

A. Copy these words on your paper. Next to each word, write two more words that rhyme with it.

1. boat   3. night   5. dog   7. chair
2. cool   4. cup   6. child   8. clown

B. Write a short poem that uses rhyme. Use the rhyming words at the ends of the lines.

Alliteration

Alliteration is another sound pattern. **Alliteration** occurs when consonant sounds are repeated. Tongue twisters are built on alliteration. Here's a famous example: Peter Piper picked a peck of pickled peppers. Can you think of others?

Here's a poem that uses alliteration. Listen while your teacher reads it to you.

THE SNAKE

A snake slipped through the thin green grass
A silver snake
I watched it pass
It moved like a ribbon
Silent as snow.
I think it smiled
As it passed my toe.

—KARLA KUSKIN

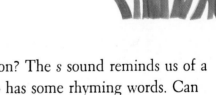

Can you hear the alliteration? The *s* sound reminds us of a snake hissing. The poem also has some rhyming words. Can you find them?

Guides for Hearing the Sound Patterns in Poetry

1. Look for rhyme. Rhyme occurs when words have the same ending sound.
2. Look for alliteration. Alliteration occurs when consonant sounds are repeated.
3. Find out if those sounds form patterns in the poem.

A. Write three sentences. In each sentence use alliteration. Underline the words that begin with the same consonant sound.

B. Write a short poem. Make at least two of the lines rhyme. Try to include some alliteration in the poem also.

Part 4   Hearing the Rhythm in Poetry

Poems are like music. They have rhythm. In some poems the rhythm is very strong. If you read a poem aloud, you hear the beats.

Listen while your teacher reads the poem below.

A GOPHER IN THE GARDEN

There's a gopher in the garden and he's eating all the
　onions,
and he's eating all the broccoli and all the beets and
　beans,
and he's eating all the carrots, all the corn and
　cauliflower,
all the parsley, peas, and pumpkins, all the radishes and
　greens.

At breakfast, lunch or dinnertime the gopher is no
　loafer
and he quickly will devour everything before his eyes.
He does not even hesitate to eat a cabbage twice his
　weight,
or a watermelon five or six or seven times his size.

—JACK PRELUTSKY

290

Can you hear the rhythm? Read the poem aloud yourself. Try to tap out the rhythm.

This poet fits the rhythm to the meaning of the poem. The hungry gopher starts out eating "all the onions." There are only four beats in the first line. Let's put a mark over each sound that has a strong beat.

There's a gópher in the gárden, and he's éating all the ónions.

What happens in the poem? The gopher eats more and more. He stuffs the food in faster and faster.

The poet is clever. He makes the rhythm match the meaning. The gopher crams in food, and the poet crams in beats.

By the end of the poem, the gopher has stuffed himself. The cabbage and watermelon are bigger than he is. Meanwhile, the poet has stuffed beats into the last two lines of the poem. Instead of four beats in a line, there are eight:

> He dóes not éven hésitáte to éat a cábbage twíce his
> weíght,
> ór a wátermélon fíve or síx or séven tímes his síze.

Like the gopher, the poem is almost bursting.

Now try reading the poem aloud again. It's hard to read the last two lines. The poet has packed the rhythm tightly. He wants us to know how the gopher feels.

Guides for Hearing the Rhythm in Poetry

1. Read the poem aloud. Tap out the rhythm with your hand or your foot.
2. Mark the strong beats in each line.
3. Decide whether or not the poem has strong rhythm.

Exercises Hearing the Rhythm in Poetry

A. Copy this poem on your paper. Read it aloud. Mark the strong beats in each line.

AT HOME

Mix a pancake,
Stir a pancake,
   Pop it in the pan;
Fry the pancake,—
Toss the pancake
   Catch it if you can.

—CHRISTINA ROSSETTI

B. Discuss the rhythm of the poem. Answer these questions.

  1. Is the rhythm strong?
  2. Do the beats form a pattern?
  3. Does the rhythm seem right for the meaning of the poem?

C. Think of a lively subject. Write a short poem that has strong rhythm. Mark the strong beats in each line. Change words to make the beats into an even pattern.

Chapter 25

Writing a Report

You are reading a book about dinosaurs. You read something interesting. You would like to know more about it. You think others in the class might like to know about it, too. What can you do? You can prepare a report.

In this chapter you will learn how to write a three-paragraph report. You will learn about the following:

Pre-Writing	Choosing a subject
	Gathering information
	Making a plan
Writing	Writing a report
Revising	Revising for ideas
	Proofreading a report
	Sharing a report

To prepare a report, you need many skills. Some are skills you have already learned. You may need to learn some new skills, too. This chapter will help you. It will teach you the skills you need to prepare a good report.

Part 1 What Is a Report?

You can learn about a subject in many ways. One is by reading books. You can share what you learn in many ways, too. A report is a good way to share information about a subject.

Here is an example of a report.

WHAT CAUSES WIND

Wind is air moving from one place to another. Some air moves because it is pushed. This is what happens when you turn on a fan or blow out a candle. Most air moves because of differences in temperature. Warm air rises. Cooler air moves in to take its place.

Wide belts of wind circle the earth. They begin when air from the equator, the warmest part of the earth, rises. The air moves north and south, away from the equator. As the air cools, it begins to drop. It moves slowly toward the earth. It then moves back toward the equator. While the air is moving, the earth is rotating. This changes the path of the air.

Local winds are also created by differences in temperature. In summer, land warms up faster than water. The warm air above the land rises. Cooler air from the water rushes in. A breeze blows from water to land. In winter, land cools more quickly than water. The air then moves from land to water. Mountains, valleys, and big cities all affect temperature. Therefore, they help to create winds, too.

I got my information from these sources:

The Winds That Blow by Brenda Thompson and Cynthia Overbeck
The New Air Book by Melvin Berger
Compton's Encyclopedia, "Winds"

Studying the Example

The report is about wind. It tells what causes wind. This is the subject of the report.

The title of the report is "What Causes Wind." It tells what the report is about. It names the subject.

The report has three paragraphs. Each tells something about what causes wind. The first paragraph is about all wind. The second is about wide belts of wind. The third is about local winds. The three paragraphs include many facts about what causes wind.

The writer read about wind in three books. He gives the titles and authors of these books at the end of the report.

A report is made up of paragraphs. The paragraphs give facts about a subject.

Here is a report. Read it. Then answer the questions.

BREAKING THE PIÑATA

Breaking the piñata is a Christmas custom in Latin American countries. A piñata is a clay or papier-mâché jug. It can be made in any shape. It can look like a ship or a shoe or a bird. The outside of a piñata is decorated with tinsel and colored crepe paper. The inside is hollow. It is filled with candy and small presents. A piñata is hung from a ceiling with a rope.

One child is blindfolded. Then that player swings a stick and tries to break the piñata. After three tries, the next person gets a turn.

Someone usually breaks the piñata. The candy and presents tumble to the ground. The children scramble after them.

I got my information from these sources:
Disney's Wonderful World of Knowledge, "Holidays Around the World"
Britannica Junior Encyclopedia, "Christmas"
Childcraft, "Holidays and Customs"

1. What is the subject of the report?
2. What is the title?
3. How many paragraphs does the report have?
4. What does the first paragraph tell about piñatas?
5. What does the second paragraph tell about piñatas?
6. What does the third paragraph tell about piñatas?
7. List five important facts about piñatas and how they are broken.
8. Where did the writer's information come from?

Part 2 Pre-Writing: Choosing a Subject

Most reports will be about something you are studying. Many times you will be given a subject. Sometimes, though, you will need to find one of your own. This is how to do it.

Make a List

First, read through the chapter or unit you are studying. List the subjects you would like to know more about. Choose the three that are the most interesting.

Here is how one student began. Her class was studying the Old West. She looked through the unit. She chose three subjects:

1. The life of a cowboy
2. Pueblo houses
3. Totem poles

Use the Library

Next, find out if there is enough information on your subjects. To do this, go to the school or neighborhood library. Look for your subjects in the card catalog. You may need to look in several sections for each. For example, to find out about the life of a cowboy you might try these subject cards: Cowboy, The Old West, Ranch Life, and United States. List the titles, authors, and call numbers of the books on your subjects. Save this list. You will need to use it again.

Find the books on the library shelves. Look through them. You do not have to read them carefully. You are just getting an idea of how much information there is.

Next, read about your subjects in two or three encyclopedias. Check the encyclopedia indexes, too. Add the names of the encyclopedias, the volume numbers, and page numbers to your list of books.

You may not find much information about a certain subject. Cross that subject off your list.

You may find too much information. You will then have to think about limiting the subject. Let us say you have listed *electricity*. You have found many books about electricity. You have also found many pages about electricity in encyclopedias. You decide that this subject is too big for a short report. As you read, you think of a better subject—how a light bulb works. On your list you change *electricity* to *how a light bulb works*. Doing this limits your report. *How a light bulb works* becomes the main idea of your report.

Decide on a Subject

You now have a final list. It has three subjects. You know that there is enough information about each. You also know that there is not too much information. Choose the one subject that is most interesting to you.

A Good Subject for a Report

A good subject is interesting to you.
A good subject has enough written about it.
A good subject is not too big for a short report.

Do either Exercise A or Exercise B.

A. Look through a chapter of your science or social studies book. List three subjects that you find interesting. Check for information in the library. Cross out or change subjects if you like. Then choose one subject for a report.

B. Choose two of these subjects. Look for information in the library. If you find too much information about a subject, limit your search to one main idea about that subject. Then choose one subject for a report.

1. Recycling milk cartons
2. What coal miners do
3. Prairie dog towns
4. How deaf people communicate
5. How cheese is made
6. How a tadpole becomes a frog
7. Why dinosaurs died out
8. The Chinese new year

Part 3 Pre-Writing: Learning About the Subject

You have chosen a subject. Now you must learn about it. To do this, you must return to the library. This time you know exactly what kind of information you are looking for.

Earlier, you listed books on your subject. Find each of these books on the shelves. You can either check them out or use them in the library. Read the parts of the books that are on your subject.

You also listed encyclopedias. Read about your subject in these books, too.

Taking Notes

You will learn many facts as you read. You need to remember them. Taking notes will help you.

A good way to take notes is on 3x5 index cards. At the top of each, write where you got the information. Then write a fact about your subject. Write the fact in your own words. Do not copy the information. Write each fact on a separate card.

Here are two examples:

Note Card 1

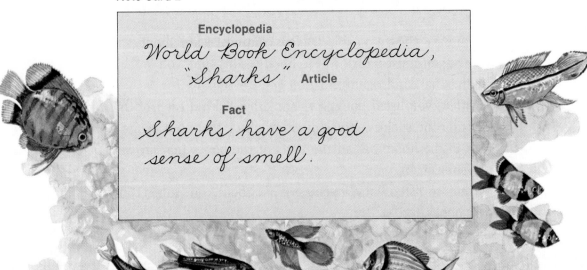

Title

Hungry Sharks by John F. Waters Author

Fact

A shark can smell blood from a wounded fish.

Note Card 2

Encyclopedia

World Book Encyclopedia, "Sharks" Article

Fact

Sharks have a good sense of smell.

Note Card 1 shows a fact learned from a book. It gives the title and author of the book. The fact is in the writer's own words.

Note Card 2 shows a fact from an encyclopedia. It gives the name of the encyclopedia and of the article. This fact is also in the writer's own words.

> You read in order to learn about a subject.
> Notes help you remember what you read.

As you take notes, you may decide that you don't want this subject after all. There may be too much information. You may have to limit the subject to a smaller idea.

There may be too little information, or you may not be interested anymore. If this happens, choose another subject. Start all over to learn about your new subject.

Exercises   Reading and Taking Notes

A. Read this paragraph. On a 3 x 5 index card write the name of the book and the author. Then write one fact that you learned. Write it in your own words.

Some squirrels build summer houses high in trees. A female squirrel first heaps up leaves and twigs. She hollows out the inside. She then lines it. She presses moss, leaves, and chewed bark against the sides. Her finished nest is soft and waterproof.

303

B. Read about your subject in books and in encyclopedias. Take notes as you read.

Part 4 Pre-Writing: Planning the Report

Planning is important. It takes a lot of thinking. You must decide what information to include in your report. You must decide what not to include. You must put your facts in order.

Rereading Your Notes

Begin your plan by rereading your note cards. Many of them will be on the same main idea. Think of questions about the main idea of your report. Write the questions on a sheet of paper. Choose three important questions that your notes can answer. Cross out any other questions.

One writer chose to report on sharks. Susan, the writer, read a book and an encyclopedia article about sharks. She decided to limit her subject to the ways that sharks find food. She reread the book and the encyclopedia article and wrote many facts on 3 x 5 cards. Then she reread her cards. She decided to answer these three questions in her report:

1. How do sharks find most of their food?
2. In what other way do sharks find food?
3. Can sharks see their food?

Sorting Your Notes

Some of your note cards will help to answer your first question. Put them into one pile. Some of them will help to answer your second question. Put them into a second pile. Put the cards for your third question into a third pile.

Some cards probably will not fit into any pile. Put them into a fourth pile. You may decide to use them later.

Fasten each pile of cards together. Use rubber bands or paper clips. Label them *1, 2, 3,* and *extra cards.*

Beginning Your Plan

Reread your note cards. Write three questions. Then sort your cards into three or four piles.

Making an Outline

An outline is very helpful. It shows what will be covered in a report. It shows the facts in the order that they will be given.

The first step in making an outline is to answer your three questions. Susan wrote these answers.

1. Sharks find food by sensing the movements of fish.
2. Sharks also find most of their food by smell.
3. Sharks can see their food, too.

The next step is to write the outline. Use your three questions as the three main topics. Use your facts as subtopics. Under main topic *I.* write the facts from the cards in pile 1. Under main topic *II.* write the facts from pile 2. Under main topic *III.* write the facts from pile 3. Arrange the facts in the order you want to give them in your report.

The third step is to write the title. The title of the outline will be the title of the report. It should tell the main idea of the report.

When Susan was planning her report on sharks, she made the outline shown on the following page.

How Sharks Find Food

Main topic   I. Sharks find food by sensing the movements of fish.

Subtopics ⟨
A. Fish cause vibrations
B. Shark hears sounds with its ears   (facts from pile 1)
C. Shark feels sounds with the hollow tubes on either side of its body

Main topic   II. Sharks also find most of their food by smell.

Subtopics ⟨
A. Shark has nose with two openings
B. Shark swims and water goes through nose
C. Shark smells blood   (facts from pile 2)
D. Shark follows smell
E. Shark finds wounded fish

Main topic   III. Sharks can see their food, too.

Subtopics ⟨
A. Shark notices moving fish
B. Shark sees in dim light
C. Shark sees in bright light   (facts from pile 3)
D. Shark hunts for food at night as well as day

Correct Form for an Outline

1. Important words in the title are capitalized.
2. Main topics are labeled with Roman numerals followed by periods.
3. Subtopics are labeled with capital letters followed by periods.
4. The first word of each main topic and subtopic is capitalized.
5. Main topics are listed one under the other.
6. Subtopics are listed one under the other.

Answer your three questions. Then make your outline. Use the three answers as main topics. Use the facts from each group of cards as the subtopics. Check your finished outline. It should follow correct outline form.

Part 5 Writing the Report

You are now ready to write your report. It is important to follow your outline. Begin by copying main topic I. This is your first topic sentence. Then complete the first paragraph. The sentences should cover the subtopics under main topic I.

Write your second and third paragraphs in the same way. First copy the main topic from your outline. Then write other sentences to cover the subtopics.

When you finish, you will have a three-paragraph report. Each paragraph will give facts. They will tell about the subject of the report.

Follow your outline when writing a report.

Exercise **Writing Your Report**

It is now time to write your report. Follow your outline closely. Be sure to use the three main topics of the outline. Use them as the topic sentences of your three paragraphs.

Part 6   Revising the Report

The next step after writing your report is revising it. Is your report as good as it could be? By rereading it carefully and changing it a little, you can improve it.

These questions will tell you what to look for as you read your report. Mark the changes in the report as you read it. Pretend you are reading it for the first time. That may help you see where the report is not clear. Maybe you will think of a better way to say what you want to say.

Guides for Revising

1. Look at the report as a whole. Is it interesting? Is it easy to understand?

2. Do all three paragraphs tell about the main idea, or subject, of the report?

3. Does each paragraph begin with a topic sentence?

4. Do all the sentences in a paragraph stick to the main idea of that paragraph? Should any words or sentences be taken out?

5. Should any sentences be added to a paragraph to make it cleaner? Do any sentences need more words?

6. Is every group of words a complete sentence?

7. Does the title tell the subject of the report? Does it limit the subject enough?

8. Compare your report with the notes you took. Did you copy the facts from your notes correctly? Are there any left-out facts that would be useful in the report?

Here is the shark report after Susan revised it. The marks tell how she wants to change what was written.

~~Sharks~~ How Sharks Find Food

Sharks, ^also^ find food by sensing the movements of the fish. ~~They~~ ^Fish^ make vibrations, or, ^sound^ waves, in, ^the^ water. A shark can hear the sound with its ears ~~and~~ it also can feel the sound. ~~It feels the sound through~~ ~~some~~ through hollow tubes the tubes can be found on ~~the~~ ^either^ side of its body.

Sharks find most, ^of their^ food by smelling ~~it~~. A shark's nose has 2 openings. ~~A shark can swim fast.~~ As the shark swims, water goes through ~~2~~ openings. The ~~shark~~ ^Animal^ picks up the smell of ~~the~~ blood from the water around him. ~~The shark~~ ^It^ follows the smell until it finds a woonded fish ~~, that is bleeding~~. ¶ Sharks can see their food, too. Sharks are good, ^especially^ at noticing moving ~~things like~~ fish.

~~Dim light is as good as bright light for sharks~~ Most sharks see as well in dim light as in bright ~~to see things in and so sharks can hunt at~~ light and so this helps him hunt for food at night. ~~night and day, too.~~

The writer made many changes. She moved the paragraph about the sharks' sense of smell to come first. Then she used this symbol, ¶, to show where the third paragraph should have been indented. Find all of her other changes.

309

Exercise   **Revising for Ideas**

Revise your report. Follow the guides on page 308.

Proofreading

After revising your report for ideas, you must proofread it. Proofreading is part of revising. You are still looking for ways to improve your report. When you proofread, though, you are looking for mistakes in form, capitalization, punctuation, and spelling. You are also looking for grammar mistakes and the wrong use of words.

Ask yourself these questions as you reread your report.

Guides for Proofreading

Form

1. Is the first line of each paragraph indented? (See page 105)

Grammar

2. Did you avoid combining sentences that should be separate? (Pages 54 to 57)

3. Is every pronoun used correctly? (Pages 77 to 87)

4. Is every verb form correct? Are helping verbs needed? (Pages 161 to 171, 180-185)

Capital Letters

5. Does every sentence begin with a capital letter? (Page 340)

6. Does every proper noun begin with a capital letter? (Pages 336 to 339)

7. Are the words in the title capitalized correctly? (Pages 342 and 343)

Punctuation

8. Does every sentence have the correct end mark? (Pages 347 to 351)

9. Are commas, apostrophes, and other marks used correctly? (Pages 352 to 362)

Spelling

10. Is every word spelled correctly? (Pages 367 to 375)

Before Susan could proofread her report, she had to copy it. She had marked so many revisions on the first copy that it was hard to read. In her second copy she changed everything she had marked for change.

Then Susan proofread the report. She found that it still had mistakes. She marked them for corrections. Here are the first and last paragraphs of the report after proofreading. Find all the corrections.

> Sharks find most of their food by smell⊙ A shark's nose has ∧2 openings. As the shark swims, water goes through ∧openings. The Animal picks up the smell of blood from the water∧around ~~him~~. It follows the smell until it finds a (woonded) fish.
>
> *two* *these* (sp) *wounded*

> Sharks can see their food, too. Sharks are (good espeecially) at noticing moving fish. Most sharks see as well in dim light as in bright light⊙ and so this helps ~~him~~ hunt for food at night.
>
> *them* *as well as day*

Symbol	Meaning	Symbol	Meaning
≡	Capitalize a letter.	⊙	Add a period.
/	Change a capital letter to a lowercase letter.	⋀	Add a comma.
		∩	Trade places.
∧	Add letters or words.	¶	Indent a line to show the beginning of a paragraph.
—	Leave something out.		

311

Look at the first copy of your report. If it is too marked-up with revisions for you to read it easily, copy it. Then proofread the report. Use the questions on page 310 as a guide. Mark your corrections on your paper.

Giving Credit

You wrote your report in your own words. However, you got your facts from books. You must list the names of the books you used.

Susan made a clean copy of her report *How Sharks Find Food*. Then she added this to the end of the report.

I got my information from these sources:
Hungry Sharks by John F. Waters
World Book Encyclopedia, "Sharks"

She underlined the title of the book. She capitalized the title of the book and the name of the article. She capitalized the name of the author. She put quotation marks around the name of the article.

Studying an Example

Here is what Susan wrote in the final copy of her report.

How Sharks Find Food

Sharks find most of their food by smell. A shark's nose has two openings. As the shark swims, water goes through these openings. The animal picks up the smell of blood from the water. It follows the smell until it finds a wounded fish.

Sharks also find food by sensing the movements of fish. Fish cause vibrations, or sound waves, in the water. A shark can hear the sound with its ears. It can also feel the sound. It does this through hollow tubes. The tubes are on either side of its body.

Sharks can see their food, too. They are especially good at noticing moving fish. Most sharks see as well in dim light as in bright light. This helps them to hunt for food at night as well as day.

I got my information from these sources:
Hungry Sharks by John F. Waters
World Book Encyclopedia, "Sharks"

Exercise **Finishing Your Report**

You have written your report, revised it, and proofread it. Now it is time to make the final copy. Use your best handwriting. Be sure to make all the changes you marked on your earlier copies.

At the end of your report, tell where you got your information. Give the titles and authors of any books you used. Give the names of the encyclopedias and the titles of the articles.

Part 7 The Process of Writing

You have learned much about the process of writing a report. This chart shows all the steps you have followed. Whenever you write, you will follow the steps of pre-writing, writing, and revising.

Steps for Writing a Report

Pre-Writing

1. Choose a subject.
   Make a list of interesting subjects.
   Look for information.
   Decide on one subject.

2. Learn about your subject.
   Gather information about your subject.
   Take notes.

3. Plan your report.
   Reread your notes.
   Write the main ideas that your notes tell about.
   Sort your notes according to the main ideas.
   Make an outline with your main ideas as topics.
   Facts from your notes should be subtopics.

Writing

1. Write a paragraph for each topic in your outline.

2. Begin each paragraph with a topic sentence.

3. Write a sentence about the subtopics.

Revising

1. Revise your report. Use the Guides for Revising on page 308.

2. Proofread your report. Use the Guides for Proofreading on page 310.

3. Make a clean copy.

4. List the titles and authors of the books you used.

Part 8   Sharing a Report

There are many ways to share a report. You might hang it on a bulletin board. You might put it into a book, along with the reports of your classmates. You might exchange your report with a partner.

Another way to share your report is to read it aloud.

When you read a report aloud, you are sharing interesting facts. Pictures can often make the facts even more interesting. You might want to use pictures with your report.

There are different ways to use pictures. You can show them while you are reading. You can hang them up beforehand. You can pass them around afterwards.

You should choose your pictures ahead of time. You should also decide when and how you want to show them.

Another part of getting ready is practicing. Stand in front of a mirror or ask someone in your family to help you. As you read your report, remember these things:

1. Stand still.
2. Look up from the paper once in a while.
3. Speak loudly enough to be heard.
4. Speak slowly enough to be understood.
5. Do not speak too slowly.
6. Stress the main facts.

Being prepared is the secret to giving a good report.

Exercise   **Sharing Your Report**

Decide with your teacher how you will share your report. You might decide to read it out loud. If so, get ready. Decide on pictures. Practice giving the report.

Chapter 26

Writing Friendly Letters

Everybody likes to receive letters. A letter tells you that someone was thinking of you. Maybe your friend wanted to share some news with you. Maybe your friend wanted to find out what you are doing.

Often you have the same reasons to write to other people. You may also want to invite guests to a party. You may need to thank someone for a present.

317

This chapter will help you to write different kinds of letters. It will show you the correct form. It will help you to enjoy writing letters as well as receiving letters.

Part 1   The Parts of a Friendly Letter

There are five main parts in a letter:

the heading	the body	the closing
the greeting		the signature

Each part is written in a certain place in the letter. The following rules will help you write each part correctly. Look at the sample letter below as you read about each part.

A Friendly Letter

Heading
512 South Webster Street
Akron, Ohio 44303
October 2, 1984

Greeting

Dear Karen,   **Body**
   Guess what?   I have a job after school! I just have to tell you about it. My older brother Dan got more customers on his paper route. Now he needs some help. I was hoping he would ask me, and he did. I'm excited. Now I can save my money for something special.
   What have you been doing? Are you still taking gymnastics? I would like to hear from you. Please write.

Closing Your friend,
Signature Pam

The Heading

The **heading** tells where you are and when you are writing.
Write the heading in the top right-hand corner. Put in this information:

> house address and name of street
> name of city, state, and ZIP code
> month, day, and year

Follow these punctuation and capitalization rules:

1. Capitalize all proper names such as streets, cities, and states.
2. Place a comma between the name of the city and the state.
3. Use the correct ZIP code.
4. Place a comma between the date and the year.

The Greeting

The **greeting** is how you say "hello" to your friend.
Write the greeting below the heading, but at the left margin. Here are some examples of greetings:

> Dear Mrs. Smith,   Hi, Robert,   Greetings, Rachel,

Follow these punctuation and capitalization rules:

1. Capitalize the first word and any proper nouns.
2. Capitalize a title such as *Mrs., Mr., Ms., Dr.,* and *Miss.*
3. Use a period to abbreviate titles of people like *Ms., Mrs., Mr.,* and *Dr.*
4. Use a comma after the greeting.

The Body

The **body** of the letter is where you talk to your friend. Always write about things that will interest your friend. Also show interest in what he or she is doing.

Write the body below the greeting. Use a separate paragraph for each subject. Indent the first line of each paragraph.

The Closing

The **closing** is a simple way of saying "goodbye."

Write the closing one line below the body. Line it up with the first word of the heading. Here are some examples of closings:

Your friend,	Missing you,	Sincerely,
Love,	Always,	Lovingly,

Follow these punctuation and capitalization rules:

1. Capitalize only the first word in the closing.
2. Use a comma after the closing.

The Signature

The **signature** is your handwritten name. Write your signature below the closing. Line it up with the first word in the closing. You may use your first name or a nickname. If you don't know the reader well, write your last name also.

320 Putting the Parts Together

All five parts of a friendly letter work together. Read the sample friendly letter again. Notice how each part is written.

A. Write the following headings correctly. Follow the rules.

1. 6589 ocean drive
   miami florida 33139
   october 4 1983

2. 2309 oakland avenue
   cairo illinois 61709
   may 20 1984

3. p o box 249
   kirby montana 59042
   january 15 1984

4. 62 west 54th street
   omaha nebraska 68132
   november 28 1983

B. Write these greetings correctly. Follow the rules.

1. dear uncle bill
2. dear grandfather
3. hi cousin marie
4. dear dr newman
5. greetings frank
6. dear miss thompson
7. dear aunt sarah
8. hi joanne

C. Write these closings correctly. Follow the rules.

1. your daughter
2. sincerely
3. missing you
4. always
5. love
6. your friend

D. Choose one of the following events. Write a letter to a friend or relative. Tell about the event in the body of your letter. Also write a heading, a greeting, a closing, and your signature.

1. You have just been given a new pet.
2. Somebody gave you just what you wanted for your birthday.
3. Your class went on a field trip.
4. Your baseball game (or another event) was rained out.
5. You were the star of your class play.
6. You just finished reading a good book.

321

Part 2   Addressing the Envelope

The envelope has two separate addresses:

1. The address of the person to whom you are writing
2. The return address, which is your address

Return Address

Michael Gilbertson
593 Shay Street
Boston, Massachusetts 02116

Address

Miss Nancy Bianconi
32 Capital Drive
Washington, D. C. 20008

When you address an envelope, follow these steps:

1. Make sure the envelope is right-side up.
2. Begin the address in the center of the envelope.
3. Put your return address in the upper left-hand corner.
4. Double-check all numbers in the address.
5. Write as neatly as possible in ink.

Exercise   Addressing Envelopes

Draw three envelopes on your paper. Address them to the people on the following list. Use real addresses.

1. A relative   3. A friend
2. Your principal, at the school address

Part 3 Writing Invitations

Invitations must be written carefully. You must include the needed information. Here are the questions you must answer:

1. What kind of activity is it?
2. Why is the activity taking place?
3. Where will the activity be held?
4. When will the activity be held? Tell the day, date, and time of the activity.

Read the following sample invitation. Find all of the necessary details.

An Invitation

> Sunset School
> 2375 St. Anne Drive
> Phoenix, Arizona 85040
> February 28, 1985
>
> Dear Mom and Dad,
>   I would like to invite you to attend our class play, "Close Encounters of the Historic Kind." The play is about the early history of our country. I play Paul Revere.
>   The play will be performed on Thursday, March 10, at 1:00 P.M., in Room 212.
>   I hope you can come.
>
>   Your son,
>   Marvin

Write invitations for two of the following events. Put in all five parts of a letter. Be sure to include all of the necessary details about the activity. You decide who should be invited.

1. A birthday party
2. A band concert
3. A picnic
4. A weekend visit
5. A surprise party
6. An overnight visit

Part 4   Writing Thank-You Notes

Thank-you notes are a special way of being polite. A thank-you note shows that you appreciate someone's gift. You write a thank-you note when you have been a guest. A thank-you note shows that you are grateful. It shows your appreciation for someone's kindness. Always write the thank-you note as soon as possible.

Read the thank-you note on the following page. Notice that it is short and sincere. Notice, too, that the heading may be shortened to just the date.

324

November 9, 1985

Dear Grandmother,
The sweater you sent me for my birthday is really nice. It fits perfectly and I like the colors in it. I know it will keep me warm when I'm playing hockey.
Thank you for remembering my birthday in such a nice way.

Your granddaughter,
Christy

Exercise   **Writing Thank-You Notes**

Write thank-you notes for two of the following reasons.
Write your notes carefully and neatly. Follow correct punctuation
and capitalization rules.

1. Thank your neighbor for helping you fix your bike.
2. Thank your aunt and uncle for the birthday gift.
3. Thank your friend for the surprise party.
4. Thank your neighbor for letting you spend the night.
5. Thank your uncle for helping you with a school project.
6. Thank your grandparents for the Christmas gift.

325

Chapter 27

Writing Business Letters

A business letter is different from a friendly letter. It has a different purpose. You are writing to someone you do not know. You are usually asking for something.

The business letter is written to request information. It is also written to order materials. You write a business letter when you need information for a report. You also write a business letter to request items shown in newspapers, magazines, or catalogs.

Part 1 The Parts of a Business Letter

The parts of a business letter are similar to the parts of a friendly letter. However, a business letter has one added part. Read the following sample business letter carefully.

A Business Letter

Heading

317 Broadway Avenue
Madrid, Iowa 50156
May 2, 1986

Inside Address

Dr. Paula Maynard
Dental Associates Building
7852 Kelsey Boulevard
Madrid, Iowa 50156

Greeting

Dear Dr. Maynard:

Body

Our class is writing a book about careers. I am writing about dentists. Since you are my dentist, I thought you might help me. Do you have any information that I could use in my report? If you do, please send it to me by May 12.
Thank you very much.

Closing

Respectfully,

Signature

Juan Gomez

Juan Gomez

The Heading

The heading for a business letter is the same as the heading for a friendly letter.

The Inside Address

The **inside address** is the address of the company to which you are writing. It is the same as the address that goes on the envelope. Sometimes the inside address includes a person's name. Here is a sample:

Ms. Janet M. Purcell, Manager
The Olson Company
Olson Building
62 West 45th Street
Omaha, Nebraska 68132

Write the inside address below the heading, and at the left margin. The rules for punctuating and capitalizing the inside address are the same as the rules for the heading.

The Greeting

The greeting in a business letter is more formal than the greeting in a friendly letter. Sometimes you don't know the name of the person to whom you are writing. If you don't know the person's name, use one of these suggestions:

Dear Sir or Madam:
Dear Ladies and Gentlemen:

Write the greeting one space below the inside address, and at the left margin. Use a colon (:) at the end of the greeting.

The Body

The body of a business letter is short. State your business clearly and include these details:

1. What you are writing about
2. Why you need this information
3. When you need this information

The body of the business letter should be written in paragraphs. Indent the first word of each paragraph.

The Closing

The closing for a business letter is more formal than the closing for a friendly letter. Here are some sample closings:

Very truly yours,   Sincerely,   Respectfully,

As in the friendly letter, write the closing below the body, and in line with the heading.

The Signature

A business letter should be signed clearly with the full name of the writer. Sometimes the writer's name appears twice to make sure it can be read. To do this, skip four spaces below the closing. Then print your name. In the space between, write your name. Here is an example:

Respectfully,

Susan Martelli

Susan Martelli

Writing Business Letters

A. Write the following inside addresses correctly on your paper. Follow the punctuation and capitalization rules carefully.

1. ebony, jr.
   820 south michigan
   chicago illinois 60605

2. kdfw-tv
   400 north griffin
   dallas texas 75202

3. learning stuff
   p o box 4123
   modesto california 95352

4. japan air lines
   5 world trade center
   new york new york 10048

B. Write the following greetings correctly on your paper. Use the proper capitalization and punctuation.

1. dear dr stewart
2. dear ladies and gentlemen
3. dear miss romirez

4. dear sir or madam
5. dear senator ward
6. dear reverend moore

C. Write a business letter to one of the following TV networks. Ask for information about your favorite TV actress or actor or TV show. Use the rules for each part of the letter. Use the sample letter on page 328 as a guide. Write neatly.

American Broadcasting Company, Inc.
1330 Avenue of the Americas
New York, New York 10019

Columbia Broadcasting System, Inc.
51 West 52nd Street
New York, New York 10019

National Broadcasting Company
30 Rockefeller Plaza
New York, New York 10020

Part 2 Addressing the Envelope

The envelope for a business letter has two addresses. The return address is written in the upper left-hand corner. The address of the company to which you are writing is placed in the center of the envelope. Suppose you are writing to a particular person at the company. Include the name of that person in the address.

**Envelope
for a
Business Letter**

Luke Christopher
512 Hollister Road
Cleveland Heights, Ohio 44118

Ms. Pat Donovan
Walt Disney Productions
500 Buena Vista
Burbank, California 91505

Exercises Addressing Business Envelopes

A. Choose three of the companies or offices listed in Exercises A and C on page 331. Then draw three envelopes on your paper and address them correctly. Use your own home or school address as the return address.

B. Look up the name and address of three of the following businesses. Use your local telephone book. Draw three envelopes on your paper and address them correctly. Use your own home or school address as the return address.

1. a pet store
2. a toy store
3. a record store
4. a hospital
5. a drug store
6. a department store
7. a locksmith
8. a shoe store

Chapter 28

Using Capital Letters

Capital letters are a certain kind of letter used in printing or handwriting.

$$A B C D \qquad a B C D$$

You use capital letters only in particular places in your writing. For example, you normally use a capital letter at the beginning of a word, not in the middle. When you begin a word with a capital letter, you **capitalize** that word. Using capitals is called **capitalization.**

There are rules that tell when to capitalize words. This chapter presents some of those rules.

Part 1   Names of People and Pets

Nouns are names of persons, places, and things. A **common noun** is the name of any member in a group of persons, places, or things. You do not capitalize a common noun.

woman   city   car

A **proper noun** is the name of a particular person, place, or thing. Capitalize every proper noun.

Betsy Ross   Little Rock   Dodge

Begin every proper noun with a capital letter.

Words that name people always deserve special attention. Here are some guides for capitalizing these words.

Names of People and Pets

Capitalize the names of people and pets.

Angela   Carlos   Toto

Capitalize each word in a person's name.

Abigail Adams   George Washington Carver

Initials

An **initial** stands for a name.

Capitalize an initial and put a period after it.

Wilda H. Martinez   S. I. Hayakawa

Titles and Their Abbreviations

Many people have words like *Miss, Doctor,* or *Mayor* written before their names. These words are called **titles.** Titles in names are capitalized. Here are some examples of titles:

Miss Burke	Senator Percy	Reverend Jackson
Doctor Quinlivan	Judge Chin	Mayor Hatcher

Some titles have short forms. A short form of a word is called an **abbreviation.** Abbreviations for titles are capitalized and marked with a period.

Mister = Mr.   Mistress = Mrs.   Doctor = Dr.

The title *Ms.* has no long form. It is always capitalized and ends with a period. The title *Miss* has no short form. Do not end *Miss* with a period.

Capitalize titles and their abbreviations when you use them with names. Put a period after every abbreviation.

The Word *I*

Usually pronouns are not capitalized. However, the pronoun *I* is an exception.

Always capitalize the word *I*.

Exercises   **Using Capital Letters in Names**

A. Copy these names. Change small letters to capital letters where they are needed.

1. ms. rita figueroa
2. president wilson
3. thomas a. edison
4. shirley temple black

5. dr. salk
6. ella t. grasso
7. queen elizabeth
8. mr. spock
9. roberto clemente
10. emily dickinson
11. miss muffet
12. captain hook

B. Copy the following sentences. Change small letters to capital letters where they are needed.

1. ms. evergates sent a letter to senator sanchez.
2. The lawyer listened to judge baker.
3. carla and i made cupcakes.
4. luke skywalker destroyed the death star.
5. dr. dolittle talked to animals.
6. charlie brown has a dog named snoopy.
7. chris evert lloyd plays tennis.
8. The people elected governor rhodes.
9. joanne and i visited the milwaukee public museum.
10. clark kent changes into superman.

Part 2   Names of Particular Places and Things

Like names of people, the names of particular places and things may have more than one word. When a name has more than one word, you capitalize every important word in the name. Do not capitalize little words like *the, of,* or *in.*

the Rio Grande   the Statue of Liberty

Here are some particular places and things that need to be capitalized.

1. Capitalize names of days, holidays, and months. Capitalize their abbreviations, also.

Sun.	Wed.	Jan.	Oct.
Mon.	Thurs.	Feb.	Nov.

However, do not capitalize the names of seasons, such as *fall*.

2. Capitalize names of buildings and streets. Also capitalize abbreviations for such words as *building, street, road,* or *avenue* when they name particular places.

Symphony Hall	East 128 Street	E. 128 St.
Prudential Bldg.	Skyline Drive	Skyline Dr.

3. Capitalize names of cities, states, and countries.

Cleveland, Ohio	Osaka, Japan
Kansas City, Missouri	Mexico City, Mexico

Capitalize abbreviations for these names, also. When you use the two-letter abbreviations for states, capitalize both letters.

Illinois = IL   New Mexico = NM   Washington = WA

4. Capitalize names for people of particular countries.

Americans   Chinese   Russians

Exercises   **Using Capital Letters for Particular Places and Things**

A. In the following list, there are some common nouns and some proper nouns. Copy each noun. Capitalize each proper noun.

1. library
2. halloween
3. the liberty bell
4. city

5. miami, florida   9. the franklin street bridge
6. mexicans   10. river
7. grant avenue   11. the grand canyon
8. august   12. weekend

B. Copy the following sentences. Use capital letters where they are needed.

1. Carol moved to vermont.
2. The building is on union street.
3. My birthday is in december.
4. Mary poppins floated into london.
5. We drove across the golden gate bridge.
6. My family camped in yellowstone park.
7. Donna enjoyed the mark twain museum.
8. Doug watched the fireworks on the fourth of july.
9. I want to visit disneyland.
10. Christopher columbus is a famous italian.

Part 3 First Words

The rules given so far in this chapter tell about capitalizing certain words. In the rest of the chapter, you will learn that any word will be capitalized if it is written in certain places.

1. Begin every sentence with a capital letter.

Ector built a birdhouse.
Did Maureen plant these flowers?
Call the fire department!

340

2. Capitalize the beginning of every direct quotation.

When you write the exact words that somebody said, you are **quoting** that person. The words are a **direct quotation.**

Usually, when you write a direct quotation, you also write words to explain who said it. These words may come before or after the quotation.

My mother asked, "Are you ready?"

"Are you ready?" my mother asked.

Notice how the capital letters and quotation marks (" ") set off the direct quotation.

3. Capitalize the first word in most lines of poetry.

Snow makes whiteness where it falls.
The bushes look like popcorn balls.
The places where I always play
Look like somewhere else today.
—MARIE LOUISE ALLEN, "First Snow"

4. Capitalize the first word in the greeting of a letter.

Dear Lillian,   Dear Ms. Kwan,   Dear Sir:

5. Capitalize the first word in the closing of a letter.

Your friend,   Sincerely,   Yours truly,

Exercises   **Using Capital Letters in First Words**

A. Copy the following poem and letter. Capitalize them correctly.

1. the ostrich is a silly bird,
    with scarcely any mind.
  he often runs so very fast,
    he leaves himself behind.
      —MARY E. WILKENS FREEMAN,
        "The Ostrich Is a Silly Bird"

2. dear Jodie,

   yesterday was an exciting day. it was my birthday. my mother sent me to the store. when I came home, all my friends jumped up from their hiding places. they yelled, "surprise!" my friends had planned a surprise party! we had a good time.

   $$\text{your friend,}$$
   $$\text{Gina}$$

B. Follow the directions for Exercise A.

1. how doth the little crocodile
     improve his shining tail,
   and pour the waters of the Nile
     on every golden scale!

   —LEWIS CARROLL, "The Crocodile"

2. dear Mr. Sendak,

   i enjoy your books very much. my favorite is the story about Pierre. it's funny when he says "i don't care" to everyone.

   yours truly,
   Allen

Part 4   Titles

Capitalize the first word, the last word, and any other important words in a title.

Do not capitalize a little word such as *in, of, for, a, the,* or *by,* unless it comes first or last.

Little House in the Big Woods (book)
The Lord of the Rings (movie)
"The Little Mermaid" (story)

Put quotation marks around the titles of short works, like stories, poems, television programs, and reports. Underline the titles of long works, such as books, movies, and magazines. When they are printed in books, these titles are set in italics instead of being underlined.

Exercises   Using Capital Letters in Titles

A. Copy the following titles. Capitalize them correctly. Copy the quotation marks and underlining.

1. <u>star wars</u> (movie)
2. <u>caddie woodlawn</u> (book)
3. "sleeping beauty" (story)
4. "the today show" (television program)
5. "the pied piper of hamelin" (poem)
6. "collecting stamps" (report)
7. "the electric company" (television program)
8. "jack and the beanstalk" (story)

B. Follow the directions for Exercise A.

1. <u>black beauty</u> (book)
2. "the walrus and the carpenter" (poem)
3. "goldilocks and the three bears" (story)
4. <u>e. t.</u> (movie)
5. <u>highlights for children</u> (magazine)
6. <u>my father's dragon</u> (book)
7. "life of the plains indians" (report)
8. "paul revere's ride" (poem)

C. Choose eight books in your room or library. Write the titles and the authors' names. Then write the titles of two movies you have seen. Underline all the titles you list for this exercise.

More Exercises — Review

Using Capital Letters

A. Using Capital Letters in Names

Copy the sentences. Change small letters to capital letters where they are needed.

1. ms. davin called dr. walters.
2. louisa may alcott wrote many books.
3. gail and i eat lunch together.
4. alexander graham bell invented the telephone.
5. The medal was given to officer brent.
6. The poem was written by phillis wheatley.
7. Look up the phone number for ramon m. rivera.
8. miss chin teaches piano lessons.
9. My cat's name is fluffy.
10. No one sees count dracula during the day.

B. Using Capital Letters for Particular Places and Things

Copy these sentences. Use capital letters where they are needed.

1. I met many french people in paris.
2. The concert is on friday, august 3.
3. My father drove down chester avenue.
4. The pilgrims landed at plymouth rock.
5. We sailed on the ohio river.
6. Sherry flew to houston, texas.
7. Eric's address is 10 clinton street.
8. I made a card for mothers' day.
9. The team from central school won the game.
10. My grandfather was born in kunsan, korea.

C. Using Capital Letters in First Words

Copy the following poem and letter. Capitalize them correctly.

1. a mouse in her room scared Miss Dowd.
   she was frightened and screamed, very loud.
   then a happy thought hit her—
   to scare off the critter,
   she sat up in bed and meowed.

   —ANONYMOUS

2. dear Aunt Gwen,
   thank you for the sweater. it was a wonderful gift. i showed it to my mother. "that is the most beautiful sweater I have ever seen," she said. i like your gift very much.

   your grateful niece,
   Dottie

D. Using Capital Letters in Titles

Copy these titles. Capitalize them correctly. Copy the quotation marks and underlining.

1. "yogi bear" (television program)
2. children's digest (magazine)
3. the phantom tollbooth (book)
4. alice in wonderland (book)
5. "ali baba and the forty thieves" (story)
6. "wynken, blynken, and nod" (poem)
7. the jungle book (movie)
8. "how the leopard got its spots" (story)
9. a hundred and one dalmatians (movie)
10. "here comes the band" (poem)

Chapter 29

Using Punctuation Marks

Part 1 The Period

The **period (.)** is used in several different places. Most often, it is used at the end of a sentence.

1. Use a period at the ends of statements and most commands and requests.

The period lets you know that the sentence has ended. If you are reading aloud, the period tells you to drop your voice.

Statements — You can see the Liberty Bell in Philadelphia.
Joe likes sports.

Commands — Measure two cups of flour.
Don't touch the wet paint.

347

2. Use a period after an initial in a name.

An **initial** is the first letter of a name. It is used to stand for that name. The letter is always capitalized. It is always followed by a period.

P. L. Travers   J. C. Penney

3. Use a period after many abbreviations.

An **abbreviation** is a short form of a word. It is usually followed by a period. Here are some common abbreviations that are followed by periods:

Titles		Geographical Terms	
Mister	Mr.	Road	Rd.
Mistress	Mrs.	Washington	Wash.
(no long form)	Ms.	New York	N.Y.
Doctor	Dr.	South	S. or So.
Reverend	Rev.	Post Office	P.O.

Measures		Other Terms	
inch(es)	in.	Junior	Jr.
foot (or feet)	ft.	Company	Co.
ounce(s)	oz.	continued	cont.
pound(s)	lb.	Sunday	Sun.
dozen	doz.	December	Dec.

Not all abbreviations use periods. Here are some abbreviations that do not use them:

Zone Improvement Plan   ZIP
miles per hour   mph
metric measurements such as *km* (kilometer)
two-letter state abbreviations used in addresses, such as
    AL (Alabama), *AZ* (Arizona), *ND* (North Dakota)

Do not use abbreviations in writing regular sentences. They should be used only in special forms of writing, such as lists, addresses, and arithmetic problems. For example, in a report you might write this:

The museum is on Euclid Boulevard.

If you wrote to the museum, you could write this in the address on the envelope:

Euclid Blvd.

In general, the only abbreviations you should use in sentences are titles with names, *A.M.* and *P.M.*, and *B.C.* and *A.D.*

4. Use a period after each numeral or letter that shows a division of an outline. Use Roman numerals for main ideas. Use capital letters, in alphabetical order, for details related to the main ideas. Begin each idea, also, with a capital letter.

Money of Different Countries
I. Mexico
   A. Centavos
   B. Pesos
II. England
   A. Pence
   B. Shillings
   C. Pounds

Exercises **Using Periods Correctly**

A. Copy these sentences. Use periods where they are needed.

1. Meet me at 1:30 P M on Monday
2. Marisa swims at the Y W C A
3. Mr A B Price teaches art

4. The first printing press was made in 1438 A D
5. Dr J Wellington spoke to our class
6. School begins at 8:30 A M
7. Ms M Shaw works for the Halby Company
8. I woke up at 6:00 A M today

B. Copy the following phrases and outline. Use periods where they are needed.

1. So Green Rd	8. Sports
2. six lb, two oz	I. Summer Sports
3. Jordan Co	A Baseball
4. Washington, D C	B Tennis
5. Sun, Aug 5	C Swimming
6. 5 ft, 7 in	II. Winter Sports
7. 55 mph	A Ice Skating
	B Skiing

Part 2 The Question Mark

A **question mark (?)** is used at the end of every question. If you are reading aloud, the question mark tells you to raise your voice.

Can you come to my party?
How much is three times four?

Use a question mark at the end of every question.

Exercises **Using Question Marks Correctly**

350
A. Copy these sentences. Use either a period or a question mark at the end of each sentence.

1. What time is it
2. Where is Mr. Lu

3. I like strawberry ice cream best
4. How much does this notebook cost
5. The wind blew the tree down
6. When does the movie start
7. Melissa picked these daisies
8. Victor made a hand puppet
9. Can you roller skate
10. Did anyone see the accident

B. Follow the directions for Exercise A.

1. Are you waiting for the bus
2. Polly painted her bike
3. Raymond lost his furry gloves
4. Did you like the play
5. Carla locked the door
6. Would you mail this letter
7. Where is the Big Dipper
8. How many newspapers did you deliver
9. Larry fed his dog
10. Who won the race

Part 3   The Exclamation Point

An **exclamation point (!)** is used at the end of every exclamation and after any command that shows strong feeling. If you are reading aloud, the exclamation point tells you to show surprise, fear, or other strong feeling in your voice.

What a scary movie that was!
Watch out for traffic!

351

Use an exclamation point at the end of an exclamation or a command that shows strong feeling.

A. Copy these sentences. Use a period, question mark, or exclamation point at the end of each sentence.

1. What a good time we had
2. Look out
3. The snow is very deep
4. Who can solve this problem
5. Wait on the corner
6. How much do you weigh
7. Brian washed the windows
8. Call the police fast
9. May I talk to Jenny
10. Write neatly

B. Follow the directions for Exercise A.

1. Put your key in a safe place
2. When is your birthday
3. Come quickly
4. Has the mail come
5. Darryl played his new record
6. How cold this room is
7. We watched the fireworks last night
8. Gina showed me her poster
9. What an exciting game we saw
10. This store sells pet turtles

Part 4 The Comma

352

The **comma (,)** signals a pause in a sentence. If you are reading aloud, the comma tells you to pause briefly.

In this Part you will learn about eight ways you should use commas.

1. Use a comma in dates, to separate the day of the month from the year.

Paul Revere made his famous ride on April 18, 1775.

If the date is written in the middle of the sentence, place a comma after the year, also.

On April 26, 1777, Sybil Ludington warned her neighbors of a British attack.

2. Use a comma to separate the name of a city from the state or country in which it is located.

Tulsa, Oklahoma   Taxco, Mexico

If the name is written in the middle of the sentence, place a comma after the state or country.

Battle Creek, Michigan, is famous for its cereal companies.

Exercise   **Using Commas Correctly**

Copy the following sentences. Put in commas where they are needed.

1. My mother was born on December 19 1952.
2. Many cars are made in Detroit Michigan.
3. Many travelers visit Honolulu Hawaii.
4. Tokyo Japan is a crowded city.
5. The skating rink was opened on October 15 1980.
6. We moved to Ohio on August 14 1982.
7. On July 21 1969 Neil Armstrong walked on the moon.
8. Erica visited Denver Colorado last summer.
9. It snowed very hard in Buffalo New York.
10. On June 5 1981 my brother graduated.

3. Use a comma to set off the name of a person spoken to.

Tom, can you throw a fastball?
I found your sweater, Gail.

4. Use a comma after *yes, no,* or *well* at the beginning of a sentence.

Yes, I remember that story.
No, the answer to the problem is not seven.
Well, we did our best.

5. Use a comma to set apart words in a series.

Two things do not make a series. There are always three or more in a series.

Laura and Don played basketball. (No series)
Laura, Don, and Carol played basketball. (Series)

6. Use a comma after the first complete thought in a sentence with two thoughts. The comma is placed before the word *and, but,* or *or.*

Darren washed the dishes, and Rosa dried them.
They looked, but they couldn't find the needle.
Hurry up, or we'll be late.

Exercise   Using Commas Correctly

Copy the following sentences. Put in commas where they are needed.

354

1. Fred ran fast but he could not catch the bus.
2. Will you help me Steve?
3. Jackie ate a sandwich a banana and two cookies.
4. No I have not read that story.

5. Diane cut out the picture and Janet pasted it in the scrapbook.

6. The Science Fair will be held on May 18 1984.

7. Eat the ice cream now or it will melt.

8. Willy found a marble a penny and a tack in the box.

9. Yes Carl does own a camera.

10. The team played in Atlanta Georgia last night.

7. Use a comma after the greeting of a friendly letter and after the closing of every letter.

Dear Anita,   Sincerely,

8. Use a comma to set off a direct quotation from the rest of the sentence.

"This is a good book," Nels reported. (Quotation first)
Pearl asked, "Is it a true story?" (Quotation last)

Notice that the commas were placed before the quotation marks in both examples.

Exercises   **Using Commas Correctly**

A. Copy the following sentences. Use commas where they are needed.

1. We can go swimming or we can play baseball.

2. "I earned twenty cents" Timmy told us.

3. Well this is a surprise.

4. Marsha Peter Frank and Kim saw the accident.

5. Connie can you play the piano?

6. The train stopped at Flagstaff Arizona.

7. Phil shouted "We won!"

8. Did you enter the contest Ramon?

9. We saw lions tigers and leopards at the zoo.

10. The mayor was elected on March 4 1983.

B. Copy the following letter. Use commas where they are needed.

> Dear Tammy
>   Our team won the football game yesterday but we almost lost. Cliff caught the football. Then he started running the wrong way! We all yelled "Cliff turn around!" Suddenly he started running the other way. He scored a touchdown! Yes it was an exciting game.
>   Your friend
>   Tina

Part 5   The Apostrophe

The **apostrophe (')** is used for two different purposes. If you are reading aloud, the apostrophe has no effect on how you say the word in which it appears.

The Apostrophe To Show Possession

A **possessive** is a word that shows ownership or possession.

To form the possessive of a singular noun, add an apostrophe and an s.

The coat that belongs to Dolores is Dolores's coat.

The jacket that belongs to her brother is her brother's jacket.

To form the possessive of a plural noun that does not end in s, add an apostrophe and an s.

356

The shoes that belong to women are women's shoes.

The antlers of deer are deer's antlers.

To form the possessive of a plural noun that ends in s, add only an apostrophe.

The boots that belong to hikers are the hikers' boots.

The collars of dogs are dogs' collars.

Do not use apostrophes with possessive pronouns.

ours   hers   his   theirs

Exercise   Using Apostrophes To Show Possession

Make these words show possession. Write the possessive form.

1. mother	5. children	9. players
2. class	6. ladies	10. sheep
3. friends	7. men	11. doctors
4. Andrea	8. robin	12. boys

The Apostrophe in Contractions

A **contraction** is a word made by combining two words, and leaving out a letter or letters. An apostrophe is used to show where one or more letters have been left out.

Here are some contractions that are used frequently:

isn't	is not	it's	it is, it has
aren't	are not	I'm	I am
don't	do not	I've	I have
can't	cannot	they'll	they will
hasn't	has not	we're	we are
won't	will not	you'd	you would
wouldn't	would not	he's	he is, he has
shouldn't	should not	she's	she is, she has

357

Writing Words with Apostrophes

Wherever you use an apostrophe in cursive writing, do not connect the letters before and after the apostrophe. The apostrophe should separate the two letters.

I've   it's   won't

Exercises **Using Apostrophes Correctly**

A. Write each of the following phrases as a contraction.

1. could not	6. have not
2. he will	7. they will
3. she is	8. he has
4. cannot	9. would not
5. they are	10. I have

B. Each of the following sentences needs one apostrophe, either for a possessive or a contraction. Number your paper from 1 to 10. Find each word that should have an apostrophe. Copy the word, putting in the apostrophe where it should be.

1. Theyre studying together.
2. Where is Dans pen?
3. The baby shouldnt be left alone.
4. The magicians trick fooled everyone.
5. Goldilocks fell asleep in the baby bears bed.
6. Youd enjoy this movie.
7. We lost Jacks softball.
8. The team isnt giving up.
9. The robots eyes glowed.
10. Theyll meet us at your house.

Part 6 The Colon

There are several uses for the colon (:). Here are two of the uses.

1. Use a colon after the greeting in a business letter.

Dear Sir: Dear Ms. Meyer:

2. Use a colon between numerals that tell the hour and the minutes.

9:40 A.M.   7:00 P.M.

Remember to use periods in the abbreviations A.M. and P.M.

Exercise   **Using Colons Correctly**

Copy this business letter. Use colons where they are needed. Use periods correctly in the abbreviations A.M. and P.M.

April 21, 1984

Dear Mrs. Jones
   As you know, the prince held a ball at the palace from 800 P M to 200 A M last Friday night. However, a young lady ran from the palace in a hurry at 1200 A M. She left behind one glass slipper. The prince and I will be coming to your house tomorrow between 145 P M and 200 P M to try the slipper on any young woman living at that address.

Sincerely yours,
Sir Percy,
Prince Charming's
Private Secretary

359

Part 7   Quotation Marks

Quotation marks (" ") are used to set off direct quotations and certain titles. A **direct quotation** means the exact words a person says.

1. Use quotation marks before and after the words of every direct quotation.

Margie said, "I want to be pitcher."

"Then I'll play catcher," Jerry agreed.

Follow these guides when you write direct quotations.

Guides for Writing Quotations

1. Only the speaker's words are placed inside the quotation marks.

2. A direct quotation begins with a capital letter.

3. If the quotation comes at the end of the sentence, put a comma before the quotation. The end mark for the sentence usually is placed inside the quotation marks.

   Ira called, "Here comes the helicopter."

4. If the quotation comes at the beginning of the sentence, put the end mark for the quotation inside the quotation marks. Put the end mark for the rest of the sentence at the end of the sentence.

   "Can you swim fifty yards?" Bert asked.

   "Your lemon pie is delicious!" my mother exclaimed.

   "This cat is so friendly," Inez said.

Notice that the third example has a statement inside the quotation marks. In this situation, use a comma instead of a period to set off the statement from the rest of the sentence.

2. Put quotation marks around the titles of poems, stories, and other short works.

"Pecos Bill and the Tornado"   (story)

"Barbara Frietchie"   (poem)

"All About Bears"   (student report)

Exercises   Using Quotation Marks Correctly

A. Copy the following sentences. Use quotation marks where they are needed.

1. Spring is finally here! exclaimed Pat.
2. The story called The Fox and the Grapes is a fable.
3. Christine read the poem The Highwayman.
4. When do we eat lunch? asked Nancy.
5. I wish you could come, Francis said.
6. Richard's report is called My Hobby.
7. Mark said, I can fix your watch.
8. The sky is falling! shouted Chicken Little.
9. My favorite story is Rip van Winkle.
10. Tanya said, I like your new dress.

B. Follow the directions for Exercise A.

1. I like to dance, James said.
2. Baseball in Japan is an interesting report.
3. Marta asked, Where should we meet?
4. We need a quart of milk, my mother said.
5. Our class recited the poem called The Swing.
6. Windwagon Smith is a good story.
7. Alice shouted, Watch out for the wet paint!
8. Jeff's report is Our First President.
9. How old are you? asked Sylvia.
10. We all enjoyed the poem Casey at the Bat.

Part 8   Underlining

Underlining is used in writing to mark titles of long works.

Underline the titles of books and other long works.

When these titles are set in print, they are in *italics*.

<u>*Roosevelt Grady*</u> (book title in writing)

Roosevelt Grady (book title in print)

<u>Cricket Magazine</u> (magazine)

<u>Planet of the Apes</u> (motion picture)

Exercises   Using Underlining Correctly

A. Copy the following titles. Underline them.

1. Mary Poppins (book)
2. The Wizard of Oz (book and movie)
3. Pinocchio (book)
4. National Geographic World (magazine)
5. Benji (movie)
6. Half Magic (book)
7. Sports Illustrated (magazine)
8. Fantasia (movie)

B. Copy the following titles. Use quotation marks or underlining as needed.

1. The Village Blacksmith (poem)
2. Peter Pan (book)
3. The Lion and the Mouse (story)
4. How To Make a Puppet (report)
5. Willy Wonka and the Chocolate Factory (movie)
6. Amazing Stories (magazine)

More Exercises — Review

Using Punctuation Marks

A. Using Periods Correctly

Copy the following sentences. Use periods where they are needed.

1. My mother shops at the H L White Store
2. I read a poem by A A Milne
3. A L Tilman owns the hardware store
4. King Tut ruled Egypt around 1340 B C
5. Ms Warfield will meet you at 9:00 A M
6. The children's librarian is Anna F Wong
7. Rev Roberts works in our neighborhood
8. The movie begins at 7:30 P M
9. Columbus landed in America in A D 1492
10. Teresa visited Dr Harvey

B. Using Question Marks Correctly

Copy these sentences. Use either a period or a question mark at the end of each sentence.

1. Which paper is yours
2. Denise has a cold
3. Did you bake these cookies
4. Where is my hammer
5. May I borrow your bike
6. Juanita plays the drums
7. What is Barney's telephone number
8. The washing machine is broken
9. The dog barked
10. Would you like some lemonade

363

C. Using Exclamation Points Correctly

Copy these sentences. Use a period, question mark, or exclamation point at the end of each sentence.

1. Answer these questions
2. Where is the post office
3. Jason sings very well
4. Yuriko helps in her mother's restaurant
5. What a colorful picture you painted
6. Jean listened to the news
7. Who is pitching in today's game
8. What a good idea you had
9. Can you hear me
10. Run for your lives

D. Using Commas Correctly

Copy the following letter. Use commas where they are needed.

Dear Donna

We are having a good time on our trip. We are now in San Diego California. We went to the zoo today. Well I never saw so many animals. My mother asked me "Which animal did you like the best?" I liked the monkeys polar bears and seals. Donna I will write you more about our trip soon.

Sincerely
Jan

E. Using Apostrophes Correctly

Number your paper from 1 to 10. Find each word that should have an apostrophe. Copy the word, putting in the apostrophe where it should be.

1. Id like to meet your father.
2. The principals office is down the hall.

3. Charleys kite is caught in a tree.
4. Emily isnt feeling well.
5. Hes painting the house.
6. The lions teeth are sharp.
7. Kevin borrowed his brothers skateboard.
8. Carrie wont tell our secret.
9. The dogs tails are wagging.
10. Ive kept my promise.

F. Using Colons Correctly

Copy this business letter. Use colons and periods where needed.

Dear Mrs. Perkins

Pronto Bus Company is happy to take your class to the zoo. The bus will be at your school at 845 A M. The bus will leave the school at 9 00 A M, and arrive at the zoo at 9 30 A M. We will leave the zoo at 4 30 P M, and return to your school at 5 00 P M.

Sincerely yours,
Ms. Ellen Carpenter

G. Using Quotation Marks and Underlining Correctly

Copy the following sentences. Use quotation marks and underlining as needed.

1. That ice is thin! Sally shouted.
2. Martin said, I have three goldfish.
3. I gave a book report on The Enormous Egg.
4. Kathy and I acted out the story of Rapunzel.
5. On the Road to St. Ives is a funny poem.
6. May I play outside? Regina asked.
7. Ned finished his report All About Cowboys.
8. Holly watched the movie King Kong.
9. Debbie said, Follow me.
10. I have a new jacket, Chico said.

Chapter 30

Improving Your Spelling

This chapter will show you how to study difficult words. It will also give you some important rules for spelling easier words.

Part 1   Plan Your Study of Spelling

Sometimes a word is difficult for you to spell. There are some things you can do to make the word easier for yourself. When you do these things often, they become **habits.**

Habits for Improving Your Spelling

1. Make a habit of looking at words carefully.

367

When you come to a new word, be sure you know its meaning. If you are not certain, look up the word in a dictionary.

Practice seeing every letter. When you see a new word, or a tricky word, like *government*, look at all the letters.

2. When you speak, pronounce words carefully.

Some words are spelled wrong just because they are pronounced wrong. You may leave out the sound of certain letters. Then in writing you will probably leave out those letters.

Here is a list of words that are often pronounced wrong. The letters in dark print are left out. Be careful to say each letter. Then you will remember to write each letter.

1. reg**u**lar	4. gen**e**ral	7. po**e**m
2. Saturday	5. ru**i**n	8. vi**o**let
3. prob**ab**ly	6. diff**er**ent	9. fin**al**ly

3. Find out your own spelling enemies and attack them.

Look over your past papers. Make a list of the misspelled words. Also keep a list of new words that are difficult for you. Study these words until you can spell them correctly.

4. Find memory devices to help with problem spellings.

Some words do not follow regular spelling rules. In these cases, think of a **memory device** to help you. A memory device is a trick, or a catchy sentence about the word, that you can remember easily. The device tells how to spell the word.

friend—She is a fri**end** to the end.
believe—Never bel**ie**ve a lie.
piece—Take a **pie**ce of pie.

5. Proofread what you write.

368

To make sure that you have spelled all words correctly, reread your work. Check it carefully, word for word. Don't let your eyes race over the page and miss misspellings.

Steps for Mastering Difficult Words

When you notice that a certain word is difficult for you, study that word by itself. Give it all your attention. If you take the time to learn it correctly once, you will save yourself the trouble of correcting it many times. Follow these steps to master a specific word.

1. **Look at the word and say it to yourself.** Pronounce it carefully. If it has two or more syllables, say it again, one syllable at a time. Look at each syllable as you say it.

2. **Look at the letters and say each one.** If the word has two or more syllables, pause between syllables.

3. **Copy the word.**

4. **Close your eyes and picture the word in your mind.**

5. **Without looking at the word, write it.**

6. **Now compare what you have written with the word in your book or list. See if you have spelled the word correctly.** If you have, write it once more. Compare it with the correct spelling again.

7. **If you have misspelled the word, notice where the error was.** Then repeat steps 3 through 6 until you have spelled the word correctly three times in a row.

Exercise   Developing Good Habits

Here are some words that are often pronounced carelessly and then misspelled. Look at each letter of every word. Pronounce the words correctly to yourself. Write the words in alphabetical order. Check your spelling.

February	different	government	library
numeral	remember	interesting	family

Part 2   Rules for Spelling

Many words follow certain rules. Studying the rules should help you with these words. Here are the most important rules.

Adding Prefixes

A **prefix** is a syllable that is added to the beginning of a word to change its meaning. Here are some common prefixes and examples of their use.

Prefix	Basic Word	Modified Word
re (again)	heat	reheat (heat again)
dis (not)	like	dislike (not like)
un (not)	lucky	unlucky (not lucky)
in (not)	formal	informal (not formal)
im (not)	proper	improper (not proper)
pre (before)	heat	preheat (heat before)
mis (incorrectly)	dial	misdial (dial incorrectly)

When you add a prefix to a word, the spelling of the word stays the same.

Adding the Suffixes *-ly* and *-ness*

A **suffix** is a letter or syllable added to the ending of a word that changes it in some way. For example, the suffix *-ly* added to an adjective changes it to an adverb.

Adjective	Adverb
A *bright* star was shining.	A star was shining *brightly*.
Pat had a *real* adventure.	Pat had a *really* adventurous trip.

When you add the suffix *-ly* to a word ending with *l*, you keep both *l*'s.

The suffix *-ness* added to an adjective changes it to a noun.

Adjective	Noun
Jay's writing is *neat*.	He is known for his *neatness*.
The storm was *sudden*.	We were surprised by its *suddenness*.

When you add the suffix *-ness* to a word ending with *n*, you keep both *n*'s.

Exercise Adding Prefixes and Suffixes

Find the misspelled word in each of these sentences and spell it correctly.

1. The movie was realy exciting.
2. Ken mispelled a word.
3. My stubborness gets me into trouble.
4. Jennifer poured the milk carefuly.
5. I am disatisfied with this product.
6. The pictures were hung unnevenly.
7. This card trick is actualy very easy.
8. Robin rerote her paper.
9. I missunderstood your directions.
10. Sheila droped the ball through the net.
11. It was the wetest spring in years.
12. John was feedding my bird while I was away.

Adding Suffixes to Words Ending in Silent *e*

Notice what happens when you add suffixes beginning with vowels to words that end in silent *e*.

fame + ous = famous   have + ing = having

When you add a suffix beginning with a vowel to a word ending in silent *e*, you usually drop the final *e*.

Now see what happens when you add suffixes beginning with consonants to words that end in silent *e*.

care + less = careless   state + ment = statement
nine + ty = ninety   love + ly = lovely

When you add a suffix beginning with a consonant to a word ending in silent *e*, you usually keep the final *e*.

The following words are exceptions to these two rules:

truly   argument   ninth   judgment

Exercise   Adding Suffixes Correctly

Add the suffix given for each word. Write each new word in a sentence.

1. dream + er
2. paste + ing
3. use + less
4. wise + er
5. safe + ly
6. true + ly
7. hope + less
8. red + est
9. grace + ful
10. drop + ed
11. break + ing
12. fine + est

Adding Suffixes to Words Ending in *y*

See what happens when you add suffixes to words that end in *y* following a consonant.

silly + er = sillier   funny + est = funniest
happy + ness = happiness   worry + ed = worried

When you add a suffix to a word that ends with *y* following a consonant, you usually change the *y* to *i*.

However, the *y* is not changed when the suffix *-ing* is added.

bury + ing = burying   reply + ing = replying
cry + ing = crying   hurry + ing = hurrying

Notice, too, what happens when you add suffixes to words that end in *y* following a vowel.

pay + ment = payment   buy + ing = buying
player + er = player   destroy + ed = destroyed

When you add a suffix to a word that ends with *y* following a vowel, you usually keep the *y*.

The following words are exceptions: *paid, said.*

Exercise   **Adding Suffixes Correctly**

Add the suffix given for each word. Write each new word correctly.

1. play + ing
2. joy + ful
3. happy + ly
4. pay + ed
5. lazy + ness
6. fast + er
7. buy + ing
8. study + ed
9. enjoy + able
10. stay + ed
11. lovely + ness
12. carry + ed
13. easy + est
14. pity + ful
15. pretty + er

Doubling the Final Consonant

What happens to these words when you add suffixes?

hop + ing = hopping   thin + er = thinner
sad + est = saddest   tap + ed = tapped

You can see that the last letter is doubled when suffixes beginning with a vowel are added to these words. Notice that these are one-syllable words with a single vowel and a single consonant after the vowel.

Words of one syllable, ending with a consonant following one vowel, double the final consonant before adding *-ing, -ed, -er,* or *-est.*

The final consonant is not doubled after two vowels.

train + er = trainer   feel + ing = feeling

Exercise **Doubling the Final Consonant**

Add the suffix given for each word. Write each new word.

1. mad + er   5. stop + ed   9. dream + er
2. keep + ing   6. man + ed   10. squeal + ing
3. red + est   7. break + ing   11. wet + est
4. thin + est   8. rub + ing   12. look + ed

Spelling Words with *ie* and *ei*

For many years, people have had trouble remembering whether *i* comes before or after *e* in certain words. This old rhyme helps many girls and boys with the problem.

> *I* before *e*
> Except after *c*,
> Or when sounded as *a*
> As in n*ei*ghbor or w*ei*gh.

The words below follow the rules in the rhyme.

1. believe   3. receive   5. weigh
2. niece   4. ceiling   6. eight

However, these four words do not follow the rule.

either   neither   seize   weird

Exercise   **Writing Words with *ie* and *ei***

Write a sentence for each of the *ie* and *ei* words listed above. Underline the *ie* and *ei* words.

Part 3 Words Often Confused

Homonyms are words that sound the same or nearly the same. They have different meanings and are usually spelled differently. Because they sound so much alike, people often write the wrong homonym.

It will help you in your writing to know about some homonyms that are used often and are easily confused. Then you will be careful to write the correct homonym for the meaning you have in mind.

Here are six sets of homonyms. Read their definitions. See how they are used in the sentences.

> **its** shows ownership or possession.
> **it's** is the contraction for *it is* or *it has.*
>
> > The dog wagged *its tail.*
> > *It's* going to rain.
>
> **your** is the possessive form of *you.*
> **you're** is the contraction for *you are.*
>
> > *Your* blue jeans are dirty.
> > *You're* my best friend.
>
> **hear** means to listen to.
> **here** means in this place.
>
> > Can you *hear* the music?
> > Please come *here.*
>
> **their** means belonging to.
> **there** means at that place.
> **they're** is the contraction for *they are.*
>
> > *Their* house is painted blue.
> > We will meet *there.*
> > *They're* going to the zoo.

right means proper or correct. It also means the opposite of left.

write means to form words with a pen or pencil.

> Sam gave the *right* answers.
> Dora tied her *right* shoelace.
> W*rite* your name on the paper.

to means in the direction of.

too means also or very.

two is the whole number between one and three.

> My father is going *to* the store.
> This soup is *too* hot.
> Elizabeth has *two* pencils.

Exercise   Using Homonyms Correctly

Read these sentences. Choose the correct homonym in the parentheses. Write it on your paper.

1. Turn (right, write) at the next traffic light.
2. I'm going to (right, write) a letter to Sue.
3. Dick has (to, too, two) blisters.
4. The telephone is over (their, there, they're).
5. Ron didn't (hear, here) the alarm.
6. The children lost (their, there, they're) gloves.
7. (Its, It's) time to go home.
8. Tell me when (your, you're) leaving.
9. Please wear (your, you're) raincoat.
10. The cat scratched (its, it's) ear.
11. Someone is (hear, here) to see you.
12. Debbie is going (to, too, two) Miami.
13. (Its, It's) on my desk at school.
14. It was (to, too, two) dark for taking pictures.
15. I saw (their, there, they're) new dog last night.

More Exercises — Review

Improving Your Spelling

A. Developing Good Habits

Here are some words that are often pronounced carelessly and then misspelled. Look at each letter of every word. Pronounce the words correctly to yourself. Write the words in alphabetical order.

vegetable	library	poem
separate	interested	hundred
introduce	different	surprise

B. Using the Spelling Rules

Find the misspelled word in each of these sentences and spell it correctly.

1. Miss Goldsmith received two letters from her neice.
2. Althea was unnable to stop her bike.
3. I am hopeing my painting wins first prize.
4. Ernesto studyed for the test.
5. Kathy and Vincent shared the reward equaly.
6. It is two late to go to the movie.
7. Martha is truely sorry about the accident.
8. The baby wieghs seven pounds.
9. I saw there new dog last night.
10. The bird built it's nest of mud.
11. Niether of us won the race.
12. Where is you're dictionary?
13. The car waitted at the red light.
14. Mrs. Cahn usually knows the write answer.
15. The players rushed onto the field.

Index

a, an, the, 216—217, 224, 270, 342
  in book titles, 270, 342
  before nouns, 216—217, 224
Abbreviations
  capitalization of, 319, 337—339
  lists of, 348—349
  periods with, 319, 337, 348—350, 363
Accent mark, 151—152, 155
Action verbs, 157—158, 160, 174
Addresses
  business letters, 328—329
  envelopes, 322, 332—333
  friendly letters, 319
Adjectives, 211—225
  a, an, the, 216—217, 224
  comparisons with, 218—221, 225
  in descriptions, 244—247
  kinds of, 214—215, 224
  in phrases, 244—246
  in sentence patterns, 222
Adverbs, 227—233
  comparisons with, 231—233
  list of, 229
Alliteration in poetry, 289—290
Alphabetical order
  card catalog cards, 269—272
  dictionary words, 144—146
  encyclopedia articles, 277—279
  fiction books, 264—265
  indexes, 275
and, or, but, 56—59, 354—356
Announcements, making, 128—129
  guides for, 129
Apostrophe, 356—358, 364—365
  in contractions, 169—171, 357—358, 364—365
  in cursive writing, 72, 358
  in possessives, 71—73, 75, 87, 356—358, 364—365
Articles. *See a, an, the.*
Articles in encyclopedia, 277—279
Author, defined, 264
Author card, 269—270, 272

Base word, 7—12
be, forms of, 167—168, 176
  See also is, was, are, were.
Body of business letter, 328, 330—331
Body of friendly letter, 318, 320—321
Book report, 263, 273—274
Books, finding and using. *See* Library.
Business letters, 327—333

Call numbers of library books, 267—272
Capitalization, 335—345
  first words, 340—342, 345
    of outlines, 306, 349
    of poetry lines, 341—342, 345
    of quotations, 340—341, 345, 360
    of sentences, 36, 50, 54, 57—58, 340
  I, 337
  letter parts, 319—321, 329—331, 341, 345
  proper nouns, 66, 319, 336—340, 344
  rules for, 335—345
  titles
    of persons, 319, 337—338, 344
    of written works, 306, 310—311, 342—343, 345
Card catalog, 269—272
  author cards, 269—270, 272
  subject cards, 269, 271—272
  title cards, 269—272
Characters in story, 258—261
Clean copy, 121, 201, 203, 247, 314
Closing in letters, 320—321, 330
Colon, 359, 365
  in greeting of business letter, 329, 359, 365
  in writing hours and minutes, 359, 365
Comma, 352—356, 364
  with adjectives, 213
  with city and state or country, 319, 353, 355, 364
  after complete thoughts in sentences, 56—57, 354—356
  in dates, 319, 353, 355

in letter parts, 319—321, 330, 355—356, 364
with name of person spoken to, 354—356, 364
in quotations, 355—356, 360, 364—365
in series, 354—355, 364
rules for use, 352—356
after *yes, no, well,* 354—355, 364
Commands, 37—39, 50, 347, 351, 364
exclamation point with, 37, 351—352, 364
period with, 37, 347, 364
Common nouns, 66—67, 74
Comparisons
with adjectives, 218—221, 225
with adverbs, 231—233
Compositions. *See* Descriptions, writing; Paragraphs, writing; Reports, written; Stories, writing.
Conjunctions. *See and, or, but*
Context, defined, 2
Context clues to word meanings, 2—6, 13
definition, 2—3, 6, 13
example(s), 5—6, 13
restatement, 4, 6, 13
Contractions,
apostrophe in, 169—172, 357—358, 364—365
defined, 169
lists of, 169, 357
negatives, 171—172, 177
Conversation, carrying on a, 28—29
guides for, 29

Declarative sentences. Statements.
Definition as context clue, 2—3, 6, 13
Definitions in dictionary, 153—155
Descriptions, writing, 235—247
arranging details in order, 240—242
choosing a topic, 238—239
revising, 246—247
using details, 243—246
Details
in descriptions, 239—247

in paragraphs, 196—197
in stories, 261
Dewey Decimal System, 266—268
Dictionary, 143—155
accent mark, 151—152, 155
alphabetical order, 144—146
definitions, 153—155
entries, information in, 150—155
entry words, 144—155
guide words, 148—149, 155
respellings, decoded by pronunciation key, 150—152, 155
schwa symbol (ə), 151
syllables, 151—152, 155
Direct quotations. *See* Quotations.
Directions
following, in tests, 205, 208
giving, 130—131
guides for, 131
Disagreeing politely, 139—141
guides for, 141
Discussion, group. *See* Talking in groups.
Double negatives, 171—172, 177

Editing. *See* Revising, Proofreading.
Encyclopedia, 277—279
English, standard, 16—17, 21
Envelopes, addressing, 322, 332—333
Example(s) as context clue, 5–6, 13
Exclamation point
with commands, 37, 351—352, 364
with exclamations, 38, 351—352, 364
Exclamations, 38—39, 50, 351—352, 364
Exclamatory sentences. *See* Exclamations.
Experience, writing about. *See* Narrative paragraph.
Explanatory "why" paragraphs, 249—255
arranging reasons, 254—255
giving reasons, 252—253
understanding fact and opinion, 250—251

Fact and opinion, defined, 250—251

379

Fiction books, 264—265, 267
    how to find, 264
    reporting on, 273—274
Formal standard English, 16—17, 21
Friendly letters, 317—325

General words, 244
Glossary, 263, 276
good, bad, forms of, 221, 225
Greeting in letters, 319, 321, 329, 331
Guide words in dictionary, 148—149, 155

Haiku poetry, 285—287
Handwriting, value of legibility, 121, 203, 247
Heading in letters, 319, 321, 324, 329
Helping verbs, 161—166, 175—176
Homonyms, 376—379

I,
    capitalization of, 337
    in place of nouns, 78
    as subject, 80—83, 85—86, 90, 168
    verb forms with, 168
I and *me, we* and *us,* 85—86
Imperative sentences. *See* Commands, Requests.
Indenting first line of paragraph, 105, 202, 309—310
    in letters, 320, 330
Index
    in encyclopedia, 278—279
    in nonfiction books, 263, 275—276
Informal standard English, 17
Information,
    finding in books, 269—273, 275—279
    gathering for reports, 301—303
    giving credit to sources of, 312—314
Initials, 336—338, 348—350, 363
Interrogative sentences. *See* Questions.
Introductions, making, 24—27
    guides for introductions, 25, 27
Invitations, 323—324
Irregular verbs
    defined, 184

list of, 185
past forms of, 184—185
is, was, are, were, 167—168, 176
Italics
    in dictionary entries, 153
    underlining for, 312—313, 343, 345, 362, 365

Language, levels of, 15—21
    slang, 18—21
        guides for using, 20
    standard English, 16—17, 19, 21
        guides for using, 17
Letters, 317—333
    business, 327—333
        capitalization in, 329—331
        parts of, 328—331
        punctuation in, 328—331
        sample, 328
    friendly, 317—325
        capitalization in, 319—321
        parts of, 318—321
        punctuation in, 319—321
        sample, 328
        invitations, 323—324
            sample, 323
        thank-you notes, 324—325
            sample, 325
Library, 263—279
    call numbers, 267—272
    card catalog, 269—272
    Dewey Decimal System, 266—268
    encyclopedia, 277—279
    fiction books, 264—265
    making a book report, 263, 273—274
    nonfiction books, 265—268
Linking verbs, 222
Listening skills. *See* Speaking and listening skills.
Listening to learn, 132—133
    guides for, 133

Main idea in paragraphs, 105—114. *See also* Topic sentences.

Main verbs, 161—162, 165—166, 175—176

me, us, her, him, and *them,* 83—84, 91

Memory devices for spelling, 368

Modifiers
  adjectives, 211—225
  adverbs, 227—233
  defined, 212

more, most
  with adjectives, 220—221, 225
  with adverbs, 231—233

Narrative paragraphs, 195—203
  choosing a topic, 196—198
  making a clean copy, 203
  making a plan (organizing), 199
  proofreading, 201
  revising, 201
    guides for, 201
  writing a narrative paragraph, 200
Natural order in descriptions, 241—242
Negatives, 171—172, 177
  double, 171—172, 177
Negative words, 97—99
Neutral words, 97—100
no-words, *not*-words. *See* Negatives.
Nonfiction books,
  finding in library, 265—268
  reporting on, 273—274
  using for information, 275—276
Note cards for written reports, 302—305
Notes, pre-writing,
  for descriptions, 239
  for paragraphs, 115—117
  for reports, 302—303
Notes, thank-you, 324—325
Nouns, 61—75
  common, 66—67, 74
  plural, 68—70, 72, 75
    rules for forming, 69—70
  possessive, 71—73, 75, 356—357, 358, 364—365
  proper, 66—67, 74, 319, 336—340, 344

  capitalization of, 66, 319, 336—340, 344
  in sentence patterns, 89, 173
  singular, 68, 71
  as simple subjects, 64—65, 89

Object pronouns. *See me, us, her, him,* and *them.*
Opinion and fact, defined, 250—251
Opinion in "why" paragraphs, 249—255
Outlines, 305—307, 349—350
  sample, 306, 349

Paragraphs, writing, 103—121
  adding to the main idea, 109
  choosing a topic, 115
  definition of a paragraph, 104
  making a clean copy, 121
  making a plan, (organizing), 117
  proofreading, 118
    guides for, 119
  reviewing topic sentences, 111
  revising, 118—120
    guides for, 118
  symbols for revising and proofreading, 119
  taking notes, 116
  telling the main idea, 107
Parts of speech. *See* Adjectives, Adverbs, Nouns, Pronouns, Verbs.
Past forms of verbs, 182—185
Period, 347—350, 363
  in abbreviations, 319, 337, 348—350, 363
  in initials, 348—350, 363
  in outlines, 306, 349—350
  with quotation marks, 360
  in sentences, 36—39, 50, 54, 57, 347, 363—365
Phrases, in descriptions, 244—246
Plural forms. *See* Nouns, Pronouns, Verbs.
Poetry, enjoying, 281—293
  alliteration in, 289—290
  haiku, 285—287

hearing sound patterns in, 288—290
    guides for, 289
identifying the speaker in, 282—285
    guides for, 284
refrain in, 284—285
rhyme in, 288—290
hearing the rhythm in, 290—293
    guides for, 292
seeing pictures in, 285—287
    guides for, 287
Positive words, 97—101
Possessive nouns, 71—73, 75, 356—357,
    358, 364—365
Possessive pronouns, 87—88, 91
Predicate of the sentence
    complete, 40—42, 50—51, 173
    simple, (the verb), 44—46, 51
Prefixes, 7—9, 13, 370—372
Present forms of verbs, 180—181
Pre-writing,
    arranging information
        in a description, 240—242
        in an explanatory paragraph,
            254—255
        in a narrative paragraph, 199
        in outline form, 305—307, 314
        in a story, 260
    choosing a topic
        in descriptions, 238—239
        in narrative paragraphs, 196—198
        in paragraphs, 115—116
        in reports, 295, 299—301, 314
        in stories, 260—261
    making an outline
        in reports, 305—307, 314
    planning
        in narrative paragraphs, 199
        in paragraphs, 117
        in reports, 295, 304—305, 314
        in stories, 260—261
    taking notes
        in paragraphs, 116
        in reports, 295, 301—303, 314
Process of writing, 314. See also Pre-
    writing, Writing, Revising.

Pronouns, 77—91
    I, me, we, and us, 85—86
    me, us, her, him, and them, 83—84, 91
    in place of nouns, 77—79
    plural forms of, 78
    possessive forms of, 87—88, 91
    singular forms of, 78
    as subjects, 80—82, 89—90
Pronunciation key in dictionary, 145,
    150—152, 155
Proofreading,
    as a step in revising, 314
    of paragraphs, 118—120, 201—203,
        247
        guides for, 119, 202
    of reports, 310—312, 314
        guides for, 310
    for spelling, 369
    of stories, 261
    symbols, 118—119, 311
Proper nouns, 66—67, 74, 319,
    336—340, 344
Punctuation, 347—365
    in letters, 319—321, 328—331
    in outlines, 306, 349—350
    See also Apostrophe, Colon, Comma,
        Exclamation point, Period, Question
        mark, Quotation marks, Underlining.

Question mark, 37, 350—351, 363
Questions, 37, 39, 50, 350—351, 363
Quotation marks, 360—361, 365
    with direct quotations, 341, 355,
        360—361, 365
    with titles, 312, 343, 345, 361, 365
Quotations
    direct, 340—342, 355—356, 360—361
    guides for writing, 360
    punctuation with, 341, 355—356,
        360—361, 365

Refrain in poetry, 284—285
Regular verbs, 182—184
    past forms of, 182—184

Reports, written, 295—315
  choosing topic for, 299—301
  gathering information for, 301—303, 314
  limiting topic, 300
  main ideas in, 304—309, 314
  note cards for, 302—305
  outline for, 305—307
  paragraphs in, 297—298, 307—309, 314
  planning, 304—307, 314
  pre-writing, 295, 299—307, 314
  process of writing in, 314
  proofreading, 310—312, 314
  reading aloud, 315
  revising, 308—309, 314
  sharing, 315
  sources, giving credit to, 312—314
  subjects for, finding, 299—301, 314
  title of, 305
  topic sentences in, 307—308
Requests. See Commands.
Restatement as context clue, 4, 6, 13
Return address, 322, 332—333
Revising
  descriptions, 246—247
    checking details and order, 246
    making a clean copy, 247
    proofreading, 247
  narrative paragraph (telling what happened), 201—203
    guides for revising, 201
    proofreading, 201
  paragraphs, 118—121
    guides for revising, 118
    proofreading, 118
      guides for, 119
    symbols used in revising, 119
    making a clean copy, 121
  reports, 308—312
    guides for revising, 308
    proofreading, 310—312
      guides for, 310
      symbols used in, 311
  stories, 261

    proofreading, 261
    steps in revising, 261
Rewriting. See Revising or Clean Copy.
Rhyme in poetry, 288—290
Rhythm in poetry, 290—293
Roman numerals, 306, 349—350
Run-on sentences, 54—55, 58

s', 's. See Apostrophe, in possessives.
Salutation. See Greeting.
schwa symbol in dictionary, 151
Sentence patterns
  N LV Adj, 222
  N V, 89, 173
  word order and meaning, 47—48
Sentences, 31—59
  commands, 37—39, 347, 351—352, 364
  complete, 32—35, 49—50
  complete predicate in, 40—45, 50—51, 173
  complete subject in, 40—45, 50—51, 89
  declarative. See Statements.
  end punctuation in, 36—39, 50, 347, 349—352, 363—364
  exclamations, 38—39, 351—352, 364
  imperative. See Commands.
  interrogative. See Questions.
  kinds of, 36—39, 50
  parts of, 32—33, 40—46, 49—51
  questions, 37, 39, 350—351, 363
  requests. See Commands.
  run-on, 54—55, 58
  simple predicate (verb) in, 44—46, 51
  simple subject, 43—46, 51
  statements, 36, 38—39, 347, 363
  stringy, 57—59
  topic, 107—114, 117, 197, 200, 250, 252—255, 307—308
  writing good sentences, 53—59
Setting in stories, 258—261
Signature in letters, 320—321, 330—331
  printed form in business letters, 330

383

Simple predicate (the verb), 44—46, 51.
See also Verbs.
Simple subject, 43—46, 51
   nouns as, 64—65, 89, 173, 222
   pronouns as, 80—82, 85—86, 90, 168
Singular forms. *See* Nouns, Pronouns,
   Verbs.
Slang, 18—21
Sources of information, giving credit to,
   312—313
Speaker in poetry, 282—285
Speaking and listening skills, 123—133
   making announcements, 128—129
   giving directions, 130—131
   listening to learn, 132—133
   using the telephone, 124—127
   See also Conversation; Introductions;
     Reports, reading aloud; Stories,
     telling; Talking in groups.
Specific words, 244, 246
Spelling, 367—379
   habits for improving, 368
   memory devices, 369
   proofreading, 369
   rules for, 370—379
     adding prefixes, 370
     adding suffixes, 182, 218—220,
      371—375
     words with *ie* or *ei*, 375
   steps to master, 369
Standard English, 16—17, 21
State-of-being verbs, 159—160, 174, 222
Statements, 36, 38—39, 347, 363
   period with, 36, 38—39, 50, 54, 57,
     347, 363—364
Stories, telling, 187—193
   getting people to listen, 190
     guides for, 190
   high point of the story, 188—189
   parts of the story, 188—189
   shaping the story, 188—189
     guides for, 189
   telling a "what" story, 191
   telling a "why" story, 192—193
Stories, writing, 257—261

characters in, 258—261
details in, 243
order in, 258, 260—261
prewriting, 260—261
proofreading, 261
revising, 261
setting in, 258—261
steps for, 261
subjects for, 257—261
Stringy sentences, 57—59
Subject cards in card catalog, 269,
   271—272
Subject of the sentence
   complete, 40—45, 50—51, 89
   simple, 43—46, 51
     nouns as, 64—65, 89, 173, 222
     pronouns as, 80—82, 85—86, 90,
      168
Subtopics in outlines, 305—307
Suffixes, 10—13, 182, 218—220,
   371—379
Syllables, as shown in dictionary entries,
   151—152, 155
Synonyms, 94—98

Table of contents, 263, 275—276
Talking. *See* Speaking and listening skills.
Talking in groups, 135—141
   disagreeing politely, 135—137,
     139—141
     guides for, 141
   sharing ideas, 136—138
     guides for, 137
Telephone, using the, 124—127
   guides for, 126
Telling about what happened. *See*
   Narrative Paragraphs.
Tests, taking, 205—209
Thank-you notes, 324—325
Title cards in card catalog, 269—272
Titles
   capitalization of, 306, 310, 312—313,
     319, 337—338, 342—343, 345
   of persons, 319, 337—338, 344
     abbreviations, 337—338, 348—350

of written works, 306, 312—313, 333, 342—343, 345
    quotation marks with, 312, 343, 361, 365
    underlining for italics, 312, 343, 362, 365
Topic sentences
    defined, 107
    in description, 236, 245
    in explanatory paragraphs, 250, 252—255
    in narrative paragraphs, 197, 200
    in paragraphs, 107—114
    in reports, 307—308
Topics in outlines, 305—307

Underlining titles for italics, 312, 343, 345, 362, 365
Usage,
    of adjectives,
        comparative and superlative forms, 218—221
    of adverbs,
        comparative and superlative forms, 231—232
    avoiding double negatives, 171—172
    distinguishing between homonyms 376—377
    of pronouns
        as subject, 80—82
        in parts of the sentence other than simple subject, 83—84
    of verbs
        irregular verbs, 184—185
        subject-verb agreement, 167—168, 176

Verb, the (simple predicate), 44—46, 51. *See also* Verbs.

Verbs, 157—185
    action, 157—158, 160, 174
    agreement with subjects, 167—168, 176, 180—181
    defined, 44
    forms of, 167—168, 180—185
    helping, 161—166, 175—176
    irregular, 184—185
    kinds of, 157—160, 174
    linking, 222
    main, 157—158, 161—162, 165—166, 175—176
    past forms of, 182—185
    present forms of, 180—181
    regular, 184
    in sentence patterns, 89, 173, 222
    separated parts of, 165—166, 176
    state-of-being, 156, 159—160, 174, 222

Word parts, 7—13, 370—379

Writing. *See* Descriptions, Explanatory Paragraphs, Narrative Paragraphs, Paragraphs, Reports, Sentences, Stories.

you,
    and verb forms, 168
    understood in sentence, 37

ZIP code, 319, 348

Editorial Director: Joy Littell
Senior Editor: Patricia Opaskar
Managing Editor: Kathleen Laya
Assistant Editor: Elizabeth M. Garber
Director of Design: Allen Carr
Assistant Designer: Mary MacDonald

Acknowledgments

William Collins Publishers, Inc.: For the dictionary excerpt reproduced on page 145, from *Webster's New World Dictionary for Young Readers*; copyright © 1976 by William Collins + World Publishing Company, Inc. Thomas Y. Crowell, Publishers: For "I Look Pretty" from *Honey, I Love and Other Love Poems* by Eloise Greenfield; copyright © 1978 by Eloise Greenfield. Dodd, Mead & Company: For a selection from *The Top of the Pizzas* by Bill Basso. Follett Publishing Company: For a selection from *The Wheel of King Asoka* by Ashok Davar; copyright © 1977 by Follett Publishing Company, a division of Follett Corporation; used by permission. For "A Modern Dragon" from *Around a Toadstool Table* by Rowena Bennett; copyright © 1967 by Follett Publishing Company, a division of Follett Corporation; used by permission. Harper & Row, Publishers, Inc.: For "First Snow" from *A Pocketful of Rhymes* by Marie Louise Allen; text copyright © 1957 by Marie Allen Howarth. For "The Snake" from *In the Middle of the Trees* by Karla Kuskin; copyright © 1958 by Karla Kuskin. Macmillan: For "A Gopher in the Garden" from *A Gopher in the Garden and Other Animal Poems* by Jack Prelutsky; copyright © Jack Prelutsky, 1966, 1967; reprinted with permission of Macmillan Publishing Co., Inc. Gabriela Mistral: For "You Have Me" from *Selected Poems of Gabriela Mistral*, translated by Langston Hughes; English translation copyright © 1957 by Indiana University Press; reprinted by permission of Joan Daves. William Jay Smith: For "Toaster" from *Laughing Time* by William Jay Smith, published by Atlantic, Little Brown, 1955; copyright © 1955 by William Jay Smith; reprinted by permission of the author. World Book—Childcraft International: For an excerpt from *The World Book Encyclopedia*; copyright © 1980 by World Book—Childcraft International, Inc. Remy Charlip: For a selection from *Harlequin and The Gift of Many Colors* by Remy Charlip and Burton Supree; text copyright © 1973 by Remy Charlip and Burton Supree; all rights reserved; published by Four Winds Press, New York, New York.

Photographs

Cover Photo Researchers: Howard Uible

Magnum: René Burri, ii; Woodfin Camp: Jeffrey Foxx, xiv, 76; James L. Ballard, 14, 22, 30, 60, 122, 134, 142, 156, 178, 204, 248, 262, 294, 327, 334, 346; Paul Fusco, 52, 102, 226; John Wehrheim, 92; Ian Berry, 187; Burt Glinn, 195; Burk Uzzle, 210, 234; Bruce Davidson, 256; Erich Hartmann, 280; Wayne Miller, 316; Charles Harbutt, 354.

Illustrations

Kip Lott, 2, 3, 4, 5, 38, 62, 63, 95; Linda Gist, 7, 9, 10, 11, 43, 44, 45, 71, 72, 73, 87, 98, 114, 196, 197, 228, 260, 307, 312; Rodica Prato, 12, 36, 109, 165, 169, 170, 172, 191, 245, 291, 292; Len Ebert, 17, 18, 19, 21, 64, 113, 138, 150, 159, 166, 167, 180, 232, 268; Greg Hergert, 24, 26, 28, 32, 34, 35, 40, 80, 81, 85, 94, 97, 124, 126, 127, 128, 129, 130, 231, 333; Karen Ackoff, 37, 147, 152, 264, 267, 329; Sam Courser-Stearns, 54; Ken Izzi, 56, 57, 131, 188, 206, 217, 269; Bill Schmidt, 67, 68, 101, 189, 192, 193, 252, 253; Leslie Robin, 99, 110, 240, 242; Richard Harvey, 104, 107, 139, 141, 149, 218, 282, 283, 289, 293; Steve Sullivan, 108, 163, 251, 278, 279, 288, 303, 321, 324; Yoshi Miyake, 116, 117, 121; Gary Cooley, 137; Bob Masheris, 199, 203, 274; Wayne Bonnett, 214, 215, 216, 230, 236, 238, 297, 298, 299, 300, 302; Steve Bates, 259, 260. "The Shaman's Dance" by Pitalouisa, by permission of the West Baffin Eskimo Co-operative, © 1970, 270. Photo of Lakeland Terrier, from *The World Book Encyclopedia* © 1980, World Book—Childcraft International, Inc. 277. David Sharp, Ken Izzi, and Jeanne Seabright: mechanical artwork and handwriting.

386